Music Therapy, Sensory Integration
and the Autistic Child

of related interest

Music Therapy Research and Practice in Medicine
From Out of the Silence
David Aldridge
ISBN 1 85302 296 9

Clinical Application of Music Therapy in Developmental Disability, Paediatrics and Neurology
Edited by Tony Wigram and Jos de Backer
ISBN 1 85302 734 0

Art Therapy with Children on the Autistic Spectrum
Beyond Words
Kathy Evans and Janek Dubowski
ISBN 1 85302 825 8

Music Therapy – Intimate Notes
Mercédès Pavlicevic
ISBN 1 85302 692 1

Music Therapy in Context
Music, Meaning and Relationship
Mercédès Pavlicevic
ISBN 1 85302 434 1

Music for Life
Aspects of Creative Music Therapy with Adult Clients
Gary Ansdell
ISBN 1 85302 299 3

Autism – The Search for Coherence
Edited by John Richer and Sheila Coates
ISBN 1 85302 888 6

Bright Splinters of the Mind
A Personal Story of Research with Autistic Savants
Beate Hermelin
ISBN 1 85302 932 7

Music Therapy, Sensory Integration and the Autistic Child

Dorita S. Berger

Jessica Kingsley Publishers
London and Philadelphia

BS

First published in the United Kingdom in 2002 by
Jessica Kingsley Publishers Ltd
116 Pentonville Road, London
N1 9JB, England
and
325 Chestnut Street,
Philadelphia, PA 19106, USA.
www.jkp.com
© Copyright 2002 Dorita S. Berger
Foreword © copyright Donna Williams

Library of Congress Cataloging in Publication Data
A CIP catalog record for this book is available from the Library of Congress

British Library Cataloguing in Publication Data
A CIP catalogue record for this book is available from the British Library

ISBN 1 84310 770 7

Printed and Bound in Great Britain by
Athenaeum Press, Gateshead, Tyne and Wear

10/29/03

In memory of my parents, Charlotte and Leon Schneck —
two special people who taught me to inquire

Contents

Foreword

Mind and consciousness are like a gradual sunrise that takes time to come up. In the meantime, we are not stagnant, waiting for life to happen. We map everything, letting information processing take care of itself. We map rhythm and pattern, the pitch and volume, the form and flow of movements around us, of objects, places, of people. This is the music of life and we feel it with our bodies, long before we identify mind with self, this is the realm of sensing, and we all began there. Some of us stay here longer than others. As a person diagnosed with autism, I am one of those people.

Music has a particularly special place in the foundations we all came from. Whether we hear it in the footsteps with which an individual crosses the floor, the visual rhythm with which someone holds and puts down a glass or the flow and shifts of how someone sits in their own body, music in its broader sense is everywhere, and it is our first language.

Music has the most important of all places in the lives of those who find the realm of the mind a place of rusty cogs and heavy effort – the stuff of overload, shutdown, information processing delay and the sensory chaos that ensues. Such is the stuff of developmental conditions like those in the autism spectrum. Like those I have lived with personally all my life. Music has the convincing power to restore order in chaos, to reassure that in spite of an absence of sensory cohesion, that something whole and wonderful, flowing and consistent still exists outside of us in the world we might otherwise give up on as being non-user-friendly. It is a place where those who struggle to keep up with the rate of information, left meaning-deaf, meaning-blind at the time of incoming information, still can meet with others in a form of communication and a state of involvement I call Simply Being. More than this, when haywire chemistry tells you that emotion and connection with others signal the threat of death, in music there is at least one social realm that remains safe, indirectly confrontational and accepting of the right to "lose oneself" as an act of self-calming in order to stay.

Music was an exceptionally important part of my life, not just in the unprocessed patterns around me (I couldn't understand three sentences in a row until I was nine) but in the form of classical music, 60s rock and roll, blues and TV jingles and theme songs. The emotional journeys of classical music gave me an experience of emotion no degree of severe exposure anxiety could later erase. I heard people through it. It helped me stand the music of their voices in spite of the chaos. It gave me a basis for sequencing. Rock and roll gave me humor and stored lines, blues gave me a comedian's timing. The TV jingles and theme songs formed the main content of my personal language – a language speaking in "feel", "theme" and "topic" and although it may have been part of me being seen as crazy and disturbed (it was the 60s–70s and autism wasn't well known) it was the bridge to the language I have today.

Music therapy is about building a safe space, a meeting place, somewhere to feel equal, a foundation of experience in which to remember in our bodies a spectrum of emotion and connection with a process of connection among others equally being in their own space. Music therapy can be modulated and defies the confines and rigidity of social convention. Through song, we can address topics where directly confrontational language dare not go (or would not be tolerated with meaning on-line). Used with people with severe exposure anxiety, it can be used as the Pied Piper, the musician giving small doses, as though purely for his or her own sake, playing hard to get and always leaving the activity with the person wanting more. It can be modulated to show that those in the directly confrontational self-in-relation-to-other world, can also be indirectly confrontational in a self-owning way, demonstrating life is not so black and white but has a whole spectrum in between.

Donna Williams BA Hons, Dip Ed.
Author of five books, including the international bestselling autobiography
Nobody Nowhere *and* Autism and Sensing: The Unlost Instinct

Preface

Music therapists have long known that entering the brain through the auditory system is a key to obtaining automatic brain attendance and response. Music's ability to stimulate the limbic system's release of emotions and moods is well documented. Until recently, music therapy goals for the autistic population were primarily concerned with encouraging "connectedness", communication, socialization, and emotional and psychological improvement. But are these goals enough to instigate permanent changes in behavior that can be generalized into other situations?

Music's potential impact on a wider range of physiologic problems is often overlooked or considered a by-product. In fact, physiologic changes resulting from music interventions can be a major factor in bringing about a feeling of well-being. The apparent inability of the autistic brain properly to encode, decode, integrate and coordinate simultaneously a plethora of sensory information appears to be at least one major cause for erratic behaviors and ill-adaptive responses. The interactive sensory systems include tactile, vestibular, proprioceptive, visual and auditory information processing. It is an area in which music interventions can have major impact in perpetuating functional adaptation.

In observing autistic and other alternative behavioral responses to given situations, it is essential to ask why the observed behaviors exist in the first place. What is happening with the "atypical" system of behavioral responses that music interventions can impact? How can a process as abstract as music order the senses to integrate and induce *cenesthesia* – a sense of sensory balance and physical well-being?

This book is designed for music therapists, parents, teachers and health clinicians – those who are raising, teaching and working with populations functioning in alternative ways to those that are generally considered to be "normal". Although there may be reference throughout to "dysfunctional" actions on the part of autistic persons, I ask the reader to consider that in all probability, we are all somehow dysfunctional in some way, and that the term "dysfunctional" actually defines very little.

The subject of this book is music – theories about why it works, and what its potential role in human adaptation implies, especially as a clinical intervention for autistic and other diagnosed populations. Aspects of physiologic function and information processing that contribute to the state of sensory integrative adaptation are discussed, and ways in which music can foster functional adaption are considered.

Also discussed is the important role of the music therapist's knowledge of physiology in shepherding atypical human systems towards the state of sensory integration – the state of cenesthesia. My theory suggests that when sensory integration and functional adaptation become the *primary goals* addressed by music therapy, the overall sense of well-being for the autistic and other diagnosed systems will be an inevitable by-product. Connectedness, socialization and emotional, psychological and cognitive improvements are predicated upon the body and brain feeling comfortable and at ease with itself and its environment.

As this book progresses, the reader will discover that "functional" and "appropriate" are not the same things. Furthermore, these terms are defined by each individual system, as each system's own unique response to navigating through life comfortably. *Comfort* is a personal element. What is "comfortable" for one may not be for another. Therefore we must establish at this point that no person can determine for another what is "appropriate", "adequate", "comfortable" or "acceptable" behavior. *Comfortable* for whom? *Acceptable* according to what laws and standards?

Through knowledge of physiologic function, sensory systems and sensory information processing, the music therapist is able to examine and understand more astutely how music might address sensory processes that are unique to each autistic or other special needs person. Parents, clinicians, and teachers are better able to understand why music therapy is such an important intervention.

Armed with a broader understanding of how the human body works, the music therapist can target precise clinical goals and interventions complementing and augmenting goals of related therapies, including speech pathology, physical and occupational therapy, and emotional, psychological, cognitive, behavioral, social and play interventions.

Specific rhythmic, instrumental, vocal and movement activities, stimulated by prescribed prompts, and unique activities devoted to mind-body preparatory balance exercises, when undertaken, can ultimately result in auditory-visual integration, reflexive motor planning, rhythmic internalization, mind-body coordination, sequencing skills, task organization, and adaptation to sound environment.

As the reader progresses through the information presented on the following pages, he or she will do well to keep in mind that a sense of well-being is predicated upon a body feeling physiologically balanced. Integration of the sensory systems ultimately promotes intuition, cognition, self-identity, esteem, and traditional holistic goals of music therapy, including visual contact and communication. To achieve this through music therapy is to promote well-being.

Several chapters in this book present some rather complex elaborations. These have been included to provide the reader with a broad scope of human physiologic function that can be impacted upon by music. When the elements of music are understood in context with physiologic information processing and brain function, the role of music in human adaptation becomes tangible. For parents, therapists and administrators involved with special needs populations, this "technical" information can also provide the justification and terminology often sought for the acquisition of music therapy services.

Appendix A reprints an article co-authored by Dr Daniel J. Schneck and myself, titled "The Role of Music in Physiologic Accommodation: Its Ability to Elicit Reflexive, Adaptive, and Inscriptive Responses". It originally appeared in *IEEE Engineering in Medicine and Biology Magazine*, Vol. 18, No.2, March/April 1999, an issue devoted entirely to the role of music in human function.

Finally, this book is not a recipe book of music "tasks". Tasks are not therapy. Rather, music therapy is an approach to solving a physiologic or psychologic problem through understanding possible causes creating the problem and considering how music, through its elements, can be applied as a targeted intervention to alter the issue.

At seminars I present, I am often asked to provide activities that can address the problems discussed in this book. My response is always the same: if one is a professional clinician or educator, then one can absorb and internalize the information herein, and use one's creative instincts and knowledge to develop interventions based on the understanding of physiology and the body's engineering of a patient. If one is a parent, then one is not qualified to administer music therapy, so having a list of activities would be insufficient in addressing specific issues. A consultation with a music therapist would be advisable. A therapist, after all, not only knows what exercise to provide and how, but also *when* and *how much* to provide.

I would like to thank my dear colleague, Dr Daniel J. Schneck, for instilling in me a strong sense of physiologic understanding through our many personal conversations uniting music with aspects of human adaptation and biomedical engineering. I would also like to thank my colleagues in allied therapy areas who provide me with, and continue to turn to me for, information to help link music and the work of music therapy to their areas of physiologic understanding.

I especially thank my patients, whose struggles to survive and understand a very complicated universe continue to stimulate my thinking, challenge my assumptions of human behavior, teach me to see life from many novel perspectives, and demand that I be the best clinician I can be.

CHAPTER I

Introduction: Who Defines "Appropriate"?

Most societies live within established systems of stated or assumed laws governing group social behavior. Humans, like other pack animals, rely on groups for survival. Regardless of levels of sophistication and cultural development, every group seems to manifest expected "norms" of participation, written or unwritten.

For the human animal, the expectation is that a person wishing to function cooperatively and comfortably within their social group will "follow the rules" of the pack and behave accordingly. Therefore, in our Western societies, we are quiet in libraries, respect our elders, eat with implements and dishes, sleep in beds, sit or stand when told to do so, and so on. Mom, Dad and teacher are happy, as are neighbors, extended family members and God.

One assumption is that all "normal" or "typical" or "acculturated" human beings will eventually learn the rules of the group and behave as expected. But what if that does not happen according to plan? Suppose personal behavior, in its most "natural" form, is actually more a matter of physiologic needs rather than socially established "rules". This begs another question: for whose benefit are rules designed?

Another assumption is that the group understands the needs of the individual, and that the individual, equally, understands and therefore wishes to comply with the rules of the group in order to be accepted. Obviously, at least in the case of diagnosed individuals, that assumption can be erroneous.

Imagine yourself in the following circumstances. You are in an alien culture, one which neither your brain nor body can understand or interpret. The pressures pushing/pulling on your body are so overwhelming you have difficulty navigating from one point to another. The road seems to be going downhill…no…uphill…or maybe sideways? Sounds around you seem to be a myriad of vocal squeaks and squeals and whirrs and hisses; people seem to have similar faces and odd characteristics, strange and unidentifiable expressions. You are grabbed and prodded by others; their arms wave at you, demanding things – what? Fragments of color and shapes float before your eyes; bodily parts seem to belong someplace, but where? Is that arm connected to *your* body?

You are hot, no, cold. It is crowded. It is noisy. There seems to be no reference for spatial directions; you recognize little. People talk *at* you. It's gibberish. You try to communicate. *They* don't understand. You don't understand what *they* want. *They* are upset. *They* physically manipulate you.

Your system is confused, frightened, in a state of panic. You emit strange vocal sounds, cover your eyes, agitate, flail your arms, move in confusion, lose your balance, run and hide. You are afraid. Fear puts your senses into "survival" mode, ready to protect you from harm. Your vision is peripheral, taking everything in; your hearing is ambient, hearing all sounds at once, from far away, in strange sequences. You run, spin, shout, cover your ears, look to hide from all of this in an effort to feel safe. You are especially afraid of those who are after you demanding that you SIT! LOOK at them! BEHAVE in ways you do not understand.

What sense can you make of this place? Are you comfortable? Do you feel good about yourself? Would you want to connect with these aliens or rather, run from the pack? You seek solace in solitude and live by your own rules. In your own world. Are you less a person?

The fact is, we tend to assume that being human – being a "person" – means having the capacity to learn and abide by the rules of the group, regardless of physiologic determinants, and that those "rules" can be applied similarly to everyone. This is clearly not the case. One's physiologic function determines the rules and needs of the game. To assume otherwise is naively to impose methods of behavior on systems that simply cannot function like those of others, of the "pack". In effect, it is like demanding that a goldfish learn to live within a group of tuna! (Tuna live in salt water; goldfish (carp) are freshwater fish.)

Insight into aspects of physiologic and sensory function which may be contributing factors to behavior is of vital importance to understanding how to work with and educate the atypical population. The behaviors describing responses to the alien world as noted above may be termed *atypical* for "normal" human earth-dwellers but are quite *typical* behaviors of persons within the autistic spectrum: persons who are, in effect, living on an alien planet, as their systems evaluate it – a world for which their physiology is perhaps not effectively operational.

What's in a "label"?

Consider this: there are really only two types of persons on this planet – the diagnosed, and the *un*-diagnosed! Therefore we might need to adjust our opinions about what is *appropriate* and *functional*, since we are all probably *dys*functional, or *a*typical, in some manner, at some time. The determination of what is "normal" has not been derived through empirical scientific data, but rather has been mostly theorized through anecdotal observation of behaviors. And, as a matter of fact, many of these theories are highly culturally (pack) specific and not necessarily universal. Since the world-at-large is often unwilling to accept data that is not scientifically proven, perhaps we need to be equally unwilling to accept anecdotal information regarding what is "normal" behavior. Normal for whom? Are the words "normal" and "typical" interchangeable? (Perhaps "normal" is as normal does.)

Consider the possibility that atypical and unusual behaviors are, in fact, *typical adaptive responses* of each individual system to incoming sensory information that the brain may not have encoded, decoded or interpreted according to the "norm". It then becomes imperative to understand what the behaviors imply about the function of that body.

For instance, a "normal" person with a "typical" headache would be irritable, antisocial, impatient, intolerant of loud sounds, non-conversant, unfocused, and so on. These behaviors would not be labeled *in*appropriate because they are *appropriate for that body's current physiologic condition*. Once a serious illness is ruled out, the behaviors are allowed to run their course. Indeed this person is not "labeled" and the condition is (fortunately) temporary. But what if the condition were to be permanent? Would behavioral expectations change and attempts be made to alter these behaviors despite the physiologic reasons for their presence in the first place? It would seem more beneficial to discover the cause and develop a remedy for the *reasons* behind certain behaviors.

Consider Randy, an eight-year-old child with Fragile-X syndrome. He is non-verbal and his behaviors closely resemble those of autism. Randy had a habit of humming continuously as he propelled himself down a corridor or long stretch. Rather than asking why Randy was humming, staff at his school insisted that the humming was a "stim" (a self-stimulation) which had to be discontinued. They proceeded to take measures that could interrupt the humming. However, when they did so, the interruption of the humming distressed Randy and also disrupted and inhibited his movement flow.

As the consulting music therapist, I was asked to look into this issue and develop methods which would eliminate Randy's movement humming. After meeting with Randy for 45 minutes three times a week during a six-week assessment period, I noted that he hummed only when he was engaged in extended movement such as propelling himself down a long corridor. I speculated that perhaps there was a physiologic reason for his humming. After all, he did not simply sit and hum, rock and hum, or play an instrument and hum. The humming seemed directly related to his propulsion in space.

When I discussed Randy's situation with my physiologist colleague, Dr Daniel Schneck, he suggested I might check which pitch Randy was humming to see if that might provide a clue to the behavior. I discovered that Randy was humming a pitch within the frequency of "B" to "C#" (C-sharp) in the middle register of the piano. Those frequencies, Dr Schneck conjectured, could be within the range of frequencies of the alpha-gamma motoneurons that trigger movement. This suggested a possible relationship between the humming and muscular frequencies. Dr Schneck speculated that perhaps the humming was somehow assisting the child's movement in a continual flow through large spaces. Perhaps, too, it was a kind of navigational echo-system like those used by some animals (such as whales) to negotiate movement through space.

Whatever it was that Randy's brain was doing remains unclear, but the end result was that with the humming "crutch" Randy could navigate the corridors quite efficiently. I strongly recommended not tampering with Randy's need to hum, since it clearly was not an attempt to "make noise", be disruptive, defiant, or otherwise uncooperative. In the end, after music and allied forms of therapies had intervened to alter Randy's navigational efficiency over long stretches of space, the need to hum eventually extinguished itself.

It took more than a year to repattern that aspect of Randy's sensory insecurity. I introduced the recorder (a blowing instrument) for Randy to use in long stretches of walking, as well as in music therapy interventions. In addition I recommended a kazoo, a mouth instrument which requires humming into in order to derive sound, as a way of redirecting his humming into a "socially acceptable" behavior. The recorder and kazoo were also used by the speech pathologist and occupation therapist to give Randy's brain more tonal feedback and sound vibrations in breathing and movement activities. He seemed to enjoy the kazoo most.

After more than a year, even if the kazoo was inadvertently left behind and was not part of his walk, Randy did not hum! In other words, when the hum had been redirected into a musical function, Randy's humming into the kazoo helped his system "relax" and allow higher level processing to teach the brain that humming was useful in making the kazoo play. Thus without the kazoo, the need to hum seemed to evaporate.

Whether the humming was related to his movement is still unknown. However, the redirection of humming into an enjoyable music-making event did appear to play a role in reorganizing his sensory system in some way. Collaborative interventions also aided his vestibular and visual systems to regulate, ultimately eliminating Randy's need to hum (audibly).

At a later level Randy preferred to play the recorder (into which one simply blows rather than hums). Thus music therapy could still assist in helping Randy's breathing and oral-motor systems become organized and prepared for expressive language learning.

Yes, it is true that human survival is based on "functional" behavior in response within the "norm" to given circumstances. But the terms "functional" and "norm" refer to the manner in which a specific system has adapted its unique survival strategies (according to *its* "norm") in negotiating this planet. "Functional" and "normal" are relative to the system which is applying the behavior in order to fulfill its particular needs – individually! Thus, while one person may be able successfully to "modulate" quickly from, let us say, a disappointing situation, another may require minutes, hours, days, to achieve the same level of balance as person number one. Both the rule book and jury are out on what time-span is "correct" for adaptation, what the adaptation "should" be, and who determines the rules.

What determines "right" and "wrong" responses?

Many observable behaviors are defined and interpreted by persons outside of the situation – persons who, meaning well, generally find certain behaviors to be unconventional, inconvenient, intrusive and stressful to deal with, and determine that these must be modified for the good of the persons with atypical responses. "Right" and "wrong" ways of behaving are basically determined by socio-cultural (pack) standards rather than scientific givens. Furthermore, societies seem to be primarily involved with *cognitive* literacy, often omitting intuitive/instinctive learning and placing physiologic and emotional well-being on the back burner, if considering them at all.

The question is, who benefits from the altering of autistic behavior? Is it truly the autistic person, or is it the others? Both? Equally? And what price does the diagnosed ("labeled") person pay for the "benefit of others'? Persons with the label "autistic", such as Donna Williams, Temple Grandin and others, have often stated that the benefit to them seemed to be far less than the benefit to society – the pack.

For the most part, my work in music therapy has sought to alter concepts and attitudes concerning "appropriate" and "acceptable", ideologies which seem to be largely based upon erroneous assumptions governing what and why certain "behaviors" should be this or that way. Concepts of "shoulds" focused upon eradicating "alternative" behaviors may often be more detrimental than helpful to the "labeled" person. Again we need to know: for *whose benefit* are we altering someone's behavior?

When human behavior is approached from the physiologic understanding that everything done by the brain and body *is done for a reason*, and when therapists, parents, educators, caregivers investigate those reasons more fully, then interventions can be designed more astutely. Goals aimed at obtaining "appropriate" and "acceptable" ways of responding may not necessarily benefit the diagnosed person.

In other words, the possible cause of a behavior needs to be assessed and understood first, before a determination can be made as to how, or even if, attempts to alter behaviors need to be undertaken. It is not enough to simply rely on the generic label "autism" and set out to alter autistic behavior. After all, *"autistic" behavior is the only way in which that particular physiologic system has learned to respond and adapt to its environment.* Behavior is the *symptom* of a problem, not the problem itself!

By studying what certain behaviors might designate physiologically, and how the senses are implicated, it is possible to apply interventions that directly address those sensory and physiologic issues. This, in turn, may automatically influence and alter behavior. Interventions informed with physiologic knowledge can help the uncomfortable system readapt its ways of dealing with stimuli, enabling new and alternative response options for the brain and nervous system to ponder. This may be said of any physiologic distress, whether temporary or enduring.

Thus, the primary therapy or educational goal in any number of situations, conditions, syndromes or diagnoses, must initially be relative and proportional to the perpetuation of *physiologic comfort* – a level of cenesthesia in which the senses and physical attributes of the body cooperate – before any altered forms of "functional" behavior can be sought or even attained. "Appropriate" is defined by each body individually.

The brain does not know that it does not know

As you read through the information in the following chapters, bear in mind that the brain only knows what it knows from encoding, decoding and interpreting incoming sensory information. *The brain only deals with information it receives and is equipped to interpret.* It does not know what it does not have. It does not know that it is *supposed* to have or do something, nor how its body is *supposed* to act in certain circumstances that appear alien to that brain. (If you are born blind and visual energy is not transduced to arouse the visual cortex, then your brain does not know that it is *supposed* to see. In other words, your brain does not know that it has no eyes!)

For example, my brain does not know that my sensory system does not have electro-receptive sensors with which to decode electric fields discharged from other beings. So my brain, unlike that of a shark, which can decode electric fields generated from other fish, resorts to other methods to detect the whereabouts of other humans. We use the cortex (see Chapter 2) and its cognitive (externally learned) information to build machinery and technology that tell us the information that our own brains cannot process on their own.

My human brain also cannot decode the extremes of high pitches that any dog can hear. My brain does not know that these frequencies even exist, because my auditory sense is neither detecting nor transmitting (transducing, i.e. converting to electrical impulses) this sensory information. (And if it is and my human brain doesn't know what to do with it because it has no way of encoding or decoding the information, it will ignore and discard it!) Again, we build technologies to detect these frequencies so we can at least perceive their design visually on a screen.

Human adaptation to the planet has developed survival strategies based only on the information the human brain receives and can process. The manner in which incoming information is processed, discussed in later chapters, determines the resulting behavior.

First and foremost, the brain is concerned with survival of the body. It will call for *any* response that directly addresses physiologic safety and comfort. Unfortunately for autistic and other atypical persons, those responses do not always correspond with socially approved behaviors.

If decoding and interpretation systems are somehow unusual (compared to "typical" universal standards of responses), this will impact upon resulting behavior. For instance, the brain may not be able to redirect nervous energy away from hand flapping to, let us say, gum chewing or cigarette smoking (which, by the way, are stimming actions of sorts!) or stretching, or even leg shaking. Spinning may be the brain's only way to test its vestibular system and help the body become centered.

The brain may not be able to decipher the meaning and organization of fragmented visual and auditory information it receives in order to tell the eyes to gaze directly into someone's face, or the ears to focus on verbal language while tuning out unrelated sounds. In fact, *autistic behavior is "normal" for that system* and atypical for us! It is important to remember that *we* are the foreign culture and language to which *they* are being asked to adjust and adapt!

The clinician, educator and caregiver working with diagnosed populations, especially clinicians and persons with some understanding of basic physiologic function, will tend to question what is being witnessed and will approach interventions from a much broader, informed perspective.

Although the information discussed throughout this book mainly addresses autistic characteristics, much of what is included can also be applicable to a broader spectrum of atypically functioning populations. These especially include older adults, brain-damaged and Alzheimer's sufferers, persons with syndromes such as Rett, Down, Cornelia de Lange, Williams, ADD, and populations with neuro-physiologically atypical function. The information given here can also be applied to individuals with the psycho-physiologic emotional problems that often result from some multisensory systems malfunction.

CHAPTER 2

Aspects of Autism

Many myths exist about the anomaly labeled "autism" that continually beg clarification. We now know that autism is *not* a "childhood" disorder, although it can appear as early as 20 weeks in the womb and is generally clearly evident by the age of two. Autism is *not* a psycho-emotional disorder resulting from a "frigid" mother. Autism is *not* a behavioral problem requiring conformity.

Autism is a *neurologically atypical* manner of function, with genetic and sensory-motor implications. There appear to be atypical brain structures in persons with autistic symptoms that can be detected in utero, or after birth (Frith 1989, pp.1–15). However, it is still unclear whether an atypical brain structure is a contributing factor of autism, or rather, whether autistic neurologic processes create the altered brain structures. Nevertheless, it is clear that the "frigid parent" theory is not valid, and what appears in childhood as autism remains throughout life.

Autism is a *developmental* disorder often referenced under the term Pervasive Developmental Disorder (PDD). The term *pervasive* means that delays in certain areas of development will impact, along the line of growth, upon other areas of development, compounding the deficits of function. Because it is a developmental disorder, autistic symptoms inherent in a particular personality will appear different at different ages, some aspects fading away with growth stages while others begin.

Autism is a *spectrum disorder*, meaning *there is not one way of being autistic.* Autistic characteristics range from the genius savant who can perform complex calendar calculations but cannot add two plus two, to high-functioning scientists, authors and artists, to minimally functional, non-verbal individuals with severe retardation. Each and every individual diagnosed as being autistic demonstrates completely unique attributes on the continuum of the disorder. For reasons as yet unknown, the disorder is prominent in male children, with only one out of every five autistic child being female (Siegel 1996, pp.21–2).[1]

General characteristics of autism

Characteristics in the autism continuum as defined in various medical references and autism literature, may be summarized as follows:

- inability to formulate normal affective relationships (autistic "aloneness"; social ineptitude; etc.)

- desire for sameness, repetitive routine, structure (ritualistic behaviors)

- self-stimulation (stimming) activities such as flailing hands or arms, unusual vocal sounds, odd body movements

- internal preoccupation and fantasizing

- disturbed or inappropriate affect; visual avoidance

- echolalia; speech deficits; lack of language

- intellectual dysfunction; retardation (slow mental function, inability to generalize or conceptualize, etc.)

- sensory-integrative dysfunction; dyspraxia (motor-planning dysfunction)

---

1   Dr Siegel describes Rett Syndrome, which occurs only in females, as a genetic disorder akin to autism. She states, "Between the second and fifth or sixth year of life, when Rett's syndrome is usually first diagnosed, the girl may also meet diagnostic criteria for autism or PDD because of a marked lack of social relatedness and the presence of other features of autism. Rett's syndrome is included as a non-autistic PDD because its cause is not otherwise known, and because, for the period of time that the child with Rett's syndrome has autistic signs, she may benefit from teaching approaches used for autistic children."

- communication deficits – lack of speech, lack of vocal inflection, inappropriate verbal responses, etc.

- unique "splinter" skills, such as perfect pitch, photographic memory, genius calculation capacity, etc.

and other related and observable displays of atypical responses.

Asperger Syndrome, (Siegel 1996)[2] generally a higher level of function, but with autistic implications, has no apparent clinical delays in language, basic cognitive development, adaptive behaviors or self-help skills. Asperger Syndrome includes, in addition to many of the aforementioned autism characteristics:

- qualitative impairment in social interaction skills (lack of sharing ideas and interests; failure to develop peer relationships; lack of social or emotional reciprocity)

- defiant behaviors; inability or unwillingness to follow or comply with instructions.

These characteristics represent generally visible means of identifying and arriving at the diagnoses referred to as autism and related PDD disorders. But these aspects by no means specifically characterize any single way of being autistic. In fact, if taken out of context, one could probably ascribe many of the above features to any individual deemed "normal" or "typical"!

One of the actualities of autism, however, is the existence of often profound neurobiological impairment contributing to the altering and inaccuracy of sensory information processing, coding and interpretation by the brain. This distresses the system's ability to formulate adequate adaptive responses (functional adaptation) to the environment in which it must function, resulting in many of autism's characteristics described above.

---

2   In Chapter 1, "Defining Autism: PDD, and Other Disorders" the author refers to Asperger Syndrome as a related but higher functioning autistic disorder without the language or cognitive retardation seen in autism. These children appear "normal but odd". AS children are often misdiagnosed due to the factor of normal "appearance". Socially, issues are similar to autism.

Thus most if not all aspects of autism may actually be the results of the system's confusion. It may be said, in fact, that these characteristic behaviors are the adaptive responses of the autistic system to its environment, based upon the given input and how the brain has processed and interpreted the information. How would the brain know that the given stimuli and interpretation thereof are incorrect?

As stated in Chapter 1, the brain only deals with, codes and interprets information it receives, in whatever manner this information is received. The brain does not know what it does not know! Let us take a closer look at two of the above characteristics of autism and explore some possible sensory-systemic reasons for resultant behaviors.

Autistic "aloneness"

One can formulate hundreds of reasons why, psychologically, someone might prefer to be "alone". Donna Williams, an autistic woman of great insight and individuality, reminds us (Williams 1998, pp.118–19) that: "Identity is about how we recognize ourselves in relation to others. Those who are monolingual and monocultural, either in the system of sensing or the system of interpretation [of sensory information] will have a very different sense of identity." She further states that: "The primarily sensory being exists in a world of all self with no simultaneous sense of other, or all sense of other with no simultaneous sense of self. Because of this, the sensory being may never know the concept of loneliness."

What Donna Williams seems to imply is that alternative sensory processing, and the manner in which sensory information is interpreted (or not interpreted) by the brain, determines how one understands one's self and how that self relates to "other" persons or things. Considering questions raised previously regarding what determines "appropriate", let us now ask: What can a person with autistic sensory processing gain from "connectedness"? Is that system prepared to process this kind of input?

In order for one to understand concepts of "alone" or "lonely", one needs to intuit, identify and derive meaning from being with "other". Further, if that need for "other" is limited or non-existent, then who really has the *need* to modify the state of aloneness to one of "connectedness"?

Perhaps it is only therapists, educators, caregivers, those of us who under-stand and *want* connection, who have the emotional need to connect.

On the psycho-emotional level, we probably do not understand nor fully accept the concept that another being does not have needs for connec-tion similar to our own. So, meaning well, we often try to superimpose our own attitudes and needs, ones that we consider essential to our own well-being, upon the atypical system that neither requires, wants nor appre-ciates it.

Recall that the brain – the mind – seeks only what it needs for survival. At the primal level, even the most severely disabled being seeks the connec-tion to a caregiver. However, there is a difference between seeking the con-nection with another for the purpose of physical survival needs, and seeking the psycho-emotional connection for symbiotic and intellectual purposes.

The state of being connected subsumes the emotional need to be with another. This presupposes that an awareness and identification of similari-ties and differences between *self* and *other* exists. Also implicated is the ability to perceive and understand concepts of states-of-mind of self and other: reading affect, understanding body language, anticipating other's thoughts and needs, and so on.

Above all, emotional connectedness requires the sensory perception of self and other, and the identification of other as a contributor to self. Also required is an awareness and establishment of self body image, and the need for external reference and validation. These elements come into play when seeking personal connection to another person. Added to this is knowing the "rules" of give and take, sharing ideas, seeking the opinions of another, sensing group safety, and making "meaning" out of connection.

Dr Stanley Greenspan (1998) discusses several fundamental develop-mental skills and the impact of sensory misinformation upon the ability to engage in relationships with others. Among those fundamental learning attributes are the factors of self body image, and the ability to create complex gestures and find meaning in gesture and body language of others.

When there are severe sensory misinterpretations, for example if someone else's touch or voice evokes fear, if balance is precarious, if there is visual and auditory fragmenting of information, if there is no tangible "sense of self", it would be nearly impossible to read another's body language or affect. Being "alone", then, is just being the way things are. "Alone" is, after all, a term we outsiders attribute to a state of being. It may have no real meaning to someone on the autistic spectrum (and many other diagnoses).

Before attempting to redirect "aloneness" into "connectedness", the *psycho-emotional* piece entwined with the *sensory* pieces need to be examined and understood. Interventions that help integrate physiologic functions with psychologic behaviors must be carefully orchestrated. One might investigate what and how "connectedness" can be imbued with sensory/psychologically meaningful information that makes emotional sense to the child or adult being treated or taught, and that can later be generalized into adaptive behaviors. The fear factor must be dealt with first, and that implies a reorganization of sensory information toward functionally adaptive, stressless interpretations.

Desire for sameness and structure

Before we take a closer look at some of the sensory processing issues implicated in autistic behaviors, let me reiterate the importance of first reducing a system's physical distress in order to allow the brain to process information as calmly as possible. One of the problems plaguing a brain that is registering erratic, inaccurate and confusing sensory information is an inability to codify, generalize, and apply what previously may have been functional responses to a new but similar situation (i.e. the ability to generalize a response to other areas). If that presents a problem, then obviously, *sameness* – keeping things as much the same as possible – is of utmost importance. (If you have memory problems recalling where to find your keys, don't you want to have them in the same place each time?)

Sameness is an essential ingredient to functioning comfortably. Ritual provides comfort within repetition of the known. Elements of "surprise" and "unknowns" do not generally yield calm reactions but rather fear, confusion, anxiety, tension, insecurity. Is it any wonder, then, that "sameness" and "structure" – routine and ritual – are imperative in helping atypical sensory systems get through a day?

When we look at our typical manner of going through a day, what do we find? Clocks to let us know exactly where in the flow of the day we are;

calendars to keep track of days, months and years; file cabinets in alphabetical or numerical order to help us locate things easily; the routines of meals, hygiene, love; the rituals of spirituality; and so on.

What happens to our systems when we meet up with surprises and changes? Observe your own physical and emotional reactions the next time someone brings a surprise guest home for dinner! What transpires in your nervous system when you cannot locate the keys you surely placed on *that* table? How do you feel when you are late, or when you are waiting for someone else who is late? Physiologic anxiety requires no cognitive pre-planning. You do not "prepare" to be nervous. It happens instinctively. And no, it is not necessarily a rational response.

Most of us require the safety of sameness, ritual, repetition. Many of us tend to be perseverant in one way or another.

When the sensory system is registering and interpreting coordinated incoming information reliably, there is a good chance that an efficient response will take place and be repeatable in resolving problems with minimal stress. The response can then become generalized, tagged for reference (by the hippocampus), and filed in memory for recall if and when similar circumstances arise at another time. In short, having once been surprised and having successfully adjusted, modulated, to resolve (in an accommodating manner) the problem of the unexpected, there might be less stress when another similar unexpected situation repeats itself. The key word here is *modulation*, that is, how the system is able to move easily and quickly from stress to coping in order not to be affected by a situation for longer than necessary.

However, if sensory information is registered, interpreted and logged incorrectly, modulation can take much longer, and each surprise dinner guest will elicit the same initial response of stress and inability to modulate (cope) quickly in order to problem-solve. This tends to result in entirely different problem-solving behavior each time. Therefore, sameness — placing a toy in the same exact place each time, arranging items in a specific way, following a repetitive schedule, and so on — is a vital component in eliminating the stress of having to "adjust" to each new (even if similar) circumstance.

Sameness and ritualistic behaviors foster comfort. A situation is dependable in its sameness. Reliability and repetition are ingredients inherent in animal adaptation to environmental forces. The central difference between typical and atypical requirements regarding sameness, ritual, and repetition, is the inability of the atypical system to modulate adequately and efficiently when things do not adhere to similar routines. In the first case, the system adjusts quickly while in the latter more time and processing is required in order to reformulate functional responses. Meanwhile, the atypical system is greatly distressed physiologically, becoming intolerant and volatile psychologically and emotionally.

Learning to translate autistic behavior

Discussing some aspects of autism in this manner is by no means an effort to explain away certain behaviors or dismiss concerns regarding responses that are atypical. It is, however, a way of translating the meaning of autistic conduct into possible sensory/physiologic etiology. If we accept the hypothesis that what the brain does, it does for a reason, then we must also assume that every behavior results from some form of physiologic prerequisite. Unreliable interpretation of sensory information in autism actualizes as behavioral havoc which, in the opinion of that atypical brain process, *is* a functional response although perhaps quite inefficient in the larger scheme of things within our culture.

This is not to say that aspects of autistic reactions cannot or should not be altered to provide more efficient options *for that individual system*. Surely any body will function more efficiently when stress and fear are reduced and maintained at a minimal level. The exploration of sensory issues implicated in the autistic demeanor confronting a therapist, parent, educator, is meant to widen the scope of observation in order to help effectively intervene and provide readaptive options to address the etiology.

Music therapy in the realm of autism's sensory interpretation mismanagement, particularly as it relates to functional adaptation, plays an important role in providing repetitive stimuli which aim to "teach" the brain other possible ways to respond that might be more useful in the long run. First, however, we need to understand which senses we are talking about, what physiologic adaptation means, what the basic elements of music contain, and how they can be applied in sensory treatment.

In the next chapter, information about sensory integration will help the reader link many aspects of autism to physiologic complexities.

References

Frith, U. (1989) 'What is Autism?' In *Autism: Explaining the Enigma*. Cambridge, Mass.: Blackwell.

Greenspan, S.I. (1998) *The Child with Special Needs: Encouraging Intellectual and Emotional Growth*. Reading, Mass.: Addison-Wesley Longman, Inc.

Siegel, B. (1996) *The World of the Autistic Child: Understanding and Treating Autistic Spectrum Disorders*. New York: Oxford University Press.

Williams, D. (1998) *Autism and Sensing: The Unlost Instinct*. London: Jessica Kingsley Publishers.

Recommended reading

Gillingham, G. (1995) *Autism: Handle with care! Understanding and Managing Behaviour of Children and Adults with Autism*. Arlington, Tex.: Future Education, Inc.

Grantin, T., Scariano, M.M. (1986) *Emergence: Labeled Autistic*. Novato, Calif.: Arena Press.

Hart, C.A. (1993) *A Parent's Guide to Autism: Answers to the Most Common Questions*. New York: Pocket Books/ Simon & Schuster.

Jordan, R., Powell, S. (1995) *Understanding and Teaching Children with Autism*. New York: Wiley & Son.

Kozak, F.M. (1986) *Autistic Children: A Working Diary*. Pittsburgh, Pa.: University of Pittsburgh Press.

Powers, M.D. (1989) *Children with Autism: A Parent's Guide*. Rockville, Md.: Woodbine House.

Schopler, E. and Mesibor, G.B. (eds) (1993) *Autism in Adolescents and Adults*. New York: Plenum Press.

Siegel, D.J. (1999) *The Developing Mind: Toward a Neurobiology of Interpersonal Experience*. New York: The Guilford Press.

CHAPTER 3

Aspects of Sensory Integration

Two simple truths can be stated about life on this planet. First, all life must display *functional adaptation* to environmental forces (i.e. gravity, energy, biochemical and gaseous influences, sights, sounds, tastes, heat, cold, etc.) in order to survive.

Second, all animal life adapts by coding *adequate sensory stimuli* – some in the form of electrical frequencies (vision, hearing), others non-electrical (smell, taste, heat, etc.) – and converting these into *sensory action potentials* (electrical impulses) that travel to the brain through the central nervous system (CNS) for processing.

In effect we animals are like FM receivers, converting electrical impulses into functional circuitry which stimulates the nervous system into sending messages to the brain calling for appropriate adaptive responses. Of course, "functional" responses are based upon how the brain has interpreted the information in the first place in order to help the system understand and resolve the issue efficaciously. Recall that the operative word *appropriate*, as stated earlier, applies to each physiologic system *individually*.

All animals, including human beings, use a two-way process in managing information:

- input enters and goes *to* the brain via *sensory neurons* (the *afferent* nervous system);

- output comes *from* the brain to the body via *motor neurons* (the *efferent* nervous system).

A human being has some 12 billion neurons! For input transactions we come equipped with *receptors* in the form of sensory receiving organs that pick up energy (electrical frequencies, heat, etc.) and transmit them to central processing – the brain (like a radio picking up waves). Thus:

- eye receptors pick up and transduce light frequencies
- ear receptors pick up and transduce audio frequencies
- muscle receptors are sensitive to stretches and contractions producing transmissions to the brain, notifying it where the muscles are and what they're doing; and so on.

A constant stream of electrical impulses flows through sensory receptors along the spinal cord up to the brain. This is *sensory input*.

The spinal cord, brain stem, the organs in the paleoencephalon (including the reticular activating system (RAS), amygdala, thalamus, hypothalamus, hippocampus, cerebellum, etc.), and the neo-cortex (the brain's cerebral hemispheres – the gray matter) register (encode), decode and use sensory input to interpret conditions and send messages back to the system for modulated responses assuring safety and well-being. Once signals are registered and interpreted instinctively, our cognitive brain later recognizes and labels the results psychologically (cortical level) as being:

- conscious awareness
- body postures
- motor planning
- memories
- knowledge
- movement coordination
- feelings
- learning
- perception
- ideas
- problem solving

and other recognizable states which we have learned to label and categorize.

Sensory integration is the system's process of taking in and organizing billions of bits of uncoordinated sensory input. These are organized into cohesive whole pictures that enable the brain to know what is happening. The brain and nervous system then apply this information towards commanding useful, functionally adaptive responses to meet existing conditions. This is how and why animals survive. Sensory integration involves sorting, logging and assigning priority order to sensory information so that an "efficient" response to resolve a problem can be delivered. These activities often involve the whole brain, old and new.

Another way of understanding this phenomenon is to equate "integration" with sensory interpretation and coordination, as suggested by Donna Williams (1998). In fact, sensory input is actually the simultaneous stimulation of every major sensory system, all the time, non-stop! Bodies are continuously bombarded with millions of sensations all at once, the majority of which the brain either ignores in the first place, or discards immediately after determining their usefulness for safety.

In the typically responding system, internal and external sensory stimuli are dealt with in a manner deemed functionally adaptive to a situation. We will learn more about this later when we look at aspects of physiologic information processing relative to functional adaptation (see Chapter 4). For now let us consider the process of brain function at the instinctive, intuitive level and see how sensory information travels through the afferent central nervous system to the brain.

Our emotional brains

Joseph LeDoux (1998) and Dr Daniel Schneck (1997), among others, remind us that when studying sensory processing it is important to understand that humans, like other animals, are first and foremost emotional respondents to the environment. The major and most fundamental concern of our brains is safety and survival. This necessitates a quickly activated feedback control system responding from the intuitive/emotional instinct level of survival. Anything that the brain senses or assesses as detrimental to safety and survival will receive top priority. Everything else will have to wait, including thinking and reasoning!

Fear of a threat to survival is the strongest emotion in the vertebrate kingdom. This means that before one can consider thought processing and cognitive brain function (cortical), one must look at brain function at its most primal sub-cortical level and see how sensory information, especially in relation to the fear factor, is dealt with at the very outset.

The journey begins

All information entering the biologic system, whether externally or internally stimulated, travels up the central nervous system within the spinal column into the *paleoencephalon* (the "old brain" – some 500 million years old). At the top of the spinal cord, the information reaches a very thick, net-like bundle of nerves, called the *reticular* (meaning "net-like") *activating system – RAS*.

The RAS extends through the *medulla* (the one-inch piece of brain stem that is the evolutionary core of the brain and the primitive site of survival instincts such as fight-or-flight), and the *pons Varolii* ("Varolio's bridge", named after Costanzo Varolio), which contains important motor and sensory nuclei for several cranial nerves. The RAS extends into the short *mesencephalon* (mid-brain).

Perception begins with the RAS. This mass of net-like nerve cells continuously sifts through hundreds of millions of pieces of incoming information that converge upon it. It is the first place where decisions are made as to what information will be distributed to other regions of the brain, what will require further processing in the *neo-cortex* (the "new" brain, only five million years old), and what information will simply be discarded as "useless" to the system.

Only that information that the RAS considers appropriate for further processing – because it is essential, unusual, potentially dangerous, action-provoking, interesting, arousing, or whatever else the RAS uses as criteria for evaluating information – will pass through the gate and be forwarded to other levels of the brain for further processing. (Approximately 75 per cent of incoming sensory information is discarded!)

The RAS is the brain's gate-keeper. It can also be likened to a sieve, through which information gains access to other parts of the organ.

Nothing reaches higher level processing without first passing through the RAS.

The RAS controls arousal, attention and awareness. How we interpret, respond or react to information stimuli, whether internally (organically) precipitated (muscle sensations, itches, cramps, hunger, fatigue, etc.), externally stimulated (light, sound, heat, environmental factors), or cognitively conjured (as feelings, attitudes, concepts, thoughts, beliefs), is first managed by the RAS.

From RAS to Ring

Next in line to receive information, after the RAS has determined that further input is required, are the *thalamus*, (the "inner room", the interior anatomical location of this large, oblong mass of brain organ located at the rear of the fore brain), and the *limbic system*. The term "limbic system" derives from its ring-like arrangement bordering the top of the brain stem, where the top of the spine connects with the brain and where the RAS components are located (*limbus*, edge or border). Here decisions are made concerning whether or not information will be passed along.

Everything that follows in the body depends on what the thalamus and ring (*th-ring*) decide. Two particularly important organs in the system are the *amygdala* (Latin for almond-shaped tonsil), which assesses emotions (and permanently records fear), and the *hypothalamus* (meaning below the inner room), which sorts and makes decisions about all the incoming sensory information, determining what will happen next with the information.

If the RAS is the "sieve" of the paleoencephalon, the thalamus, amygdala, and hypothalamus are its chief sensory/emotional reception centers. The amygdala, thalamus, and hypothalamus are in constant communication with each other, assessing the nature of incoming information and responding to fear. As long as these organs are processing "fear-induced" information, whether real or invented, the system will be in the continuous upheaval of the fight-or-flight mode. Nothing will reach higher portions of the cognitive brain (neo-cortex) until the fear and danger issues are abated.

The RAS and thring regions are intimately connected with each other and all other parts of the brain. From here originate principal motor output pathways that connect with other portions of the limbic system, major glands (pituitary, adrenal, etc.), and higher regions of the brain (neo-cortex). The paleoencephalon serves not only to maintain all life-support systems within a body, but also to control all other regions of the brain, including those dealing with cognition at the cortical (intellectual) level.

The hypothalamus is strategically situated right at the center of the limbic system. Working as a team, the *thring* (thalamus + limbic system – especially the amygdala) appraises virtually all incoming information, calling for responses ranging from immediate and instantaneous (to a life-threatening situation) to relaxed (to a pleasant and non-threatening situation). When information is perceived by the amygdala to be unsafe, the system calls forth reflexive, automatic, emotional responses, known as *fear responses*. These include alerting the major pituitary gland to summon the thyroid, adrenal and all other available emergency units to activate survival elements (pounding heart, hyperventilation, sweat, brisk movements, peripheral auditory and visual alertness, etc.).

This is done without "cognitive" input; it happens on the instinctive level. The brain does not involve intellectual processing, which takes too much time! Before a being knows what's happening, or even that something is happening, the heart is already pounding, and sweat, adrenalin and cortisol are gushing into the system, along with a variety of other chemical stimulants (catecholamines) supporting the fight-or-flight response.

Here is a simple example of this fear-induced instinct. You are listening to a lecture and suddenly your name is called. You are asked to stand up and respond to a question. Your heart is already racing, palms sweating, knees shaking. Confusion abounds. The question, mind you, is a simple "what do you think?" but the sudden state of alertness upon hearing your name called has sent the amygdala, thalamus, hypothalamus into an alarmed state. All this happens *before* you can rationalize the situation and talk yourself into fearless calm. Fear is the animal's primal survival instinct.

In the case of autism, the flight-or-fight response is quite predominant, probably owing to an inability of the RAS and the limbic system accurately to assess and interpret incoming sensory information in relation to fear of danger. A large portion of sensory stimuli assaulting an autistic system appears as dangerously threatening. That system is unable to register, modify and assess information comprehensively and reasonably.

Even common events such as a cough, sneeze, or gas pains can trigger fight-or-flight responses in systems that are not interpreting information adequately. Remember that sensory input, regardless of whether it is externally or internally induced, if not dismissed, *will* call for response. For most of us, the brain accepts the cough or sneeze as not especially threatening, and we respond by noticing and modulating away from the message (except, of course, in cases of chronic ailments or serious diseases).

For the autistic system, the brain, in dealing only with what it receives and the manner in which it receives and perceives it, seems not to have the ability to register sensory stimuli properly in order to modulate appropriate responses. Fear responses prevail. Thus, for instance, tactile defensiveness, auditory and visual discomforts, and balance problems elicit avoidance and other pertinent behaviors. The cognitive (intellectual) brain – the neo-cortex – does not have much of a chance to become appropriately engaged when the system is stuck in the fight-or-flight mode determined by the paleoencephalon.

The pendulum of the process swings back and forth from amygdala to thalamus to hypothalamus, leaving no opening for the engagement of the cortex. As long as the system is in this state, the learning of information remains a major problem. The brain is simply busy elsewhere!

Filing into memory

After the RAS, amygdala, thalamus, and hypothalamus have concurred that incoming sensory information is safe, and fear is no longer a factor, then information is dispatched through the autonomic nervous system (ANS) for tagging by the *hippocampus,* another member of the limbic system. *Stimulus coding* (tagging) by the hippocampus is the process whereby all (safe) sensory information taken in by the paleoencephalon is tagged to give it temporal significance and a sense of "sequencing".

Stimulus coding is how we know where we were a minute ago. Tagging, when accurate, is done in the order in which the information arrives. Where stimulus coding is faulty or non-functional, such as in cases of autism, strokes, or brain injuries, individuals may lack a sense of time or memory, and display sensory overload. Much of the agitation of Alzheimer's and stroke victims is largely due to the sensory overload status, when the system is receiving more information than it can effectively record and file.

Sensory overload is prevalent in persons on the autistic spectrum. Their systems are constantly being bombarded with sensory inputs that seem to come into the brain with no apparent rhyme or reason – no sequence, no temporal sense and no identifiable order. There is more information than the brain knows what to do with. Short-term or sequential memory problems can also result.

The time between information first reaching the RAS and being tagged by the hippocampus is referred to as primary, short-term or "working" memory. Working memory may retain information for as long as several seconds, although the initial "print" perceived by the senses lasts as an image for only a few thousandths of a second. Furthermore, "working memory" may choose to drop or totally ignore inputs. This could contribute to the lack of responsiveness which often appears in autism, when information seems not to be getting through to the brain (ignored signals, pictures, people, language, calls, sounds, and so on). Recent research is showing that working memory may be implicated in the process of *attention*, especially focus and visual attention.

Another potential problem with improper hippocampus stimulus coding in autism is the person's need to rehearse, massage and/or otherwise confirm conflicting sensory inputs. For example, the ears may be telling something, but the optical illusion perceived simultaneously by the eyes may be telling something completely different. Or, after the hippocampus has stimulus-coded the information, primary memory may simply have passed the information along into secondary memory without giving it a cognitive thought. (Like looking at someone many times yet never registering the color of the eyes!)

Primary, secondary and tertiary memory

The transfer of information from *primary* memory to *secondary* memory and ultimately to permanent storage in *tertiary* memory involves moving up the ladder from the paleoencephalon to the higher levels of the neo-cortex where information is filed according to its particular attributes.

In the neo-cortex, information tagged in primary memory is first re-tagged and recorded, semantically, temporally or spatially, to prioritize and further identify what the system may ultimately want to do with it, if anything. At this stage, the brain still reserves the right to discard information it decides not to retain, for whatever reason. This reorganization and transfer to secondary memory may take place within 24 hours surrounding the sleep state. (Some theorize that sleep and dreaming may be associated with the process of sorting through, cataloging, filing, organizing, distributing, and storing all of the information taken in by the brain during wakeful states that has successfully graduated to this level.)

The information which the brain chooses to keep for ever is stored in tertiary (permanent) memory. It is interesting to note that information may actually wander around in the neo-cortex for months, or even years, before it finally winds up in permanent storage. Data stored in tertiary memory remains there for life, barring brain damage and similar illnesses. True, one might have to "dig deep" to recall the information, but once it is branded into memory, it will always be there.

Psychologists have long been exponents of "digging deep" to extract suppressed memories and information. Hypnosis seems to be able to extract information from tertiary memory. Permanent memory may also have some sort of abstract code which allows for generalization and association of information and responses. Much is still unknown about the cortical, higher levels of brain function.

Opening the gates to learning – the neo-cortex

In dealing with issues of sensory integration as it appears in the autistic spectrum, it is necessary to grasp elements of brain function and how sensory disorganization can contribute to a lack of well-being. Four hundred and ninety-five million years before the neo-cortex evolved to enable cognitive function, animals survived. It seems proper, then, to conjecture that *knowing* and *thinking* (cortical function) are not necessarily the precursors to behavior. *Feeling* (sub-cortical function) is.

Indeed, our five-million-year-old neo-cortex helped us ultimately to evolve language communication, mathematical reasoning, poetry, art, nice homes, fancy meals, elegant clothing, and computers! But evolutionary survival depended first, and continues to depend, upon human instinctive and emotional information processing. Knowledge, psychology, physics, electronics come only after the system has abated its fears and threats, when the RAS and *th-ring* finally allow the neo-cortex into the picture!

Touring the neo-cortex landscape

Cognition – knowing – and consciousness take place in the neo-cortex, the large, wrinkled body of gray matter above the paleoencephalon. Why this brain area developed is still undetermined. Nevertheless, it is where information goes (when allowed to) from the paleoencephalon, for storage, combination, and human consciousness.

The neo-cortex is divided into two hemispheres connected by tissue (a bridge) called the *corpus callosum*. If this tissue is severed, the left-brain literally does not know what the right-brain is "thinking"! It is currently determined that, in general, the right hemisphere of the neo-cortex controls the left side of the body, and vice versa. It is also conjectured that each hemisphere has its own function and responsibilities, and that both hemispheres are in constant communication with each other through the corpus callosum, and with the paleoencephalon through the endless networks of the nervous system. In this manner, the whole brain achieves its infinite number of high-level tasks.

The *right hemisphere* is thought to be involved with spatial perception, instinctive and intuitive perception and behaviors, face recognition, and sundry elements of sensibility. It is thought to be generally more holistic in its processing of information, assessing the whole picture. Music, creative expression and perception, and speech prosody appear to be designated, in large part, to right-hemispheric function.

The *left hemisphere* is detail-oriented. Facts, figures, language grammar and meaning, analytical tasks, appear to be predominantly left-hemispheric functions.

The geography of the neo-cortex further includes:

- *Frontal lobe*: the Chief Executive Officer of the cortex. This is thought to be the predominant area from where decisions, intellect, reason, planning, predictions, and a good deal of language processing emanate.

- *Temporal lobe*: the check-in point for music and audition. This cortical area is concerned with, among other things, sensations and cognitive meaning of sounds entering the sensory system.

- *Occipital lobe*: this area, located at the very back of the brain, receives, defines and interprets visual information. Interestingly, in the event of blindness occuring, especially at birth, the occipital lobe can ultimately be recycled and assigned other responsibilities. (A researcher discovered action in the occipital lobe of blind persons reading Braille.)

- *Parietal lobe*: this cortical area ultimately processes much of the tactile and proprioceptive information sent up from the paleoencephalon. Tactile and proprioceptive sensory systems are discussed in Chapter 5.

- *Cerebellum*: this area of the brain is actually a part of the paleoencephalon. It appears to coordinate many motor functions (motor-planning activities), apparently maintains muscle tone, and handles aspects of the vestibular system, to be discussed in Chapter 5.

The whole brain is involved in behaviors. Both the paleoencephalon and the neo-cortex can initially interact at the command of the paleoencephalon. Although the collective regions influence each other's decisions, attitudes and prospects, incoming information will only reach the neo-cortex, and the various upper lobes, if the paleoencephalon decides to allow information to progress further. This is why it is important for clinicians or educators to understand basic adaptation at the primary brain levels.

Sensory interpretation is individual

To summarize, it is through each individual's sensory receptors that the intuitive, emotional brain (paleoencephalon) receives its signals and instinctively calls for responses. Incorrect interpretation of sensory information will provoke incorrect, atypical, possibly inefficient and ineffective behavioral responses. When one is in a constant state of "fear", when one is in a perpetual state of fight-or-flight, when one is unable to make sense of the planet or of information coming into the nervous system, then one's system will be in a perpetual state of siege. This will impact upon instinctive and cognitive behavior. Responses will be those that the brain determines are expedient responses based upon what is perceived as hostile or safe.

The paleoencephalon, especially the RAS, amygdala, thalamus, hypothalamus, and later the hippocampus will ultimately determine behaviors and enable the neo-cortex to become a player. The neo-cortex and cognitive learning have no way of functioning adequately when the system has difficulty understanding and modulating a state of distress. In order to achieve functional adaptations (see Chapter 4) that bring about calmer opportunities for learning at the cognitive level, the system's errors, discomforts and stresses must first be eased.

Above all, we humans are creatures of emotion – limbic system driven. Instinctive/intuitive behavior is pre-wired as our hard-drive and does not initially have to be taught what to do. However, we are not instinctively driven by the neo-cortex (thought and cognition). The neo-cortex has to be taught what it knows. That means first we react and afterwards we think about it! As for memory, it is believed that once an event is acted upon reflexively on the sub-cortical (emotional) level, events eliciting strong emotional responses will generally be committed to long-term memory more efficiently and effectively than those elicited through passive response. (When you are excited about a circumstance or event, you will recall it better than if it just comes and goes.)

There is also an aspect of memory referred to as *memory of sensation*, which enables neural pathways to function more and more efficiently with each repeated input of stimulus. This is known as *programmed* learning, which is what music, occupation therapy and other therapies are seeking. (Remember Pavlov's dog?) This will be further referred to in Chapter 5.

The neo-cortex is the portion of the brain from which learning and cognition, language, memory, conditioned responses, and many other activities emanate. But, as we have learned thus far about the brain, if fear, anxiety, stress or discomfort are present, then nothing – no pertinent information – will be sent up to the neo-cortex by the paleoencephalon. The RAS and *thring*, the gate-keeping system, first deal with distress, safety and survival. Only when all systems function cooperatively and efficiently at that level do the gates open to higher level cognitive processing.

In examining aspects of sensory information processing, stimulus coding, sensory integration, cognitive learning and autism, an essential consideration looms clear: the first important goal to achieve for that autistic system is *a sense of calm*, a stress-free type of information processing that will allow the paleoencephalon's sub-cortical gate-keepers to pass non-threatening stimuli through to higher levels of function. In short, the threat sensations must be removed (or redirected) before learning and conformity can take place.

Consider again Randy's humming. By using recorder and kazoo to redirect the behavior, and by calling upon the making of music as an alternative to the humming, a calming of the system was accomplished, enabling the brain to try new options of function. These were then adopted as self-altered functional behaviors. Thus, although the paleoencephalon comes pre-wired, it can still be coaxed into re-evaluating incoming sensory information in order to quiet the amygdala, thalamus, hypothalamus, and other players long enough to allow the development of functional responses and the opening of the gates to higher learning.

Music, as we have seen, presents one of the most viable resources for putting the body at ease. Elements of music (Chapter 8), when appropriately applied to meet specific goals, contribute an enormous wealth of information to the limbic system, which in turn can translate into comfortable adjustments of the physiologic system. Music can immediately become a quieting factor, enabling the old brain and the sensory systems to "calm down", enjoy aspects of sensory input and dispel fear. Music does not require "interpretation". It simply provides an environment – a sound blanket – wrapping itself around the body and providing a sense of safety and security.

The human brain, since it registers auditory information as a way of processing the environment, immediately tunes into linked sound sequences and rhythm, as will be investigated in Chapter 8. The brain "tracks" sounds and generally stays tuned in for as long as sound is present, anticipating the next sound. This gives the brain and sensory systems the time to investigate safety features. But not all sounds receive the same attention. This is why a music therapist is required to help an autistic system positively redirect itself emotionally through specific music events.

Before learning about the major sensory systems, the elements of music and their impact upon the system, it is necessary to investigate the definition of "functional adaptation" in order to understand how music therapy interventions can alter a physiologic system under siege.

References

LeDoux, J. (1998) *The Emotional Brain: The Mysterious Underpinnings of Emotional Life*. New York: Touchstone Books/Simon & Schuster.

Schneck, D.J. (1997) 'A Paradigm for the Physiology of Human Adaptation.' In D.J. Schneck and J.K. Schneck (eds) *Music in Human Adaptation*. Blacksburg, Va.: Virginia Tech.

Williams, D. (1998) *Autism and Sensing: The Unlost Instinct*. London: Jessica Kingsley Publishers.

Recommended reading

Ayres, A.J. (1979) *Sensory Integration and the Child*. Los Angeles: Western Psychological Services (WPS).

Deacon, T.W. (1997) *The Symbolic Species: The Co-evolution of Language and the Brain*. New York: WW Norton.

de Fockert, J.W., Rees, G., Frith, C.D. and Lavie, N. (2001) 'The Role of Working Memory in Visual Selective Attention.' *Science 291*, 5509, 1803–1806.

Fisher, A.G., Murray, E.A. and Bundy, A.C. (1991) *Sensory Integration: Theory and Practice*. Philadelphia: F.A. Davis Co.

Fries, P., Reynolds, J.H., Rorie, A.E. and Desimone, R. (2001) 'Modulation of Oscillatory Neuronal Synchronization by Selective Visual Attention.' *Science 291*, 5508, 1560–1563.

Schneck, D.J. (1990) *Engineering Principles of Physiologic Function*. New York: New York University Press.

Thorpe, S.J. and Fabre-Thorpe, M. (2001) 'Seeking Categories in the Brain.' *Science 291*, 5502, 260–263.

Wickelgren, I. (2001) 'Working Memory Helps the Mind Focus.' *Science 291*, 5509, 1684–1685.

CHAPTER 4

Functional Adaptation Defined

Interpretation of Sensory Information = Response

In Chapter 3 it was stated that human animals are creatures of emotion first. Our instincts lie within the paleoencephalon that monitors and assesses all incoming sensory information. The brain's reception and interpretation of sensory information ultimately result in some sort of responses to the environment, based on interpretation of incoming information. Those responses may range from a simple disregard or dismissal of incoming information to highly activated emergency reactions. Sensory input and responses may, or may not, be tagged and logged by the brain's hippocampus for future reference in combination with previously stored information.

Chapter 3 also asserts that cognition and higher cortical processes occur at the discretion of the paleoencephalon's gate-keepers, which allow the information to go forward after safety to human survival is determined. What are basic human survival needs, and how does the human system monitor its safety factors?

Four basic human survival needs

In order for animal life to survive and perpetuate itself, the brain, when processing sensory information, is first and foremost concerned with satisfying two major factors: (a) survival of the *self,* and (b) survival of the *species* (Schneck 1997, pp.1–22). These two cardinal components of survival are in the domain of the paleoencephalon (old brain), the instinctive/intuitive systems continually dealing with deterrents to survival and safety.

Instinctive processes do not involve "thinking". The instinct to react in a potentially dangerous situation (whether real or imagined) is pre-programmed into the old, primitive brain. Regardless of diagnoses, all basic survival instincts function first at this sub-cortical level. Deficits at this primary level of function can be detrimental to safety and survival. If, or when, sensory information is inaccurate or the brain cannot determine such things as: where the body is in space, where its limbs are, what's up, down, level, what's hot or cold, loud or quiet, from where sound is coming, etc., then safety and survival are jeopardized. This can result in system confusion, stress and erratic behaviors.

Therefore, teaching a system to adapt (or readapt) in a more expeditious (functional) manner is of immediate concern to a clinician. It is for this sub-cortical level that information and experiences previously unsought by the brain are now devised and administered artificially by occupation, music, physical and speech therapists, among others.

In addition to the two primary survival needs that are addressed sub-cortically, human evolution has generated two supplementary psycho-social, emotional requirements: (c) the need for *self-determination* (freedom of choice), and (d) the need for *spiritual fulfillment*. These complementary components now call for the mediation of higher (cortical) brain processing. Enter the neo-cortex. Cortical activities undertake processes of cognition, recognition, thinking, recall, language and calculation, planning, and sundry psycho-emotional assignments.

In the case of diagnosed individuals, especially autism, these two more recent requirements often play a lesser role in the survival-needs picture, if they feature at all, and may or may not be of particular interest to the whole brain. Certain limited cortical activities are, of course, essential and undertaken. These include, among other things, recognizing caregivers, selecting and locating objects, establishing routine and ritual, indicating food preferences, and other cortically-specific undertakings. However, to many persons in the autistic spectrum, factors (c) and (d) may have little or no relevance. In the long run, the physiologic system of a diagnosed individual will survive regardless of whether these latter psycho-social needs are fully satisfied. (Some of us can survive without God, but none of us can survive without water!)

Functional adaptation is how the brain and body have decided to register and resolve a given situation physiologically in order to accommodate, or satisfy, some or all of the above four fundamental prerequisites of human survival. The relationship between biology and physiology can be differentiated as follows: *biology* comprises the anatomic features we are given and have in common with other animals (mouths, eyes, ears, arms, etc.); *physiology* is how biology is used by each individual system in order to accomplish survival and functional adaptation (Ornstein 1997, pp.14–16).

Adaptation is the resulting behavior that helps the brain and nervous system interpret and respond to both external and internal environmental factors in order functionally to accommodate the needs of the system in adequately sustaining itself. Adaptation is a continual process of accommodating the body's functional needs based on sensory information. It is helpful for a clinician, caregiver or educator to understand physiologic adaptation in order to clarify and validate interventions and educational goals.

Three basic levels of physiologic adaptation

There are three basic levels of adaptation in which the brain and nervous system seek to organize sensory information in order to satisfy the myriad requirements for safety, function and survival. These are referred to (in engineering terms) as *accommodations – functional adaptations* which have helped us evolve through millennia of negotiating life on earth (Schneck and Berger 1999, pp.44–53).

Through a very complicated system of *feedback control* (Schneck 1987, pp.889–900), not unlike some of the very highly engineered mechanical systems man has developed, signals are carried to and from the brain through the nervous system, monitoring and continuously calling for systems analysis and adjustments to meet survival needs.

The following sections outline the basic physiologic accommodations each individual system undergoes all the time. Understanding these various levels of adaptation will help a therapist, educator or caregiver determine interventions aimed at developing readaptive solutions for aspects of autism and other special needs purposes.

1. Immediate, short-term, instinctive reflexive accommodation
Environmental Conditions = Immediate Action Response

This primary level of adaptive physiologic accommodation employs the characteristics of the innate, inherent, natural (inborn) manner in which the body first reacts to environmental changes as recorded and interpreted by the brain through its complex system of interoception (internal monitoring) and exteroception (external monitoring).

We learned earlier that human beings are first and foremost emotional animals, and our initial sensory responses are evaluated emotionally (instinctively/intuitively) by the sub-cortical brain for safety features. When faced with any alteration of environmental conditions, whether from unfamiliar foods, higher or lower altitudes, sudden light and sound changes (flash bulbs, for instance), it is at this reflexive adaptive level of accommodation that one immediately experiences altered sensations and behaviors (fear tremors, fight-or-flight impulse = chills, quick heartbeats, blinking, etc.). It is a temporary and immediate reflexive response that will eventually abate, depending upon the extent to which the stimulus is present.

For example, you live in London at sea level. You take a trip to Innsbruck, Austria, high in the Alps. You arrive and immediately experience light-headedness and dizziness during your first day there. What's going on? Physiologically, we are monitored by a system of intero- and exteroception – non-stop input and output of internal signals from life-sustaining systems controlling things like breathing, blood flow, blood pressure and oxygen requirements, and external input from climate and atmospheric conditions, etc.

These conditions are constantly checked (through intero- and exteroception) against the body's homeostatic reference point (Schneck 1990, pp.429-513). This refers to the "constant" levels at which the individual body operates comfortably and efficiently (60 beats per minute heart rate; 120/80 blood pressure; 98.6°F body temperature are examples of homeostatic set points for an individual system). As soon as something changes, either internally (e.g. disease elevates temperature) or externally (climate, altitude, etc.), the brain, after checking "what things are supposed to be like" at the homeostatic reference point, will call for action to restore immediately the balanced, comfortable life-sustaining levels. This is why one sweats in hot weather and shivers in cold in order to maintain constant 98.6°F body temperature. (When viruses invade, the brain calls for a rise in body temperature (fever) as a way of killing them.)

As soon as you landed in the Alps, the brain received signals announcing a sudden loss of oxygen levels. The dizziness, panting, and shortness of breath were indicators of the brain's emergency call to rectify the situation. It called for immediate quickening of the heartbeat and pulse to circulate more oxygen-bearing blood to the brain and vital organs, heavier breathing to fill the lungs with sufficient oxygen, and so on.

All this was done in an effort to stabilize your system in this non-ordinary, non-referenced environment. As a result, your homeostatic set points for pulse, heart rate, body temperature, etc. required temporary readjustment, for the time being, in order to be congruent with this new situation

After a day or so at this high altitude, these new (temporary) reference points settled in to sustain your life in its current environment. Your system settled down, you survived and had a wonderful vacation. The autonomic nervous system (ANS) did not take directions from the neo-cortex in resolving this problem. The paleoencephalon took charge and, with the help of a variety of major glands and chemical excretions, was able to coax your system into a quick modulation modifying this unusual physiologic circumstance. (The "fight" response was put into action!)

Immediate altering of internal conditions must take place (readapt) at the sub-cortical level in order for a system to survive altered conditions of any kind, external or internal (you've eaten something that did not agree with you, etc.). This is referred to as temporary, *reflexive accommodation*. New set points remain in place temporarily, until such time as the system receives an "all clear" signal (you leave the high altitude of the Alps and return to London at sea level). Then the system returns to its normal (usual pre-Alps) homeostatic reference points.

Physiologic systems undergo millions of forms of reflexive accommodation, on an ongoing basis, every nanosecond, millions of times a day. This is how we deal with thirst, hunger, cold – not to mention the myriad sensations of which we are not aware. Always evaluating against the homeostatic reference point, human feedback control systems involving the brain and central nervous system check every bit of information to determine if any alteration is needed, how much, and for how long. It operates *all* the time and never shuts down.

In autism, sensory integration issues create problems with modulation at this primary reflexive accommodation level. This causes the system to remain in a threatened state for periods longer than usual, causing panic and fear attacks which increase the flow of adrenalin, cortisol and other potentially toxic chemicals, further hindering the ability of the system to "calm down". Changes of climate, geographic location, time zone, or changes in routine and foods, often affect autistic behaviors because of the requirement for extra time to make immediately accommodating adjustments.

Here is where music, a natural sedative able to induce the release of dopamine and other relaxants into the system, can play a prominent role in reducing the flow of chemicals that keep the system highly charged. Music can reduce fight-or-flight responses by calming the system down long enough to allow efficient modulation. Paired with a music environment, a new situation often becomes more tolerable and acceptable to the amygdala and organs of the paleoencephalon discussed in Chapter 3.

2. Delayed, medium-term, conditioned adaptive accommodation

Stimulus is Persistent = Ongoing Repetition of Response

The next level of adaptation, on which medicine, therapy, and education can effectively impact long-term, is known as delayed, medium-term conditioned adaptive accommodation. This median level of adaptation reflects the body's ability to alter its behavior permanently, in order functionally to readjust to more accommodating responses for its lifetime. This level of accommodation addressing physiologic survival needs becomes a *functional sensory adaptation*, with new set standards, i.e. new and permanent homeostatic reference points for the feedback control system to consult.

At this level of accommodation, adaptations remain intact for the lifetime of that system. (You've decided to become a permanent resident of Innsbruck!) A permanent conditioned response of the system (repatterning of brain networks, etc.) will have taken place (remember Pavlov?) because the constant repetition of stimulus application, both external and/or internal, referred to as *continuous disturbance*, has forced the system to adapt in order to sustain ongoing adequate survival mechanisms (Schneck 1990).

In short, something's gotta give! If the stimulus is not going away (the Alps are not reducing their height; the music is not stopping), the body will have to find a way to deal with and adjust (become conditioned) to the input, if it is to survive. A simple example of this kind of "coercion" for adjustment purposes is the administering of allergens to a system allergic to a substance. This is done in order to force the body eventually to accept and deal more functionally with the allergen. Many areas of medicine rely on this level of physiologic accommodation to obtain healthier responses, including disease-control inoculations.

The amount of persistence of a stimulus – the unrelenting application of the *continuous disturbance* – will ultimately bring about some level of functional sensory adaptation. (You will not be dizzy in the high altitudes of the Alps for ever, but will feel strange returning to sea level.) Note that here, as in every other bit of physiologic information discussed earlier, *functional* refers to *how that particular brain and body perceive "functional"*, and this is not necessarily transferable to another brain and body. For instance, while some systems functionally adapt naturally to the daily persistence of pollen irritants, others require gradually increasing doses of the pollen to bombard the system, coaxing desensitization.

Psychologically-based therapy interventions, aimed at retraining the neo-cortical thought processes by changing attitudes and opinions, subsequently urge the sub-cortical (instinctive) systems into adopting new "set points", reassessing fear potentials and reducing overall stress. These adjustments address elements of conditioned adaptive accommodation processes that bring about functional adaptation, although there may not be conscious awareness that this is what actually occurs.

To recapitulate, autistic "behavior" is that system's adaptation to what that brain registers, perceives and interprets to be threatening or non-threatening. This will determine how quickly that system will transition –*modulate*–toward or away from smooth and functional responses to changing circumstances. Ensuing responses are based upon that system's decoding and interpretation of that body's sensory processing system. Therefore, odd behaviors, stimming, hand flapping, lack of eye-contact, tactile defensiveness, are all part of that system's estimation of need. We may never know the reasons why. But we must accept that the behavior is "appropriate and functional' to preserve *that* system, even though it may not seem functional or acceptable in society or to *another* body's system.

Several children with whom I work tend to become exceedingly upset when they sneeze or cough. Apparently it is a frightening moment for these children and takes some doing to convince their brains that all is 'safe' despite the sudden outburst. On one occasion a child had such difficulty *modulating* from calm– to cough– back to calm, that we spent the rest of our session redirecting fear responses (tears, agitation, yelps) into calmness by drinking water, hearing native flute music and blowing into the recorder.

The realm of medium-term physiologic accommodation is the major area which music therapy, sensory integration therapy and various other therapy interventions address. Ultimately, the continuous application of music interventions – the continuous disturbance – through repetitive and constant music interventions seeks to urge the brain to change its precepts. Therapy "conditioning" asks the system to accept more accommodating alternatives and eventually reset homeostatic reference points in order to comply with new sensory interpretations. Both the sub-cortical and the cortical levels function cooperatively relative to continuous disturbance. The paleoencephalon and neo-cortex are in constant dialogue, each taking cues from the other (LeDoux 1998).

The unknown factor here is *how much* intervention to apply and for *how long*. In a conversation with Dr Daniel Schneck in which I asked this question, he informed me that in the case of permanent adjustment to high altitudes, it could take the body a full six months of continuous non-stop exposure to that stimulus input – that continuous disturbance – to obtain just 50 per cent accommodation! In view of this, it is important to consider how much exposure to music therapy could effectively make even minor changes. How often per week, how long per session, what extended period of time would yield sub-cortical adaptation?

In the case of our little humming friend, Randy was given a steady diet of recorder and kazoo daily, many times during the day and every time he walked down the hall. In addition, he received a minimum of three hours per week of music therapy over an 18-month period. It still took over a year for Randy's system to accommodate its reference point in order to replace the need for humming.

The question of how much is enough remains unresolved. After all, it takes the better part of 18 years of daily school, six hours per day plus homework, to teach the neo-cortex what it knows. And that is just at the cognitive (cortical) level. What can be said is that since physiologic accommodation is individual-system specific, obviously each case will take a different length of time and may require lifetime intervention.

In addressing sensory adaptation through music treatment, the music therapist must prescribe sufficient amounts of interventions that qualify as continuous disturbances urging a system to alter its mode of operation for the better. The goal would be to urge the paleoencephalon eventually to change its ways. (Forty-five minutes of exposure once a week, even over many months, will surely not be sufficient.) In some cases, it could take a lifetime before system changes are permanent. Often, maintenance programs are prescribed as ongoing intervention to support new adaptations. There is no such a thing as too much music intervention, but there could be a situation of not enough.

3. Permanent, long-term, genetically encoded (inscriptive) accommodation

Similar Conditions Persist Over Generations = Inherited Adaptation

This level of functional accommodation and adaptation implies the repeated application of continuous disturbances over centuries, which have caused the body to evolve genetic coding by writing in (inscribing) genetic alterations. These long-term inscriptive accommodations will alter the DNA and become inherited accommodations for generations to come. That is, if you decide to make the Alps your home, and your children, grandchildren, great-grandchildren, great-great-grandchildren, great-great-great-grandchildren, and more also remain in the Alps, it will become evolutionary that the DNA of your family will inscribe the appropriate homeostatic references enabling automatic accommodation of the altitude for all your future families. This will become part of your genetic family characteristics, and many generations from now your family line will inherit physiologic accommodations for living high in the Alps. It will become part of the DNA script.

All of our evolutionary, inherited physiologic human characteristics (especially those which differentiate us from other species of animal) fall into this category of adaptation, having been inscribed over millennia of evolutionary development. (We are two-legged, have little body hair, speak, have no tails, need music…) Music therapy interventions are not designed for this inscriptive accommodation level of adaptation. Furthermore, genetic engineering and the recent decoding of DNA information could alter inscriptive accommodation to change or "correct" many survival issues and genetic disorders. (For further reading on music and physiologic accommodation, see Appendix A.)

Music therapy for conditioned adaptive accommodation

Having briefly traversed the bumpy landscape of brain function and physiologic accommodation relative to human survival, let us see how music therapy interfaces with the information presented in this chapter.

Music therapy treatment for autism and other special needs populations focuses primarily on both (1) reflexive, and (2) delayed, medium-term conditioned adaptive accommodation, as do occupation therapy, sensory integration and similar interventions. By providing stimuli that employ music and music-related activities developed to be targeted continuous disturbances, music therapy endeavors to urge the system to "adapt" (repattern brain circuits) and employ new, more functionally accommodating interpretations of sensory stimuli.

Music therapy goals are concerned with helping the system encounter and coordinate responses to applied stimuli previously unavailable to that brain, or stimuli that require special focus in order for the sensory system to understand and properly coordinate the information. The goals are similar to those of other training programs. In astronaut training programs, for instance, weightlessness is simulated in order to teach the paleoencephalon how to adjust to an environment it has not previously encountered, an environment devoid of gravity and atmosphere. (Note how much easier it is for a system with autism to navigate in a swimming pool, where gravity is altered and there is less stress on the vestibular system.)

Obviously the astronaut's existing homeostatic reference points require adjustment in order to meet new external conditions. Once adjustments are in effect, they will remain until conditions change. It is known that astronauts often have great difficulty readjusting back into earth's environment. Physiologic changes that occur in space, such as brain shrinkage, muscular atrophy, etc., must be repatterned upon return to Earth.

In fact, any skills training program involves repatterning brain function in order to accommodate the system's transformation in the face of new stimuli. It is a very common undertaking. Learning to ride a bicycle involves teaching the paleoencephalon how to handle gravity and balance under new circumstances, and urges the brain to develop new self-correcting skills. The ice skater and skier also coax the brain into learning new ways of keeping the body erect and balanced.

Most, if not all, condition-training events aim to teach the paleoencephalon new things. Daily practice becomes the continuous disturbance! Singers learn to breathe in new ways, as do wind and brass players. Keyboard artists learn bilateral and fine-motor coordination skills second to none! String players learn to perform two completely different yet simultaneous tasks bilaterally, the right arm drawing a bow while the left arm and fingers negotiate intricate patterns on a finger-board. Performing fearlessly before an audience requires that the paleoencephalon learns not to view the event as a fearful, stress-inducing, fight-or-flight situation. This is why the more one performs (continuous disturbance!), the more accustomed one can become to the condition. (However, basic fear-related survival instincts are still active...palms sweat, the system shuts down digestion (butterflies in the stomach), etc.) All of these events involve changing homeostatic set points in order to accommodate new sensory information.

Music therapy goals addressing long-term permanent physiologic accommodation are designed specifically to address issues of sensory interpretation that need re-referencing. When the brain is provided with information it has not had previously, it gains an opportunity to explore new options to bring about alternative responses that serve the lifetime of an individual system more equitably.

The application of music therapy for autism theorizes that once the paleoencephalon and neo-cortex have received new information to help generate a better understanding of sensory information, a "correction" of coding mechanisms can evolve. This would result from repetitive applications of stimuli (music stimuli = continuous disturbance). The brain can then summon new and better responses, just as the brains of musicians, skaters and skiers do.

Music therapy also provides an opportunity for the brain automatically to replace "unacceptable" social behaviors with new, expeditious ones. Once physiologic stressors are reduced and the scattered system is better organized, cognitive and social learning can take place.

The need for, along with the understanding and acceptance of, music to relieve stress and calm humans is apparently already genetically inscribed as an accommodation in human physiology. There is no culture in the world that does not involve some form of music as a medium of intuitive expression. Music may perhaps even have preceded language in humans' need to communicate and seek solace for an agitated mind and body. It is therefore a natural resource which can be used successfully to address many multisensory elements relative to physiologic accommodation.

References

LeDoux, J. (1998) *The Emotional Brain: The Mysterious Underpinnings of Emotional Life.* New York: Touchstone Books/Simon & Schuster.

Ornstein, R. (1997) *The Right Mind.* New York: Harcourt Brace & Co.

Schneck, D.J. (1987) 'Feedback Control and the Concept of Homeostatis.' *Mathematical Modeling 9*, 12.

Schneck, D.J. (1997) 'A Paradigm for the Physiology of Human Adaptation.' In D.J. Schneck and J.K. Schneck (eds) *Music in Human Adaptation.* Blacksburg, Va.: The Virginia Tech Press.

Schneck, D.J. (1990) *Engineering Principles of Physiologic Function.* New York: New York University Press.

Schneck, D.J. and Berger, D.S. (1999) 'The Role of Music in Physiologic Accommodation.' *IEEE Engineering in Medicine and Biology 18*, 2, 44–53.

CHAPTER 5

Understanding Basic Sensory Systems

More than 80 per cent of the activities of the nervous system involve processing and organizing sensory information. Animal life on the planet is constantly preoccupied with maintaining itself within a gravitational, pressurized, energized world. There is much to take in and process in order for an upright body to maintain a comfort level of function within earth's environment.

We observe that it takes the human brain and physical system at least 9 to 18 months to learn to stand and balance in an upright position and begin taking steps securely. From birth to two years old, an infant's brain is furiously developing hundreds of thousands of neurotransmitters sending electric impulses to and from the brain. In human development the brain and nervous system learn about the environment by logging, organizing and storing information received from basic sensory systems.

Three basic sub-cortical sensory systems lay the foundation for the formation of body precepts, coordination of the two sides of the body, mid-line orientation, muscle tone, motor planning, attention span, emotional stability, cognition and general sense of self. The *vestibular* system monitors and maintains the body's balance against gravity; the *proprioceptive* system, continuously interacting with the vestibular system, tells the brain where the body and limbs are, what they are doing, what is needed and why. Both vestibular and proprioceptive systems are *interoceptive* (internal monitoring) processes receiving and transmitting to the brain sensory information derived in a variety of ways.

The third system interacting with the two above is the *tactile* system, which processes touch sensations from external sources (skin) and internal sources (including the tongue). The senses of *taste* and *smell* are tactile-system relatives; smell receptors are connected directly to areas of the amygdala and hypothalamus.

Visual and *auditory* systems come into play at higher levels of brain processing. Using the vestibular, proprioceptive and tactile systems, the whole brain amalgamates incoming and outgoing information to define the world. The cooperative, simultaneous workings of the five basic systems coalesce to provide the myriad of functions typical to human behaviors.

The vestibular system

Gravity is the human being's first problem! As soon as the infant floats out of the womb it is confronted by gravitational pressures. The DNA information (inscriptive adaptation) is in place to inform the brain how to cope with the sensation of falling, and how to sustain itself against gravitational forces. You will notice a newborn immediately stiffen and thrust both arms into space as a corrective reaction to the sensation of being pulled downward. This is the work of the vestibular system.

The vestibular system is a highly complex operation that interprets body position and spatial orientation *based on the position of the head*. For instance, how does the brain know that the tower of Pisa is leaning, and not you? Because, among other things, the brain knows the exact position of your head based on sensations flowing from vestibular receptors within the ears: hair cells (cristae) located in the semicircular canals (there are three), the utricle and the saccule of the vestibular labyrinth (Fisher 1991). Ocular-motor (eye) movements are immediately organized and regulated to compensate for any head tilt.

All head movements and positions (spinning, swinging, jumping up and down, running) are acted upon by the vestibular system. Within each vestibular apparatus the three semicircular canals monitor each of three planes in space: two vertical planes, and one horizontal. Head movements that we often use include side-to-side (no-no-no) movement, side-to-side (ear-to-shoulder) tilting movement of the head, and front-to-back (yes-yes-yes) movement.

As one moves the head in any of these directions the *cristae* (hair follicles) in the respective semicircular canal, which project into the *cupula* (a gelatinous wedge that is free to move like a swinging door) within a fluid known as *endolymph*, become excited, sending information to the brain describing the situation (Fisher 1991). Any head position or head movement will stimulate some combination of vestibular receptor hair cells to inform the brain about head position and the speed and direction in which the body is moving in space.

Responses elicited from stimulation of the utricle or semicircular canals "act on antigravity extensor muscles so as to elicit compensatory head, trunk, and limb movements, which serve to oppose head perturbations, postural sway, or tilt" (Fisher and Bundy 1989, p.240).

In order for the brain to understand the relationship of the body to space, vestibular sensations of gravity and movement must interact with proprioceptive sensations from muscles and joints, and visual verification to support what is sensed. This three-way interaction enables the vestibular system to interpret the orientation of the head and body so that when the eyes are looking at an object, the brain will know if it is the object, the head, or the whole body that is upright, tilted or prone, and whether it is the body or the external environment (or both) that is/are moving. (Is the floor moving and the body still, or is the body moving and the floor still? Or are both moving?)

In autistic function, sensations from these systems may not be properly received, synchronized, accurately interpreted or modulated. Thus the person might lack accurate spatial orientation or feel as if the ground is slanting, experience constant vertigo, feel groggy or disoriented, or have low muscle tone and a sense that he/she is falling.

Furthermore, certain autism-related activities that seem perseverative to us, such as spinning or toe-walking, may actually be that brain's way of trying to stabilize the body, seeking vestibular stimulation of the semicircular canal to provide movement in space that is fast and angular in efforts to develop compensatory body posture and tonic muscular reflexes. In effect, it may be that brain's functional sensory adaptation based on feedback information (see Chapter 4).

Occupation therapy often treats autism's vestibular issues by placing a child in a suspended hammock and rotating (spinning) the child in order to stimulate the semicircular canal to provide the paleoencephalon with information for producing newly accommodating vestibular feedbacks. Eventually homeostatic references will be reset for more functional physical accommodation.

The physical act of jumping stimulates the *utricle*, the linear head-movement monitoring system in the inner ear that detects linear motion and head tilts. The utricle is in the horizontal plane when the head is upright. Hair cells in each of four quadrants of the utricle are systematically oriented in different directions. As the head moves, gravitational and linear movement forces act upon the *otoliths* (calcium carbonate formations thicker than the endolymphs in the semicircular canal), which stimulate hair cells accordingly to indicate linear or tilted position of the head (Fisher 1991, pp.78–81).

In turn, tonic postural-support reactions of the legs (extending and retracting at the knees, referred to as *downhill limbs*) are called upon to correct body position and avoid loss of balance within the vertical (up and down) plane – a very complicated process which we take for granted!

To help overcome problems in this area, occupation therapy interventions include much jumping on the trampoline. This linear activity uses gravity to provide constant stimuli (continuous disturbance), promoting the tonic postural-support muscular adaptation which is needed for maintaining an upright position when landing on the trampoline.

As long as a constant rhythm is sustained in the jumping, occupation therapists observe an adaptive process in which there is less extension of the legs on the up jump, and more extension of the leg on coming down. If there is an off-balance movement, which often occurs when jumping on a trampoline, a transient break in the rhythm, velocity and direction of head movement will occur, causing an equilibrium reaction which should elicit a response to prevent falling (Fisher 1991, pp.78–81).

The more often this jumping intervention is provided (continuous disturbance), the more adaptive the response. This will carry over into other vestibular linear activities, such as running, walking, climbing. It will also stabilize body movements and this will later impact upon a variety of cognitive functions.

In music therapy interventions with children on the autistic spectrum, the use of a trampoline to aid and abet this kind of adaptation, combined with music to maintain rhythmic continuity while the brain attends to the auditory input, is an invaluable contribution. I observe that when providing piano music in pulses synchronized with the jumping child, and reinforcing the movement with supportive pulsed lyrics paralleling the jumper's speed (*"jump, jump, jump on the tram-po-line"*), rhythmic momentum of the jumper is sustained quite comfortably. This exercise also aids in the ultimate internalization of rhythm, setting new homeostatic references of adaptive motor pacing.

My observations during this activity are that the child appears to be jumping less fearfully, instinctively applying more corrective adaptive maneuvers that are appropriate to the particular balancing act, just to stay with the music momentum! The system seems to entrain to the pulsing music and words and remains in the action. I also note more energized and organized body movements immediately following this activity, with better eye-focus and motor control. It is almost as if the brain "forgets" what it cannot do, and simply goes about allowing new events to happen!

The vestibular system impacts upon the muscles of the body, helping to generate muscle tone that keeps the body upright. It organizes postural and equilibrium responses to maintain balance on two feet, supports limbs in pushing and pulling against gravitational forces, and enables motoric modulations that help keep body movements smooth.

For the autistic child with integrative dysfunction of the vestibular system, the world is a frightening place. Aside from inappropriate muscle tone, usually hypotonic (weak), the body fatigues easily, may seem clumsy, unpaced (running or wobbling) and frequently falling. A properly functioning vestibular system keeps the arousal level of the nervous system balanced. Slow vestibular stimulation (rocking) calms and stimulates utricle information; fast vestibular stimulation (spinning, rollercoaster) arouses and stimulates semicircular canal information.

With a poorly modulated vestibular system, the child may either be in a constant state of arousal (therefore stimming, twirling, running), or limp and tired from under-arousal, or perhaps even fluctuating between those two states. Vestibular system dysfunction or misinterpretation of stimuli also contributes to mid-line disorientation, directional spatial confusion of what is center, side, up, down, front, behind, under, over.

Inefficient vestibular information processing can also result in inadequate ocular-motor activity (eye movement). This can further implicate mental image retention capabilities needed to navigate space, and to learn to write letters and numbers. It can also impact upon sequential short-term memory, attention span, attention to details, and other cognitive functions.

The proprioceptive system

How does your brain know whether you are holding a crystal wine glass or a crystal paperweight? Because it receives electric telegrams from the fingers (tactile), wrist, elbow, arm muscles (proprioceptive), and your eyes, describing properties of the item in anticipation of what would be the appropriate position and energy required (motor plan) to grasp this item. With this information the brain calls upon the nervous system to inform gross and fine motor muscles how to go about holding this glass.

In effect, a motor plan (praxis) has been executed – just enough closure of the hand, just enough muscle energy, just enough bend to sustain the glass without squashing or dropping it (one hopes!) The brain has learned these maneuvers through trial and error from the beginning of its life.

This is the proprioceptive system at work, in tandem, obviously, with the vestibular, tactile and visual systems. Proprioception is, in fact, related very closely to the vestibular system. It monitors internal activities and works together with the rest of the brain to modulate movement activities (how much knee-bend is needed or is already in effect during jumping, for instance).

Sensations from muscles, joints, and organs enable the brain to interpret vestibular input expeditiously. Among proprioceptive sensations are joint and muscular contractions that send electric feedback to the brain, letting it know where the limbs are, what they are doing, where the body is in space, how much movement and body dynamics are required to execute a procedure functionally.

There are several intricate aspects to proprioceptive activity. First, the brain must consider a sort of pre-plan, what occupation therapy calls *feedforward* (Fisher 1991, pp.78–81) – anticipatory organization of information based upon what is recalled from previously experienced similar actions, and what those felt like (Chapter 3 refers to "memory of sensation"). Added to this is the brain's awareness of *current* body status from proprioceptive-vestibular-tactile-visual *feedback*. Is the body sitting, standing, lying? Is it stable, moving? How much energy is being expended?

(One holds a filled glass differently from an empty one.) Is the arm bent, hand clutched, in a cast? This information is factored into the process of devising functional applications addressing physical deportment.

Tennis, anyone? This is a perfect example of motor planning! Playing tennis successfully is contingent upon the perfect interaction between vestibular-proprioceptive-tactile-visual systems and rhythmic pacing. The activity demonstrates functional adaptation at work.

One begins with the instinct and motivation to meet and return a ball by slamming it with a racket. Having tried, depending on success or failure, the brain continues to conceive new and better methods of organizing feedforward and feedback information from internal and external stimuli, calling upon "the troops" to reach that ball in time to wallop an advantageous return to the opponent. The "memory of sensation" is built upon, becoming better and more efficient with each repetition of the stimulus. This is what practicing is all about. One's reflexes are being trained (repatterned).

In tennis, the eyes see and scan the court with the help of head movements; the brain knows the body's position from vestibular-proprioceptive information it receives (standing, squatting, swaying, holding the racket, etc.); the hand grips the racket (tactile-proprioceptive feedback), the brain recalls previous knowledge learned both sub-cortically (muscle memory) and cortically (strategy). The tennis player erupts into running with outstretched arm ready for the backhand, forehand, or kill. Yes, the brain at all levels has been *taught* something that now becomes functionally adaptive behavior in the realm of a tennis game.

The work of music and allied therapists parallels this "training" opportunity to teach, or re-teach, the whole brain to accommodate functional behaviors based on newly established homeostatic reference points relative to tennis. Instead of tennis, however, clinicians aim to teach the brain new options relative to sensory interpretation needed in navigating day-to-day situations.

Motor planning (praxis) relies directly on the interaction and integration of vestibular with proprioceptive input. When it is lacking or deficient, the autistic child has difficulty remaining stable, complying with directives (walk, run, etc.), learning to write, manipulating items, and achieving other tasks involving motor planning. New or altered sensory input must be provided to establish better references. Older adults, and victims of brain damage and strokes, often encounter motor-planning difficulties. Speech deficiencies can indicate oral-motor planning deficits involving where and how to move the tongue and mouth muscles in order to formulate words.

Many ritualistic behaviors, requirements for sameness, communication deficits, fear of new things, lack of body-scheme and spatial orientation, and other aspects of autism are attributed to proprioceptive-vestibular-visual sensory disorientation and sensory overload. In these cases, the system may always be in survival-mode stress.

The tactile system (touch)

Touch is one of the first, perhaps *the* first, sensation activated in the womb (along with hearing). Before the development of any form of cognitive expressive and receptive communication, touch informs the brain about existing external and internal conditions, from soothing to painful. It is believed that the oral areas (lips) are the first to respond to touch in utero (Lowery 1986) and that the mouth is one of the first available information sources an infant uses to explore its environment after birth (Getman 1985).

The brain processes tactile sensations through two main channels: the *protective system*, and the *discriminative system*. Occupation therapists postulate that regions of the paleoencephalon, especially the limbic system's hippocampus and the hypothalamus, are prominent players in tactile interpretation, although the role of these regions relative to tactile-motor information processing is still speculative (Royeen and Lane 1991).

In Chapter 3 we learned that the hypothalamus (where sensory information converges) and the amygdala (which assesses emotions) in the limbic system of the paleoencephalon are in constant conference regarding incoming information. Tactile information is included. It is thought that the hypothalamus is not only a kind of gate-keeper of sensory information, but may be directly related to autonomic nervous system (ANS) mechanisms that involve physical reactions to information.

Two tactile systems – *discriminatory* and *protective* – must work together in order for the body to interact in a functional, calm, and adaptive manner to ongoing touch sensations, including internal and external responses to pressure and pain. The discriminatory tactile system, of which most of us are aware, includes receptors on the skin, in the mouth and other areas of the body that transmit information about where and how the body is touched, and the external or internal conditions of the environment (hot, cold, wet, dry, windy, tasty, etc.). The protective system responds to any touch and is on high alert with those sensed by the brain as potentially dangerous. These might include exceedingly light touches (wind, insects, flies, itches), unexpected touches (the surprise element), and sensations of pain, bruises, lesions, burning, rough materials, and other touch sensations. The discriminatory system provides information about the quality of tactile input.

According to Royeen and Lane (1991, p.123), clinicians have long suspected that anxiety resulting from stress can amplify tactile and sensory defensiveness. They believe that "anxiety resulting from stress may be associated with unfounded apprehension or fear, as well as with concentration difficulties, restlessness, and other symptoms in almost any system of the body."

A hypersensitive tactile system creates the condition of *tactile defensiveness*, orally and externally, which is often prominent in autistic children. Abnormal and varied tolerance levels for pain, heat, cold, certain food and cloth textures, and inability to discriminate textures or qualities of hand-held items are also attributed to improper integration and interpretation of tactile information. Once again, keep in mind that behaviors resulting from responses to tactile input are that particular brain's "appropriate" manner of protecting what it believes to be threatening to that body, based on feedback from its homeostatic references. Children within the autistic spectrum often require therapy interventions for tactile adaptation.

Manifestations of stress and anxiety, it is postulated, are associated with limbic system structures including components of the RAS (the sieve of incoming information), the hypothalamus, amygdala, hippocampus (memory), and at higher levels, the neo-cortex. The fear response is further exacerbated by the release into the system of catecholamines, neurotransmitters, and chemicals such as norepinephrine, epinephrine (adrenaline), and others.

Royeen and Lane (1991, p.118) cite the theories of Jean Ayres regarding the possibly insufficient amounts of inhibitory components which could monitor and modulate certain types of impulse control. They state her theory that

> anxiety [is] both a cause and an effect of the predominance of the protective system and…the problem [is] self-perpetuating…a child chronically controlled by the protective system would be offered little opportunity for appropriate environmental exploration, and this might lead to delays in perceptual-motor development.

Anxiety resulting from touch sensations, it is theorized, is predicated on the system's ability to compare present input with what the brain expects the input to mean based on previous experience (and established homeostatic reference). A person *anticipates* what an embrace will be like. If a squeeze *feels* hostile because the tactile system and brain are misinterpreting the sensation, then that person will evade and be nervous in future embraces.

When *expectation* and *actuality* do not match owing to discriminatory system mis-registration of information, the system may be catapulted into a fright-fight-flight reaction. Behaviors common to tactile defensiveness include avoidance of embraces and other forms of physical contact, clothing preferences, hyperactivity, fine-motor deficits, resistance to fondling certain objects (playdough, sand, finger-paint, hand drums, etc.). Evasive responses are often observed in autism.

Music therapy's contribution in appeasing stress and anxiety in tactile defensiveness is infinite! In fact, because the brain attends to music and becomes enraptured by its constancy of melody and rhythm, the amygdala, thalamus and hypothalamus determine that the auditory input is "safe" sensory input. This tends to foster the discharge of inhibitory neurotransmitters (such as dopamine) and sedating chemicals that calm and minimize the excitability of the system. Furthermore, sound vibrations that permeate into the music environment blanket a person, providing a soothing tactile massage that the whole brain accepts as calming. Once again the brain attends to the music, eventually allaying fear and anxiety, "forgetting" for the moment its tactile sensitivities.

Since tactile information interacts with vestibular-proprioceptive and visual sensory input, aiding the reduction of tactile defensiveness becomes an important intervention from the music therapist working with autistic spectrum systems. Once this is observed and recognized, the application of tasks calling for interaction with designated musical instruments such as afuche cabasa, natural-skin hand-drums, keyboard, and other tools of music therapy can contribute to the easing of tactile hypersensitivity. The motivation to make music tends to override certain tactile discomfort.

Visual and auditory sensory systems

The other two prominent sensory systems, functioning in tandem with the above three, are the visual and auditory systems. These operate at neo-cortical levels, including areas of the temporal lobe, occipital lobe, parietal lobe, and frontal lobe. Since the 1990s were designated the "Decade of the Brain", and the development of new technology continues to enable brain mapping, much is being investigated concerning portions of the brain that show activity during auditory, visual and motor stimulation.

Despite the amassing of research in neuroscience, it is still unclear what the brain actually perceives, and specifically how, what, and why things are perceived in certain ways by atypical populations with sensory-integrative disorientation and interpretation problems. Therapists, educators and health professionals can only assume, with caution, what the situation might be regarding visual and auditory perception.

However, it cannot be taken for granted that two people receiving the same stimulus will register and perceive it similarly, or even that the same person receiving the same stimulus at two different times will perceive it similarly each time. Two people may describe the color red in completely different ways. What one describes as loud music or bright light, another may perceive as quiet or dim.

Many people observing the same incident will each describe things diversely. This is especially true of hearing, the process of which cannot be observed. It cannot be assumed that another receives, hears and perceives auditory information as the supplier of the input intended. Nor, again, that the same information heard two or more times will be perceived in the same way each time. Audio-visual tracking and memory play important roles in interpreting sounds and images.

In most cases, close observation of behavioral responses, body language and other defining behaviors will inform therapists about visual and auditory perception processes. Many responses are observable, especially those involving visual perceptions. Many are less obvious, particularly those related to auditory processing.

The visual system

There is plenty of research literature available on the physiologic workings of the visual system, so rather than describing them in detail here, I will direct the reader to some important aspects of this system in relation to sensory integration, and to assumptions often made regarding visual perception. As stated earlier, the visual system supports the vestibular and proprioceptive systems. Vision verifies what is sensed through the semicircular canals' vestibular and auditory receptors in the ears, along with proprioceptive information from muscular contractions and tactile input.

As a simple experiment, try this:

1. Stand and balance yourself on one foot. This will probably be easily accomplished and you will presumably be able to balance for a while.

2. Now, relax for a moment.

3. Balance on one foot again and as soon as you feel balanced, shut your eyes. What have you experienced?

Generally, the typical response is one of sudden loss of equilibrium. One begins to sway and experience vestibular confusion and disorientation. Shutting down visual input while standing on one foot has caused a disorientation in the brain, even though the head remained in exactly the same position as it was prior to the vision shut-down. Also unchanged was the information feedback from the semicircular canals and the proprioceptive systems. Just the elimination of visual support played a major role in confusing the brain's interpretation of the information it was receiving from the other systems. Incidentally, when a blind adult client was asked to balance on one foot, he absolutely could *not* do it!

One can postulate that much of the motor awkwardness of visually impaired persons can be partially attributed to the inability of the vestibular-proprioceptive systems to incorporate visual verification of the environment relative to body position in space. This factor is separate from the general lack of awareness of spatial dimensions, where the walls are, what's up or down, and so forth.

An assumption often made about a visual system is that *binocular vision* is operative, i.e. seeing out of both eyes at the same time, with the eyes synchronized to integrate each of two vantage points in order to unite the information into one complete picture. We learn from the field of developmental ophthalmology that in fact a lack of functional binocular vision is often a problem in learning disabilities and autism. The information being transmitted to the brain from each eye may not be uniting into one complete picture.

Binocular vision uses both eyes simultaneously, each performing specific tasks (location, distance, form, etc.) that combine to unify image attributes into one whole, unified picture. A fly sees out of each eye independently, creating fragmented, cubistic pictures. We cannot be sure that this is not also the case in certain human binocular vision deficits, especially in autism.

Added to this is the possibility that a person with autistic processing may be receiving visual information primarily through *peripheral (survival) vision*. Peripheral vision is the act of seeing out of the *sides* of the eyes rather than using full-front focus at mid-line. Children with autism that includes visual perception deficits might actually operate from continual peripheral (survival) vision. This is the vision mode that is in effect when the fight-or-flight response is activated, because survival rests upon the ability to incorporate a wide periphery of images (the complete lay of the land) in order to determine potential threat.

The disadvantage of peripheral (survival) vision is that it often includes *unmodulated* (unprioritized) visual input (everything at once), with the brain receiving a larger amount of visual information than necessary. Stress, anxiety, fear, panic, all contribute to entering the peripheral, fight-or-flight vision mode (an adaptive behavior when bombarded with confusing information). This ocular phenomenon is quite prominent in autism and many other neurologic sensory shortcomings. Much erratic behavior results from the constant presence of survival vision, when too much information is provided that cannot be functionally adaptable. In autism and populations with sensory-integration deficits, this often translates into an inability to focus, provide extended eye-contact, or remain on task.

The absence of visual *figure-ground*, a photography term connoting focus on a subject (figure) while incidental visual information becomes background (ground), is yet another variable in inaccurate visual sensory function. (Many *un*diagnosed persons have figure-ground problems!) The inability to perceive figure-ground means that the brain is receiving all visual information without priority or frame of reference for what it is important to see and what can be ignored or dismissed.

Depth-perception is contingent upon the brain's ability to determine what and how close something is in the foreground, and what, how far away and how wide the background is. Night-vision on a highway shows how difficult it can be to determine figure-ground and depth-perception in certain situations. All lights appear to be on the same plane, so greater frontal focus is required. Other ocular issues such as determination of size and shape of an object may also be implicated in figure-ground deficiencies.

These visual problems are significant contributors to autistic behaviors and to behaviors in attention deficit disorders, learning delays, Down Syndrome, strokes, and other diagnoses. They also contribute to an inability to attend visually for any length of time, distractability, visual sequential tracking, visual memory (implicated in learning to read), and a multitude of associated difficulties.

To complicate problems further, it is often the case that persons on the autistic spectrum have visual perception inaccuracies defining *spatial characteristics*. A walkway or surface that is absolutely level may be perceived as going up or downhill. This ocular-vestibular-proprioceptive illusion directly implicates motor-planning and movement behaviors. It is another example of sensory-integration problems where the brain seemingly receives information about the position of the head, but conflicting visual messages do not support vestibular-proprioceptive transmissions.

Toe-walking, observed in many children with autism, is often an indicator of this particular visual problem, implying misjudged vestibular needs. I once saw a vision therapist (in the field of developmental opthalmology) place prism glasses on a toe-walking child. The child immediately lowered his feet and began walking on the entire foot! By fooling the brain with a new perspective (virtual reality!), the doctor was able to induce an immediate correction of movement from the brain (reflexive adaptation). The theory of visual training is that with enough prismatic input, the brain will learn (permanent functional adaptation) to adjust its interpretation of incoming visual information relative to balance needs.

In sum, visual perception problems perpetuate motor-planning issues, balance problems, attention disorders and visual overload, often leading to exaggerated movements and generally chaotic behavioral anxieties. Developmental ophthalmologists have devised interventions using prism glasses to retrain the brain's assessment of what it sees and how it interprets the information. This is called *vision training*, and includes exercises and special lenses to alter and retrain the brain's translation of visual information.

One must remember, after all, that *the brain only knows what it knows* from information it receives. But the brain can be fooled long enough to learn new information in order to adapt functionally. Virtual reality games have been fooling the brain for some years. Fortunately one does not use virtual reality lenses often enough to create permanent (damaged) functional adaptation!

The information presented in this chapter should help target evaluations and the application of interventions. The better we understand some of the physiologic reasons for autistic mannerisms such as evasive eye-contact, motor-planning deficits, and behaviors related to tactile defensiveness, the more easily creative interventions can be designed to address these issues, often simultaneously.

Knowing that behaviors resulting from sensory misinterpretations have become that system's ongoing adaptive response to input guides the music therapist onto the course of resetting homeostatic reference points to influence functional adaptation. One example is the use of a xylophone in addressing vision problems. If you tell a child to play only designated tones on the xylophone, let us say D and A, the child is actually being asked to *look for* and *find* those specific tones. This involves learning to guide the arm into playing those notes (which requires looking!), motor planning to attain those sounds, tactile information from the mallet, visual information and more.

When the music therapist positions a variety of instruments around a room, all of the systems discussed in this chapter are put to use simultaneously: it requires a certain sense of figure-ground, depth perception and spatial orientation, in order to reach those instruments on time to play them with the song calling for this action. The more this stimulus is provided, the better the brain will become at developing strategies for successfully achieving the task (as in the tennis game!)

Music therapy interventions can require the making of music and moving in specific ways to incorporate the goals of altering sensory perception. Recall that the application of continuous disturbance, which might involve playing certain instruments in particular ways, or moving rhythmically to specific musical commands, will eventually perpetuate functional adaptation. Eventually, however, could be a long time, therefore consistency in applying interventions for many repetitions over longer periods of time is important.

The functions of the auditory sensory system are discussed in the following two chapters. Obviously, processing in the auditory system is the most important factor in the work of music therapy. The ability to "hear" within the act of "listening" is a key issue in successful music interventions for sensory integration. There is specialized music therapy for the hearing-impaired population, which is specific in its use of vibrational activities, discreet instrumentation and some auditory technology. However, the work of music therapy for autism and sensory integration may differ from that of therapy for the hearing-impaired, although much of the information in this book can be incorporated in any music therapy work.

Assumptions and misconceptions about the processes of auditory perception could be crucial in the work of music therapy and educators alike. For the most part, occupation therapy only minimally concerns itself with auditory sensory decoding. It is primarily through the work of music therapy, speech pathology, psychology of music, audiology, cognitive neuroscience and related fields that aspects of *audition*, the actual process of *listening to* and *perceiving* auditory information, are investigated.

Music activities engage the whole brain at both sub-cortical and neo-cortical levels and require minimal (if any) cognitive awareness. One need not "think" in order to receive and *perceive* the linked sounds of music. As a result, music therapy has the opportunity to combine a great many physiologic theories and practices into its clinical realm without, necessarily, encumbering thought processes.

Music is, after all, intuitive.

References

Fisher, A.G. (1991) 'Vestibular-Proprioceptive Processing and Bilateral Integration and Sequencing Deficits.' In A.G. Fisher, E.A. Murray and A.C. Bundy (eds) *Sensory Integration: Theory and Practice*, 71–107. Philadelphia: F.A. Davis Company.

Fisher, A.G. and Bundy, A.C. (1989) 'Vestibular Stimulation in the Treatment of Postural and Related Disorders.' In O.D. Payton, R.P. DiFabio, S.V. Pares, E.J. Protos and A.F. VanSant (eds) *Manual of Physical Therapy Techniques*, 239–258. New York: Churchill Livingstone.

Getman, G.N. (1985) 'Hand-Eye Coordination.' *Academy Therapy 20*, 261–275.

Lowrey, G.H. (1986) *Growth and Development of Children*. 8th edition. Chicago: Yearbook.

Royeen, C.B. and Lane, S.J. (1991) 'Tactile Processing and Sensory Defensiveness.' In A.G. Fisher, E.A. Murray and A.C. Bundy (eds) *Sensory Integration: Theory and Practice*, 108–133. Philadelphia: F.A. Davis Company.

CHAPTER 6

Are you Listening?
Part One: About Hearing and Listening

There is extensive literature detailing the biological attributes of the auditory system and the physiologic process of hearing. Auditory *perception* is quite another matter. How do the physiologic attributes of the auditory system come into play in the work of music therapy? What are some misconceptions about the *hearing* and *perceiving* of auditory information that could lead to misinterpretation of behavioral responses to sound, music, language and sensory processing.

Audition, the act of hearing, is predominantly a passive sub-cortical process. Sound energy and vibrations are everywhere in the environment and are quite unavoidable. Sound perception, the interpretation of sounds, is more complex. This involves an active exchange of communication between sub-cortical processes – instinct – and cortical processes, i.e. the conscious mind. Hearing and perceiving sound, from the cricket's chirp to a Beethoven symphony, are two distinctly different and complicated operations. Not one aspect of these can be taken for granted, nor ordinary assumptions made, when working with issues of sensory integration.

It is interesting to note that both the auditory and vestibular sensory systems operate through the same organ: the ear. Sound must travel through the vestibular canals in the ear, which consist of different tubes adjacent to each other, so there is an implied relationship between hearing and balance. Youngsters with recurrent ear infections, problems with ear drainage or tubes blockages in the Eustachian tubes, could encounter both vestibular and auditory problems simultaneously.

Audition – the act of hearing

The physiologic act of hearing – audition – involves three parts of the ear: the *outer ear* (pinna and auditory canal); the *middle ear*, which transmits sound waves to the inner ear; and the *inner ear*, where receptor cells transduce (convert) sound waves into action potentials (electric signals) that then travel through the nervous system to the brain. The *tympanic membrane* (ear drum) divides the outer and middle ears. The ear drum is set into vibratory motion when sounds travel along the auditory canal and bump against it.

Agitation of the tympanic membrane sets three little *bony ossicles* of the middle ear vibrating. This starts the vibrations of the *oval window* entrance to the inner ear. When the oval window vibrates, it sets the sound wave flowing through the fluids of the *cochlea* in the inner ear. The cochlea, adjacent to the semicircular canal (where vestibular sensory cells reside), is a long, tube-shaped structure coiled into the shape of a snail. This cochlea tube, into which sound vibrations enter, is accessed through the *round window* just below the oval window, and is divided into three cavities. All three cavities coil and continue down the entire length of the cochlea. Two of these inner cavities are separated by the *basilar membrane*. This membrane vibrates when fluids of the cochlea carry sound waves.

On top of the basilar membrane is the *organ of Corti*, also called "the organ of hearing", where the receptor cells for hearing reside. It is theorized that, at this point, frequency stimuli become transduced into action potentials (electric impulses). It is believed that the vibratory motion on the basilar membrane of the cochlea produces a shearing force on the receptor *hair cells*. These hair cells lie between the basilar membrane and another membrane called the *tectorial membrane*. It is further believed that this shearing force somehow results in the release of neurotransmitters.

This event sets up spiking activity in the fibers of the auditory nerve. Action potentials (electrical impulses) commute along the auditory nerve, enter through the pons Varolii (see Chapter 3), are assessed by the hypo-thalamus, thalamus, amygdala, tagged by the hippocampus, and sent off to the auditory cortex and to various file cabinets of the neo-cortical hemi-spheres for storage, comparison, referencing, and whatever else the cortex does with the information.

It's all in our heads

Sound processing happens entirely inside the head. Neither the intake of musical sounds nor their perception and interpretation is concretely observable to the eye of an onlooker. There are no visible means to observe "hearing" take place (on the conscious level) in the way one can observe eyes squinting or focusing. It is almost as if it were an imagined phenomenon. We cannot see ears "squinting" at loud or out-of-tune sounds (except for facial grimaces). Neither can we know, nor fully control, what we wish others to hear.

Auditory perception research has, at best, been able to derive some anecdotal inferences on the process of hearing perception. This places the entire scenario of music listening into a realm akin to virtual reality, where intangible auditory ambiguities trigger the senses and emotions to respond. Viewed in this manner, music might be defined as perhaps the most abstract of artistic expressions, providing no concrete directives and little or no solid information about the planet. Music is pure emotion, and as ambiguous as human emotion.

The coding of sound

What is the brain programmed to do in relation to sound stimuli? For purely survival purposes, animals must evaluate and code sounds for three specific characteristics: (a) *sound intensity*, i.e. volume; (b) *frequency*, i.e. what we have come to identify as pitch; (c) *sound location*, i.e. from where sound emanates.

When sound is first detected in sub-cortical pathways, the more intense (louder) the sound, the more neuronal firings are emitted. This action is coupled with the intensity of pitch (high, low, etc.). There is so much information entering the system at once that it requires a compression of the auditory information in order for the massive complexities to be effectively managed. Science conjectures the likelihood that the intensity of information in a single sound is not coded by single neurons, but perhaps in the pattern of firing in many neurons. In effect, one perceives in patterns of sounds. (The brain likes patterns!)

The frequency of sound defines its quality, corresponding to our sensation of pitch. The basilar membrane (see above) vibrates at the same frequency as the sound wave, along various locations. Higher frequencies distort the membranes at different locations than lower frequencies. Pitch becomes associated with *where* along the membrane a vibratory distortion usually occurs.

Sound location, that is, spatial characteristics of a sound stimulus, is coded according to temporal differences between the two ears. A snap of the finger to the left ear would be processed by the left ear slightly earlier than by the right. These variations must then be united and organized by the brain to provide an accurate sound picture. It is thought that in the paleoencephalon, somewhere between the pons Varolii and the medulla, at a site called *olivary complexes*, input from both ears is received. This is probably the first place where binaural interaction occurs. However, the appropriate integration of sound stimuli received by two ears simultaneously, or their accurate interpretation in the auditory cortex, cannot be assumed to be functionally operative in populations with sensory problems – or others, for that matter. It cannot be precisely known what or how someone's system amalgamates auditory information.

Auditory scanning

In the vision process, the eyes continually scan a scene, determining resting points that attract attention, for whatever reasons. Essentially, the eyes constantly survey (usually with back and forth ocular movements) what is before them.

The auditory process, despite the temporal nature of sound, undergoes similar scanning activities. The brain scans the auditory picture and determines relationships between pitches, intermittently resting at certain points in sound (for whatever reasons, those sounds are designated as focal points). In order to scan sound, which as we know is fleeting, short-term memory plays an important role. This enables the temporary holding of one sound long enough for the brain to reference it with another (scanning back and forth) in anticipation of the next sound event.

Auditory scanning, especially when continually linked sounds appear (as in music), is a cumulative process. The more that sound is added to the auditory picture, the more the short-term memory compiles the information, the wider the auditory scanning process becomes. Ultimately, earlier sound will be lost to new incoming information (the brain can only hold onto a certain amount of information at one time).

The auditory scanning process is one reason why no two people experience sound in the same way. In fact, if the same stimulus is given to one person several different times, each hearing will induce different "scanning" resting points, and new things will be noticed each time. Because of its temporal nature, the fleeting moments of sound become difficult to retain; if two people listen to the same sound, person A may linger on something that person B misses, although both are being exposed to the same stimulus at the same time. At least with visual information the picture is static in time and can be perceived in its entirety, with minimal changes!

Auditory input is never the same twice, even on CDs. (How many of us have had to replay a CD band in order to "catch" new things?) The auditory scanning process is an important contributor to how a patient receiving music therapy treatment will respond. Concrete information on this process is scarce, but an awareness that a scanning process takes place in audition assists a therapist in determining whether what is being presented musically is being received "musically" rather than fragmented.

Two ears, two sounds?

Music therapists, for whom the auditory system is a major player, can only speculate that certain processes are being activated. The perceived mental picture of what is presented as music, that is, the combination of elements and sound relationships organized as "music", cannot be definitively ascertained. Nor can it be fully determined whether what is being played, sung or spoken, is actually being received binaurally and coordinated stereophonically and sequentially.

Two ears on two different sides of the head receive and process auditory input differently and within fractions of a second of each other. Each ear submits auditory input for assessment of location, distance, quality, speed and other elements. The brain collates these pieces of the jigsaw puzzle, scanning and ultimately integrating the information into a whole, coordinated soundscape of the environment.

Since each ear is located differently, obviously each will detect sound differently in terms of distance, volume, and so on. This is true if stereophonic (binaural) hearing (both ears simultaneously) is intact. In sensory integration problems, this assumption may not hold true. It is often not possible to determine what auditory process is intact, and what impressions the auditory scanning process has produced.

If binaural stereophonic hearing functions at a deficit, the possibility that auditory information will be appropriately integrated and perceived becomes highly doubtful. The brain could be receiving individual bits of information from each ear at a greater than "normal" time gap, causing an inability for the brain functionally to coalesce the information into a complete auditory picture. There could be time discrepancies between the ears, incomplete information from one ear, a lack of distance calculation, dissimilar sound regulation between ears (one hears loud, the other soft), distortion of sound in one or both ears, and many more subtle problems.

Music therapists may find it difficult to know exactly which of the various music elements (rhythm, melody, etc.) is receiving attention at any given moment. Guessing that a patient hears what the therapist is providing as a musical stimulus could be problematic to the appropriateness of an intervention. The patient may have registration and perception distortions that alter the accurate hearing and processing of musical characteristics in the manner in which they are being presented. Sounds being dispensed might not resemble those being registered by the brain. Questions about auditory processing abound and presumptions often require re-evaluation.

It is more than likely that the auditory system of someone with autism is operating predominantly on *ambient (survival) hearing* (all sounds at once). This means there is an intake of peripheral rather than focused sounds, similar to eyes functioning on peripheral vision. Ambient auditory processes may place the nervous system on auditory overload because ambient (survival) hearing has no figure-ground orientation.

As in the visual system, ambient hearing means the intake of all audible sounds, from everywhere in the environment, received simultaneously and without discernment for what must be retained or may be discarded. Here again, it could be that the auditory scanning process never actually rests on a particular sound long enough for "focus" to take place.

Non-focused ambient hearing allows too much auditory information into the system. This can be problematic. Furthermore, a keen sensitivity (*hyperacusis*) to amplitude and frequency, or *dysacousia*, a condition in which simple ordinary sounds produce pain or discomfort, could create as much discomfort to the autistic system as a migraine headache. This would then have repercussions on body movement, receptive and expressive language learning, attention span, self-organization, socialization, and general demeanor. A lack of binaural stereophonic hearing further intensifies the inefficiency of ambient hearing.

Sound coding tango

The question of how the brain knows what to keep and what to discard may never be answered. What is known is that there is a constant interaction between both the old and new brain, the nervous system, and motor/tactile responses. The afferent auditory system sends information to the auditory cortex; the efferent system sends information from the auditory cortex. Upper brain processes can influence lower brain processes, which is why music therapy becomes one of the more effective interventions in potentially reprogramming auditory system functions.

Fibers from the higher levels of the auditory pathway can affect the activity of neurons lower in the pathway, and thus alter the way that subsequent sounds are coded! In an area of the lower brain there is a fiber system called the *olivo-cochlear bundle* (OCB). Fibers in this system run from the aforementioned olivary complex to the base of the hair cells inside the ear's organ of Corti (see above) and back (afferent and efferent directions). Most of the fibers from the olivary nucleus cross to reach opposite ears (although some do stay on the same side as that ear). When this crossed bundle of fibers is stimulated electrically in an efferent (from) transmission of information, activities of the auditory neurons and other fibers in the afferent (to) pathways become inhibited.

Inhibition of the afferent system implies a limit to the information reaching upper levels of the brain. This is essential if compression of complex auditory input is not effective, or an overwhelming amount of auditory input is about to flood the brain. The neurotransmitter acetylcholine, which is an inhibitory transmitter used in many other potentially agitating circumstances (like stress), is called into action at this point (gates are being closed!) Thus, the kind and amount of music therapy sound being provided becomes a very important consideration. Will the music inhibit information from reaching the neo-cortex while inducing stress hormones to be released? And is this what is being sought?

A second very important efferent (from) effect in the auditory system is something known as *middle ear reflex*. When a loud sound is present, two muscles in the middle ear are called upon to contract (reflexive adaptation) and reduce the ability of the tympanic membrane to transmit sound. It is the ear's version of the "squint", when the eyelids contract to reduce the intake of light from flash bulbs and other bright sources. If this reflex is somehow insufficient to block sound, we put our hands across our ears to help block sounds further. Music therapists keep this middle ear reflex in mind when dispensing sound information. Allied clinicians, educators and caregivers may need to consider this reflex as well, since tuning-out is a major complaint with autism.

Hearing for patterns

The problem of where auditory information actually goes is another question begging research and resolution. The latest brain mapping technologies are able to view areas in the auditory cortex and prefrontal lobe that appear to activate with certain types of auditory input. This is encouraging, although not quite providing an answer to the question of perception. What does it mean when certain areas light up? What happens to the information, and why? These and many other questions remain to be understood. Scientists assume that some auditory information comes back from the brain to the ear (through the efferent fibers in the olivary nuclei). Some auditory information apparently goes to motor areas, and some to other processing areas in the neo-cortex.

Although much about both the afferent and efferent auditory systems is still a mystery, scientists conjecture that there may be output coming from the auditory cortex in the lower temporal lobe which projects to a structure called the *insular-temporal cortex*. This structure might be receiving input from several sensory modalities in addition to sound, and could be implicated in multiple sensory integration issues. It may also play a role in temporal pattern discriminations, and may affect activities such as listening for speech patterns which evolve in complex frequencies. Detection of sound patterns, a major interest of the brain, is clearly addressed by music therapy, which could be why music is so influential in aiding the development of expressive and receptive language.

"Hearing" and "listening"

The biology and physiology of audition alone do not provide the reader with sufficient insight into auditory perception in autism. Because the process of receiving and decoding auditory information is not simple, there are several aspects of hearing and listening that require further thought when working with sensory and auditory deficits.

To begin with, as we are learning, it is not the ear but the *brain* that hears, as it is the brain that sees, tastes, and so forth. The ear is only the transmission system that picks up sound waves, in frequencies that convert into action potentials (electric impulses) and are sent back and forth. Audition is a temporal process. This means that information accumulates over time, relies heavily on primary (short-term) memory, and disappears as quickly as it appears across a time-span. It often cannot be retrieved in its exact format.

Unlike the visual arts that are static (stationary) in time, music is a temporal art form, evolving over a period of time. It moves through time as the wind moves through space. One cannot behold a completed auditory "picture" of a musical composition at once. To perceive sound as being music, one must await the note-by-note formation of the whole, like a sweater being knit stitch-by-stitch. In order to receive music information, the brain must efficiently log in *and hold onto* each sound. It must then scan, compare and determine how one sound relates to another (pattern), until it all adds up to reveal, in retrospect, a unified form. Syntax is evolutionary in nature. Language processing is a similar phenomenon.

Hearing and listening are not synonymous. Hearing is a passive act of receiving sound. The auditory system hears everything; it picks up everything within its frequency range, including external and internal sounds. The sound we think is the ocean in a shell is really air flow echoing through the shell's curves, coupled with sounds from inside our ears. We hear blood flowing, muscles releasing, air waves seeping through ear wax, and sounds of which we are not even aware. Much incoming auditory information is generally ignored or discarded once the brain has evaluated its safety and informational features. What remains becomes tagged and coded into memory by the hippocampus and sent on to the various storage and reference areas.

The brain *hears* even when it is not *listening*. There is no way to shut out sound (except a little by the middle ear reflex), as there is with vision. We cannot shut the ears to what we do not wish to hear, as we can close our eyes to visual input. In fact, vision may be the only sense in which the input is somewhat controllable at will. (Close the eyes, all light disappears. Shut the ears and one hears from inside!)

Hearing is an automatic, *involuntary* physiological response to stimulation provided in frequency waves "audible" through the ear's transmission system and processed in the brain's auditory cortex, prefrontal lobe and elsewhere. Hearing just happens, even before one is aware it is taking place. (In certain situations one could think of hearing as an ever-present background, and listening as foreground.)

Listening requires an active interaction with the sound environment. It is a voluntary, learned activity involving interplay between both cortices. The act of listening is an auditory and mental discipline learned by necessity, experience, repetition and training. It is fully instilled in humans by the time a child is eight months old, and progresses throughout life. In listening, one attends to, and for, specific auditory information.

Listening invokes conscious, cognitive thought processes tuning in for specific information. There are several other important aspects of hearing and listening that can affect behavioral responses to sound by autistic and other special needs populations (including Alzheimer's and geriatric), discussed in Chapter 7.

Dimensional hearing

There are levels and depths of human hearing and listening processes which I term "dimensional hearing". Musicians are taught to listen in multi-dimensional ways during "ear-training" stages of music education. This factor in my own training enables me now to understand how the cognitive (neo-cortical) process of listening can be effectively taught to persons with auditory integration problems. As we learned, the auditory system influences function, both excitatory and inhibitory, in many other sensory areas. Therefore the development of listening skills can play a major role in achieving functional sensory and cognitive adaptation. Specific areas of dimensional hearing often taken for granted are discussed in Chapter 7.

Auditory integration

The term auditory integration is often used in connection with autistic behaviors, language delays and learning disabilities. Auditory integration refers to the brain's ability to decode, encode, organize and interpret all aspects of incoming sound frequencies in a synchronized, simultaneous and comfortably tolerant manner. Rather than interpreting sounds as fragments of information unrelated to each other or to other sensory information, the integrated auditory system enables functional decoding, encoding, and interpretation of sound frequency input.

The integrated auditory system is also able to link, modulate, and register sounds efficiently. Auditory information is then filed accurately into memory in a manner that will enable appropriate retrieval at a later time. Knowing how complicated afferent and efferent auditory processing systems are, it is easy to understand how auditory integration dysfunction can occur. There could be a breakdown at any point in the process.

Take, as an example, learning to say "mama." This is in fact a very highly complex auditory integration function. To speak "mama" (even before any cognitive association with the word is identified by an infant) the auditory *m* frequencies must be perceived, processed and, memorized; and the auditory *ah* frequencies must be perceived, processed and, memorized. The sequenced combination of the two sounds being linked must then be perceived, processed and memorized. Once stored, these frequencies must be accurately retrieved, rhythmically looped in sequence, one to the other, and exhaled – *mmm + ah + mmm + ah*. This will produce a smoothly linked flow of pitches in the word "mama", made possible by the efficient work of the brain's oral-motor planning, breath control (we speak on the exhale) and task execution, among a myriad of other things. This is basically learned through repetitive listening, observing, recalling and imitating. All aspects must be perceived and recalled simultaneously, and in accurate relation (pattern) to each other, in order properly to sequence individual sounds into the whole word.

The area of auditory integration function has yet to be fully researched, and deficits are not always simple to pinpoint or correct. Audiologists, speech and language professionals, psychologists working in various areas, auditory integration training specialists and brain researchers in the field of cognitive neuroscience have provided some information as to the exact nature and reason for auditory integration problems, but it is inconclusive. (Although the field of auditory integration training has claimed some success in identifying and correcting certain auditory issues, results have apparently been inconsistent.)

Music therapy is obviously one of the best options in treating issues of auditory integration and interpretation, as it is for language and motor deficits. Music therapy provides sound stimuli on a persistent basis (continuous disturbance), with available sounds encompassing a wide range of complex auditory functions. We have noted that upper brain activity influences lower brain activity and vice versa. Therefore music stimuli can affect auditory adaptations. Comprehensive assessment of sound processing by the music therapist can quite accurately place behavioural reactions in perspective with auditory integration deficits.

Recommended reading

Bregman, A.S. (1990) *Auditory Scene Analysis: The Perceptual Organization of Sound.* Cambridge, Mass.: MIT Press.

Brown, T.S. and Wallace, P.M. (1980) 'Audition.' In *Physiological Psychology* ch.6, 117–146. New York: Academic Press Inc.

Dallos, P. (1986) *The Search for the Mechanisms of Hearing.* On-line reprint: CSCD@northwestern;cscd.nwu.edu, http://www.cscd.nwu.edu/public/ears/mecanisms.html (April 2001).

Deacon, T. (1997) *The Symbolic Species: The Co-evolution of Language and the Brain.* New York: W.W. Horton & Co.

Deliege, I. and Sloboda, J. (eds) (1997) *Perception and Cognition of Music.* East Sussex, U.K.: Psychology Press Ltd.

Engelein, A., Stern, E. and Silbersweig, D. (2001) 'Functional Neuroimaging of Human Central Auditory Processing in Normal Subjects and Patients with Neurological and Neuropsychiatric Disorders.' *Journal of Clinical and Experimental Neuropsychology 23*, 1, 94–120.

Grandin, T. (1995) *Thinking in Pictures and Other Reports from My Life with Autism*. New York: Vintage Books.

Gray, P.M., Kraus, B., Atema, J., Payne, C.K. and Baptista, L. (2001) 'The Music of Nature and the Nature of Music.' *Science 291*, 5501, 52–54.

Hargreaves, D.J. (1986) *The Developmental Psychology of Music*. Cambridge, UK: Cambridge University Press.

Hodges, D. (ed) (1996) *Handbook of Music Psychology*. Second edition. San Antonio, TX: IMR Press.

Holden, C. (2001) 'How the Brain Understands Music.' *Science 292*, 5517, 623.

Kaas, J.H., Hackett, T.A. and Tramo, M.J. (1999) 'Auditory Processing in Primal Cerebral Cortex.' *Current Opinion in Neurobiology 9*, 2, 164–170.

Lipscomb, S.A. and Hodges, D.A. (1996) 'Hearing and Music Perception.' In D.A. Hodges (ed) *Handbook of Music Psychology*. Second edition. San Antonio, TX: IMR Press.

Pinker, S. (1994) *The Language Instinct: How the Mind Creates Language*. New York: Harper Perennial.

Recanzone, G.H. (2000) 'Spatial Processing in the Auditory Cortex of the Macaque Monkey.' *Proceedings of the National Academy of Sciences of the USA 97*, 22, 11829–11835.

Rivlin, R. and Gravelle, K. (1984) *Deciphering the Senses: The Expanding World of Human Perception*. New York: Touchstone Books/Simon & Schuster, Inc.

Romanski, L.M., Tian, B., Fritz, B., Mishkin, M., Goldman-Rakic, P.S. and Rauschecker, J.P. (1999) 'Dual Streams of Auditory Afferents Target Multiple Domains in the Primate Prefrontal Cortex.' *Nature Neuroscience 2*, 12, 1131–1136.

Schneck, D.J. (1990) 'The Sensory Systems of Environmental and Somatic Perception.' In *Engineering Principals of Physiologic Function*. New York: NYU Press.

Schroeder, C.D., Lindsley, R.W., Specht, C., Marcovice, A., Smiley, J.F. and Javitt, D.C. (2001) 'Somatosensory Input to Auditory Association Cortex in the Macaque Monkey.' *Journal of Neuphysiology 85*, 3, 1322–1327.

Seashore, C.E. (1967) *Psychology of Music*. New York: Dover Publications, Inc.

Sloboda, J.A. (1985) *The Musical Mind: The Cognitive Psychology of Music*. New York: Dover Publications, Inc.

Tannenbaum, B. and Stillman, M. (1973) *Understanding Sound*. New York: McGraw Hill Book Co.

Tian, B., Reser, D., Durham, A., Kustov, A. and Rauschecker, J.P. (2001) 'Functional Specialization in Rhesus Monkey Auditory Cortex.' *Science 292*, 5515, 290–293.

Tramo, M.J. (2001) 'Music of the spheres.' *Science 291*, 5501, 54–56.

Williams, D. (1998) *Autism and Sensing: The Unlost Instinct*. London: Jessica Kingsley Publishers.

CHAPTER 7

Are You Listening?
Part Two: Dimensional Hearing and Erroneous Assumptions

About Jason

Jason was four years old when he entered the music therapy environment. His diagnosis was PDD/autism, with no expressive language and with undetermined receptive language capabilities. His parents complained that Jason often showed little response to being called by name. They thought he might have hearing problems but audiologists found his hearing to be "normal".

Jason's deportment showed many signs of autism, including flailing arms, facial grimaces, limited eye-contact, oblivion to environment and presence of others, motor-planning deficits, some dyspraxia (lack of motor coordination), quick and chaotic movements in space, tactile defensiveness. His parents sought music therapy because the child "seemed to indicate enjoyment of music, and could sit still when the TV was on, as long as there was music." Music-based programs and commercials seemed to keep him engaged for limited periods of time.

Despite his apparent "enjoyment" of music, however, Jason's responses in the music therapy studio were far from enthusiastic. As long as the piano was playing, with or without therapist sing-along, Jason either remained crouched in the corner or satellited about the room screaming in teary-eyed agitation. This continued over several subsequent sessions. Music did not appear to be a physiologically "soothing" situation for this child. Efforts on the therapist's part to mimic his behavior by reflecting his actions in sounds, or defining them in sung word associations (a standard recommended intervention), brought only more distress and chaotic behaviors.

Changes in volume, tempo (speed) or rhythmic pattern, or presentation of recognizable nursery songs seemed only to exacerbate the problem. Jason would hold his hands to both ears, screech some half-audible sounds, and become completely distraught; he would not come near the therapist or the piano. He simply shut down.

How could music be the answer to calming this system into eliminating fear responses if Jason's reaction was total panic and rejection of live music? His parents indicated that his hearing was fine except for possibly some, although inconsistent, hyperacusis (unusually acute hearing). At times certain peripheral sounds, noises, or whispers would cause him to become distracted, added Mom and Dad. Did he have dysacousia, a condition in which ordinary sounds produce discomfort or even pain? Was it just loud sounds that disturbed him? His parents acknowledged that his "sensitivities" were not consistently evidenced. The overwhelming noises of shopping malls certainly distressed him. On the other hand, loud sirens or cars honking seemed not to disturb him. It was also not usual for him to become startled by sudden loud sounds.

After several sessions spent exploring a variety of musical ranges, dynamics, tempi, styles, Jason showed only slight changes in his discomfort. Then, in one session some six weeks into therapy, Jason spotted a new item hanging on the instrument rack – a gong. Without delay, in a moment of apparent curiosity, he slammed the mallet at the gong, sending an unbearably loud sound around the room. The gong reverberated for quite some time. Jason smiled but did not flinch! He walloped it once again. I flinched, parents reacted, Jason laughed. He was enamored with this gong, apparently completely unfazed by its intense volume.

What was it about his hearing perception that made him scream at the piano yet become happily excited at this incredibly loud gong? Why could he tolerate this? (Was his middle ear reflex not functioning?) How did sound properties between the piano and this gong differ to his brain? What was Jason's auditory system about? What *was* he hearing?

Some common erroneous assumptions

The most important tools of music therapy directly impact upon the auditory system. In Chapter 6 we read that the complex process of hearing and sound perception cannot be openly viewed nor fully comprehended. This makes it all the more important for a clinician, teacher, or caregiver to make no assumptions regarding the process of hearing. Although it is easy to assume that a person "hears" musical information in the same manner in which it is presented, this may be a fallacy. Since auditory scanning is individual, as pointed out earlier, each person detects and "rests" upon different aspects of sonic information.

Here are a dozen possible misconceptions often harbored:

1. Music is always fun.

2. The content of a recognizable tune is being perceived by another in the same format in which it is being presented by the therapist.

3. Any instrumentation would be enjoyable and tolerable because the live interaction of music, therapist and patient is of primary importance.

4. Hearing the therapist sing is pleasant.

5. Lyrics are being understood for their associations and meanings.

6. The singing voice timbre is tolerable.

7. Singing along with a tune would add enjoyment and cognitive meaning to the experience.

8. Hearing one's name and actions expressed vocally in sung format constitutes a supportive and nurturing atmosphere.

9. Connection and closeness is needed by the patient.

10. Harmonic, rhythmic and melodic lines are being perceived as such.

11. The person will respond to the music according to the intent of the therapist.

12.   The person will automatically recognize *self* in the music-making process.

In fact, to assume that his or her music intervention has built-in success indicates an exceedingly high level of optimism on the therapist's part. Unfortunately there is more to this than meets the ear! A musical relationship is based on sound and *the ability functionally to receive and perceive sounds as they are intended*. That this is actually happening cannot be assumed! Sounds permeated by an intervention may be extraordinarily difficult to process accurately by the auditory system of a person with autism and sensory deficits.

Therefore, the obvious first step in the process of assessing behaviors and developing interventions for a person with autism is to *make no assumptions*. If any assumption were to be made, it would be that nothing is working as well as it could or should be. The fact that someone "hears" is by no means an indicator of exactly *what* they "hear". Some basic auditory integration problems that must be considered are listed below. Given all we have learned thus far about brain function, adaptation, sensory systems, and complexities of auditory processing, there is a need to investigate some of the following areas of audition when addressing autism.

Auditory tracking

Problems in auditory tracking have implications for language learning. How one sequentially tracks sounds determines the sense one makes of sound patterns. It was earlier stated that sound intake is a *temporal* experience. In this cumulative process, the brain tracks, re-creates and determines relationships between the sounds it receives, filing this information *in the exact sequence in which it was first received*, and according to individual characteristic, for later use and comparison.

The hippocampus of the paleoencephalon has the responsibility of sequentially tagging – coding – each piece of auditory input (like a hat-check girl tagging each hat and coat in the sequence in which items were received). The brain also *discriminates* between sounds, determining language sounds as being different from bird calls or music, music being a continuous looping of sounds unlike speech's stops and starts.

In the previous chapter, we touched upon the act of *auditory scanning.* Working memory (short-term, primary memory) is required in order to "hold onto" the information so that previous sounds can be linked to present ones. The auditory system scans sounds as the visual system scans sights, focusing on different items, back and forth, in and out (dimensionally), resting every now and then on certain sounds. The more sonic information is presented, the more scanning is involved.

Auditory tracking means that the brain follows, and keeps "track" of, the sequence in which each sound enters its domain, bit by bit in a linear temporal system. The sounds $m + ah + m + ah$ are tracked one by one, blended in association with each other, to be conjured later as the word *mama.* Music, perhaps even the sung version of *ma-ah-ah-mah* is tracked in this manner. One sound (pitch) followed by another and another, going up and down in inflected or "melodic" manner, related one to the other in a linear (temporal) and rhythmic design, could turn out to be a familiar tune.

Meaning, in language, is predicated upon the way sounds are perceived in sequential relationship to one another. Similarly in music, the ability to recognize tunes depends on the retention in short-term memory, and the immediate sequential reconstruction, of melodic tones *in exactly the same manner in which tones were coded upon entry* into the sensory system. In other words, we hold in short-term memory (in computer terms, our RAM) one tone in order to combine it to the next, and the next, and so on. This linear temporal tracking of auditory input is entirely dependent on the brain's ability to retain and reconstruct, in the exact sequence, what it just "heard". In effect, the listener to music or language is re-composing and repeating simultaneously, in his or her own head, the music or sentence just heard.

For a person with autistic spectrum sensory-integration disorders, this linear aspect of auditory processing, or auditory tracking, i.e. the ability accurately to follow a presented sequence, may be a crucial deficit to language learning. In fact, it should not be taken for granted that this process is operating functionally in any of us, diagnosed or undiagnosed! (Tone deafness is, among other things, an inability to track, discriminate, retain in working memory, and accurately reconstruct exact pitches in correct sequential and tonal order.)

A music therapist, educator, or caregiver cannot be certain, for instance, that the "tracking" is picking up and processing proper sequences of sounds reflective of what is being presented. What if there is such a thing as "auditory dyslexia"? There seems to be no term for a phenomenon in which sounds are retrieved in incorrect order (as in reading dyslexia). This does not mean that such a problem does not exist. I use the term *dysmusia* (different from *amusia*) to refer to an anomalous impairment of the ability to track, perceive and retrieve musical tones in relational sequence constituting a "tune". Suppose *dysmusia* causes sounds to be retrieved in reverse, non-sequential or scattered order? Suppose a child with autism *can* understand language but owing to a condition of *dysmusia*, the sequential tracking of language sounds actually skips every third sound or word, submitting incorrect information to memory for recall?

Assumptions regarding accuracy in hearing and listening must be held in abeyance when treating autism with music interventions. What appears as "musical input" to a typical person may not be musical at all to a system with auditory tracking problems.

The complexity of auditory tracking involves both receptive and expressive language deficits. Coupled with oral-motor problems in speech delays, auditory tracking may be one predominant reason why autistic children have difficulty hearing, recalling, imitating or sequencing verbal sounds. Auditory tracking also plays a role in the brain's ability to perceive whether sounds are "safe", "threatening", "essential".

Music therapy interventions can present "listening" activities focused on training the brain to listen, recall and imitate sequential sounds more efficiently. Some of these interventions are adaptations, for this population, of ear-training activities used in the training of musicians. These may involve listening for specific elements such as bass tones, inner voices, or nuances and cues calling forth certain actions. Gaining astute listening and sound-retrieval skills can also stimulate oral-motor planning for vocal sound imitation.

The challenge is to enable the transfer of music tracking abilities into speech tracking centers of the brain. If theories about brain plasticity hold true, then music, being a whole-brain activity, should be able eventually to influence both the paleoencephalon and the neo-cortex into adopting functional responses (set new homeostatic references) by patterning new brain connections for more functional auditory tracking.

The majority of non-verbal children I treat eventually begin forming word sounds. One boy, eight-year-old Marty, with whom I have been working for over four years, in two weekly 45-minute sessions, was so enthusiastic about imitating sounds that he actually began developing recognizable speech sound patterns and inflections as a direct result (I believe) of learning to track and imitate musical sounds. It was nice to share with his speech pathologist the discovery that Marty's language processing issues were based more on deficient oral-motor planning than on auditory tracking.

On the other hand, pitch memory and linear auditory tracking may be so astute that the listener has "perfect pitch". That means that the pitches heard once are recalled *exactly as memorized*, even in the absence of musical instruments for cuing the original pitch. Pitches are also memorized in the key in which a tune (or word) was originally presented, and in the exact original sequence. It is often impossible for a person with perfect pitch memory to tolerate pitches that are "off key", out-of-tune, sung or spoken by a new person, or otherwise different from what was originally presented, and this becomes a whole new kind of problem.

Ethan, a ten-year old PDD child with perfect pitch memory but limited expressive language, screamed when a song happened to be played in a key other than that in which it was first presented. To complicate things further, Ethan had difficulty recognizing common words if they were spoken in new or varied prosody or vocal timbres from the one in which he originally heard them. Sung sentences were retained and imitated accurately, but depended on the "tune" being in the same key, with the same inflections every time!

In Ethan's case, among the goals for functional adaptation was included the teaching of his brain to "tolerate" and become conditioned to the variables of alternative pitches, voices, instruments and keys. Several approaches were used and eventually he was able to allow changes. It did not alter his perfect pitch, however, which has since become an asset in his actual music training (he is a violinist).

Auditory discrimination and memory

Implicated in auditory tracking processes are auditory discrimination and auditory memory. The ability to discriminate between frequencies and timbres and to recall the exact sequence of auditory information that was initially presented may require intervention. As we now know, the hippo-campus (in the paleoencephalon) tags all incoming sensory information, presumably in the order in which it enters the central nervous system. If tagging is faulty and information is coded incorrectly, the memory and recall will obviously be faulty, non-sequential and possibly completely meaningless.

Often with autism, tagging of ambiguous sounds with little or no requirement for cognitive interpretation (e.g. music) seems more opera-tional than tagging of language sounds (i.e. word sounds). The English language employs extremely high frequency sounds (*T, F, P* being some of the highest) which the brain with auditory integration issues may be unable accurately to discriminate (differentiate) and recall. Discriminating *B* from *P, F* from *S*, is difficult enough for typical folk! There is a reason that one clarifies: "P as in Peter," "B as in boy."

Fanny, a pre-schooler with expressive and receptive language delays and cognitive deficits was brought for music therapy auditory evaluation. Mother and teachers seemed convinced that some of the child's delays were in the area of comprehension of receptive language. According to them, the child did not respond well to time-based questions involving words such as "before" and "after". Everyone involved was convinced that there was a cognitive problem. Music therapy sessions during the six-week evaluation period were focused on investigating auditory integration, expressive language and cognition.

Interventions involving repetition of sound sequences, musical cues and movement tasks, activities using instruments and singing were developed to meet evaluation goals. It soon became obvious that aside from being an excellent musician, this young child had difficulty speaking certain alphabet letters, including *L* and *F*. Fanny had as yet been unable to say her name, or fill in the word "farm" in the Old MacDonald song. During one session, I asked Fanny, "and what are you doing after music class today?" (an obvious "before" and "after" question.) Fanny answered, "I play bells and drum." Fanny's mother assumed the child simply did not understand the question.

However, based on Fanny's high-level interaction with music, her keen recognition of songs, her metronomic sense of rhythm, and her general responsiveness to interventions, it was difficult to assume she had a low level of cognitive function. She was, after all, a very bright child and musically ingenious. Her auditory tracking for music seemed intact, since she was able to follow, sing and recognize familiar tunes. However, her tracking ability for language sequences was still undetermined. Perhaps she had not *heard* the words of the question correctly?

The question was presented to Fanny once again, but in another format: "when we are done with music, what will you do?" Now, without hesitation, Fanny promptly responded, "I going to Sarah's house!" Aha! Fanny's mother was actually surprised at the response. I suggested in my report that Fanny's problem may not necessarily be one of cognitive deficit but rather of auditory processing and auditory integration deficiencies. (Recall that the brain only knows what it receives!)

Fanny's auditory tracking, discrimination, decoding and recall mechanisms would require further investigation. Quick-paced speaking patterns of parents, teachers, others, and various vocal timbres might be impeding Fanny's auditory processing. (We talk slow-speak when addressing a foreigner to help the person process and understand meaning! Perhaps we need to apply this mode to persons with auditory integration deficits as well.) To Fanny's ears, English was a foreign language, probably spoken much too fast for her brain to grasp and imitate.

Since Fanny had difficulty speaking *F*, it could also be true that she had difficulty hearing and processing the sound of *F*, especially if it appears in the middle of a word ("a*f*ter"). The *F* sound is extremely high frequency. It is possible that Fanny heard my original question as "and what are you doing *at the* music class today?" hearing "at the" instead of "after."

Auditory discrimination is one of the aspects of hearing and listening most often taken for granted. It is one of the foundations of language perception and learning, and must be investigated by music therapists working with language delays, stroke victims and others with brain damage. Unlike language, music does not challenge the neo-cortex to interpret, provide meaning or comprehend information. (It is more user-friendly than language.) Music can be coded as it is – sound events that make "sense" regardless of sequential accuracy or recall. Music is intuitively understandable and not threatening to cognitive processes when it is heard in non-threatening ways.

As a resource for auditory discrimination, music plays an invaluable role in training the ear to scan, listen for, and hear differences in frequencies, textures, dynamics and other auditory subtleties, as long as therapists are aware of potential deficits, and design interventions specifically to address these through music.

Auditory figure-ground

Figure-ground, as we learned in a previous discussion of vision, is a term borrowed from photography that refers to what we hear in the foreground while putting other non-essential sounds in the background. In her book, *Autism and Sensing: The Unlost Instinct* (1998), Donna Williams, an autistic with high-functioning cognition, refers to the issue of figure-ground not as a "dysfunction" but as an ability to *hear all sounds equally* and often in smaller fragments than is the "norm".

Although Williams considers this to be an asset, it can, nonetheless, be an impediment for someone less "cognitively" able. Many sound sensitivities in younger autistic persons are due largely to a lack of figure-ground discrimination ability – the inability of the brain to "tune out" unessential sounds. This problem makes a wall of sound unbearably difficult to manage.

To someone devoid of auditory figure-ground perception, the slightest rustle of leaves is equal to the barking of a dog, and they will be unable to discern the importance of one sound and the unimportance of the other. When a music therapist who, after all, is basically providing a "wall of sound", senses a figure-ground issue, he or she will alter the intervention to address this specific problem. It can be done in a variety of ways, from eliminating lyrics to intervening with single-sound instrumentation (solo flute, xylophone, recorder, violin, guitar, etc.), or unaccompanied voice.

The manner of intervention depends on the therapist's ability to recognize and evaluate the deficit in order to determine goals and objectives that can address the issue of urging the system to "functionally adapt" in a new manner (new homeostatic references). Auditory figure-ground games using various instruments, and music/movement activities adapted from various music education methods (e.g. Dalcroze, Kodaly, Orff) can be applied for assessment and intervention purposes.

Auditory focus

Related to auditory figure-ground orientation is the element of auditory focus. What one elects to *listen to*, *rest upon* and *hear* within a soundscape becomes the focus of the hearing process – the auditory focus. For instance, in a tune such as "The Alphabet Song", what element(s) of the song does one tune in to? The tune? The words? The rhythm? The harmony? All of the above?

Generally, when a tune is played without sung lyrics the instinct is to focus upon and track – pay attention to – the melody (in the foreground). Rhythm is instinctively internalized (foot-tapping). Harmony, for the most part becomes "background". (How many of us can sing back inner harmony voices without being trained to hear them?)

Musicians are specifically trained and adept in auditory focus skills, having learned to focus on musical details. As a result, a trained musician can usually recall many more elements of a tune than a non-trained listener who is simply allowing instinct to guide the listening.

When language and attention problems are present, auditory focus could be a cause or a result. The music therapist aware of this possibility provides interventions to evaluate and develop auditory focus skills. Such interventions could again be adaptations of ear-training and movement tasks used in the education of musicians.

Auditory depth perception and auditory sound location

These issues are self-explanatory. The first thing our brain does when it perceives sound is to determine *where* that sound is coming from and *how far* away it is. Also determined are how many different sounds there are, and what sounds are in the foreground. Dimensional hearing is a basic survival skill at the primary level of functioning. In addition to what kind of sound, the questions of where a sound is, and how near are the primary pieces of information that help determine whether one runs away or stays put (see Chapter 6).

Although it would be nice to assume that all brains function "normally" with regard to sound location and depth perception, the fact is that populations with auditory sensory deficits do not necessarily have the ability to assess accurately either the location or distance of a sound. As music therapists know, when listening to a song combining melody with harmony, the "harmony" (from the dimensional depth perception perspective) is further away, and multidimensional. Harmony maintains a vertical architectural structure, becoming a background wall made up of superimposed tones layered one upon the other, in front of which a melody dances. This structure of vertical sounds moves with the melody in a horizontal manner across time.

The superimposition of a melody, moving in a linear horizontal plane, seems to appear in the foreground. Chords add depth perspectives. The higher notes of a chord seem closer to the ear than the lower notes within a chord hierarchy. Also, lower frequencies require more audibility (volume) and focus than higher frequencies. Like figure-ground, auditory depth perception is an important influence on the learning of language.

When the brain cannot adequately determine from where the sound is coming, how much of what kind it is, how close it is, and what parts are important, the brain may simply dismiss the information or order the body to go on alert. That means stress, survival codes, cortisol and chaos. The problem with auditory-depth perception deficits is that the system is almost always in this survival alert. This fight-or-flight mode, directly related to auditory confusion, causes erratic fear responses.

Auditory integration reviewed

Before continuing into areas that involve auditory interaction with other sensory systems, let us recap problems of auditory integration as presented in these last two chapters on hearing and listening:

- There may be a *lack of binaural* stereophonic hearing.

- The system may be in a constant state of *ambient (peripheral) hearing*.

- There may be *unsynchronized auditory input*; one ear may be receiving and processing information before the other, in a greater than usual disparity which the brain has difficulty synthesizing.

- There may be poor *scanning* and a *lack of auditory focus* in relation to *figure-ground orientation*; all sounds may appear to be equally important.

- There may be *auditory tracking inefficiencies*; sounds may be heard or retrieved in a non-sequential manner (*dysmusia*); erratic tracking and skipped sounds could mean difficulty with short-term sequential memory coding.

- Auditory processing may be too slow to code appropriately the volume of information being transmitted or received.

- There may be inability to perceive certain frequencies; there may be a hypersensitivity (*hyperacusis*) or *dysacusia* to certain pitch frequencies.

- There may be *auditory discrimination* difficulties: difficulty discerning and looping sounds for language learning.

- There may be an inability to blend sounds one to another, hearing disparate sounds rather than blended, patterned groupings.

How and what one hears will determine physiologic responses and external behaviors. Sounds perceived as being fragmented, too loud, too fast, can induce fight-or-flight responses. Music therapy efficaciously addresses many of these auditory problems when these are properly diagnosed.

Jason revisited

Let us return to Jason, and to the questions that arose about his response to music. Certain questions seem obvious: Did Jason understand "Hello"? Did he actually perceive the *Hello* word as it was sung in synchrony with the piano music? Was his auditory system sequentially processing the melodic contour accurately? Was he able to separate the words in figure-ground from the piano accompaniment in background? Was he being assaulted by a wall of sound so that his middle ear reflex caused him pain? Was it something about the piano? Did he have perfect pitch and pick up that the piano was out of tune? Was it the auditory combination of both piano and voice? Timbre of the voice? Levels of frequencies? Too much melodic contour? Too high or too low or both in frequency dimension? In addition to auditory information, were the piano/voice vibrations also providing tactile and proprioceptive input, sending his entire sensory system into overload?

Since the overwhelming volume of the gong was not disturbing to Jason, consideration of volume, for the moment, could be put on hold. His parents had indicated that loud honks or sirens did not especially disturb him. Perhaps there was something about his middle ear reflex. It was also quite conceivable that sensory information from the complex nature of piano sounds might have generated overbearing stimulation, engaging several of Jason's sensory systems and causing him to seek refuge.

His auditory requirements needed further thought. Soon after his gong sound, I reached for my recorder (a blown instrument, like a flute), and began playing long, slow, mid-range tones. After a while, these long, slow tones gave way to recognizable children's tunes ("Twinkle Twinkle," etc.). Jason turned away from the gong toward me. I continued playing the recorder. His demeanor began to change as he remained interested in what this instrument and I were doing. (So perhaps pitch and instrumental timbre were issues.)

The more I played recorder, the longer Jason remained transfixed, observant, attendant. He rejected the opportunity to join in with hand instruments such as maracas, bells, claves, preferring to listen. He remained in this manner for about six minutes. At last, I thought, his system seemed to be relinquishing its survival behavior.

I continued to play the recorder as I moved toward the electric keyboard. I programmed simple sounds on the keyboard (flute, xylophone). I continued on the keyboard, playing simple improvised tunes on the simulated flute interspersed with mid-range xylophone. Jason remained in his original location, but turned to look at me as I played the keyboard. Our session continued with my playing and occasionally inter-jecting brief la-la-la sing-song non-verbal vocal sounds. Jason seemed tolerant and pacified, and remained quiet. He did not reach for the gong again during this session (although in other sessions, he did announce his preference for the gong), and did not play other hand instruments strewn about the floor. (Could he do physical and auditory activities together?)

This session concluded with guitar and a familiar tune from a popular local children's TV program, which he seemed to recognize. He seemed not to object to guitar sounds. His comfort state remained pacified and our session ended calmly. Future sessions eliminated use of the piano, and commenced with recorder; he also obtained a recorder and blew it as an initial activity. The piano has been carefully reintroduced into our sessions, but sparingly, with only unaccompanied melodic output.

The question is, why could Jason tolerate the incredibly loud gong, and the quiet simplicity of the recorder, but not the quiet piano and singing? One could say that Jason's early responses were reactions to unfamiliar or unexpected people and activities. Perhaps fear of the unknown, fear or dislike of therapist environment, or other variables had disturbed earlier sessions. This could be true, except that as many as five months after Jason's first visit, although tolerance and acceptance of the piano/song environment seemed increased with each exposure, his reaction to piano, even without song, displayed discomfort.

Recorder music continued to soothe, as did flute and xylophone sounds played either acoustically or on the electric keyboard. Jason also seemed to enjoy the strums of the guitar. Violin sounds upset him. Songs sung to guitar accompaniment were acceptable. The gong was his favorite. Drums were acceptable on occasion, although he had difficulty taking part in drumming owing to other sensory deficits, particularly hypotonic muscle tone, proprioceptive issues and bilateral coordination.

In evaluating Jason's auditory processes, some important information illuminated potential problems. When Jason's parents had alluded to his becoming highly distracted by many sounds and unable to cope with the wall of noise at the mall, it seemed conceivable that Jason operated on peripheral hearing, picking up all sounds without discriminating or blending sounds (which could also be problematic to his language learning). And, as a result of operating on peripheral hearing, Jason could potentially be lacking a sense of auditory figure-ground and the ability to control his auditory focus.

Lacking figure-ground perception, as stated above, implies functioning on ambient (survival) hearing: hearing all sounds peripherally (fight-or-flight mode) without central focus. Therefore to Jason, who was probably most often in survival hearing mode, all sounds appeared equal to his brain, creating distractions, distortions and fear. Furthermore, it could not be assumed that his binaural stereophonic hearing was functionally operative.

Since the piano provided such an overwhelming amount of auditory information permeating the room, it is not surprising that Jason was frightened and agitated. It could be that his ambient hearing took all the sound in equally, unable to differentiate between the singing voice and piano, the melody and the harmony. To Jason's brain, it might have appeared as a gigantic tidal wave of sound engulfing him – virtually an auditory assault on his system. In addition, perhaps his system was unable properly to blend the range of infinite frequency ranges of the piano.

The gong, on the other hand, was one single sound, not melodic or harmonic, with fewer discernible overtone frequencies. Also, the gong's pitches are lower frequencies that require more volume in order to be heard. This could be why Jason needed to step up volume in order to process low frequencies. Besides, the louder the volume of the gong, the longer the reverberations can be heard. (Or maybe it was the first time he had ever heard such low frequencies?) Perhaps to Jason's ears, it was not loud.

The recorder, and the simpler sounds played on the keyboard, provided "purer" tones with limited audible overtone frequencies; single voices with less texture. Pitches here are of higher frequencies, but can be processed more simply than the high and low pitches produced by an acoustic piano, which have to be blended. True, overtones are still present as part of the sound, but they are certainly not as intrusive as those from the piano.

Assessing Jason's auditory situation, I extrapolated first that Jason did have perfect pitch and all the ramifications that come with this type of memory. Second, the piano probably provided such an overload of auditory information that his brain could neither tolerate nor process the abundance of sound, whether the music was fast, slow, loud, soft, rhythmic, bland. The timbre (texture) and volume of a piano (even at its softest), combined with the resonance of the myriad overtones coming from several hundred individual piano strings (possibly out of tune) would make it impossible, even painful, for someone functioning in survival-hearing mode to ingest that much information comfortably.

Compounding the plethora of sound vibrations emanating from the instrument itself are all the residual sounds bouncing, reflecting, echoing off the walls of the studio. This would further confuse dimensional hearing processes. Add to this the intrusion of vocal frequencies (maybe also out of tune!), overtones, echoes, plus words asking the brain to define and interpret, and the entire scenario becomes absolutely unwieldy.

It is easy to see how auditory overload and system distress can occur. In self-defense, the brain simply shuts down all systems and attempts to escape the madness! Often, this behavior is mistaken for "social avoidance" (a psychologic issue) rather than *sensory overload*, a physiologic problem.

Integration of auditory and visual processes

In addition to processing auditory information, the brain must simulta neously integrate and interpret visual input. (One *hears* a sound and *sees* its source.) Essentially, senses confirm each other's situation, as was noticed in the exercise of standing on one foot with eyes closed (Chapter 5, p.74). Many school learning activities depend on auditory-visual integration. The teacher writes on the blackboard as she speaks the information. The class must simultaneously hear, see, tune out distractions.

In order to sequence and accurately to recall what is being taught in school, the brain must (be stress-free to) tag both visual and auditory infor-mation simultaneously and *in relation to* each other. When this is difficult or there is overload, the brain will shut down one or more systems in order to process another. This makes it appear as if a child is not listening or looking. (How many of us often shut down visual input when listening to music? Gaze up and away from someone's face when searching for thoughts?) This behavior, in a person with autism, does not necessarily indicate inattentive-ness. It usually signals sensory processing difficulties. Squirming and fidgety behaviors, for instance, usually connote a need for proprioceptive input (pressure to joints, muscles and body).

A music therapist will notice this occurrence repeatedly when treating autistic behaviors. The task of sensory systems to register, code, and interpret multiple information, especially auditory/visual, is very difficult.

When other sensory deficits are present as well, it becomes nearly impossible.

Marty, the non-verbal child mentioned earlier, consistently looks away while his arms are being physically prompted in a drumming task. It appears he cannot process tactile-proprioceptive information simultaneously with related visual/auditory input. He needs to shut down something, usually vision (by looking away,) in order to process something else. It happens consistently when physically prompted. He does not look away when we sing or play instruments together with no physical prompting. But when we sit together at the piano and I sing a story from a book, he looks away. It is as if he wants to take the information in only through his auditory sense.

Music therapy interventions have been able to relieve some of Marty's problems over the last several years, but it will take more time to reorder the adaptation to multiple sensory processing.

Auditory-motor coordination

Multidimensional sensory processing deficits implicate aspects of hearing and movement coordination. Although rhythm is a musculotropic stimulus able to instigate movement, the inability of a system to hear something and motor plan an adequate physical response without delay is problematic in autism and atypical systems. It means simultaneous processing of vestibular, proprioceptive, tactile, auditory, and visual stimuli. It means that the sensory system must be fully integrated and organized. The theory that this is not so with autism has already been discussed.

Music therapy is a natural way of tackling this problem. The playing of a musical instrument involves multisensory input, including proprioceptive-tactile feedback and motor planning. Beating a drum incorporates bilateral arm movements, bent elbows, hand grip of the mallets, up and down rhythmic arm pulses striking the drum, and the motivation to stay with the beat!

Marching while rhythmically beating a tambourine requires the multiple processing of motor and auditory cortices. In fact, the auditory cortex is close to the motor cortex and can influence movement through rhythm's musculotropic stimulation. However, the resulting action of marching and beating may not necessarily be organized or coordinated. Observing how the body responds to the task often discloses sensory deficits that require attention.

A great many interventions involving rhythmic internalization are very effective in addressing this issue to the best advantage of functional adaptation. Simultaneous music-movement exercises are especially beneficial. Activities similar to those designed by Jacques Dalcroze and Karl Orff (mentioned earlier) are especially beneficial in regulating and pacing the autistic system. Repeated eurhythmic tasks generate body coordination by involving movement responses to rhythm and music cues. Having to *listen for* rhythmic changes and music cues brings about auditory focus, tracking, figure-ground development, depth perception, discrimination and sound tolerance.

Also developed are upper-lower body coordination, spatial perception, mid-line orientation, vestibular and proprioceptive feedback, and much more. The more the body becomes rhythmically organized and paced (the hypothalamus seems to be the clock and rhythm organ), the more the entire functionality of the system becomes organized and manageable, because the brain can at last relax and do its other work.

Jason, our gong child, had difficulty performing several sensory tasks simultaneously. He could not fully attend auditorily if asked to participate physically, which is probably why he consistently rejected use of hand instruments or drums in early sessions. Despite the fact that Jason is quite rhythmically able, he displayed difficulty pulsing on the drum while hearing the song and simultaneously seeing his arms go up and down.

Jason could drum without looking, but when asked to observe his arm movements, he could not coordinate hearing, seeing, doing. Even now, when he listens to music, he tends to turn away from the sound. Besides visual-auditory coordination, this could also indicate a need to hear out of one ear rather than two. It is unclear.

Many music therapy interventions utilizing auditory-motor training elements successfully increase functional adaptation of proprioceptive and vestibular-visual and motor-auditory systems. When the auditory is engaged in the structured manner provided by music, it appears that other systems tend to line up in compliance. Since the motor cortex is located very close to the auditory cortex, music's stimulation of the auditory system also influences physical responses. One cannot assume, however, that just the presence of music alone will be enough to instigate physical alteration since, as we have seen, the auditory system's processing of music may display deficiencies. These auditory deficits must first be regulated before musical input can be effectively used for resolving additional sensory integration, psychological and cognitive problems.

References

Williams, D. (1998) *Autism and Sensing: The Unlost Instinct.* London: Jessica Kingsley Publishers.

Recommended Reading

Berard, G. (1993) *Hearing equals Behavior.* New Canaan, Conn.: Keats Publishing, Inc.

Berger, D.S. (1997) 'Are you listening?' In D.J. Schneck and J.K. Schneck (eds), *Music in Human Adaptation.* Blacksburg, Va.: Virginia Tech Press.

Findlay, E. (1971) *Rhythm and Movement: Applications of Dalcroze Eurhythmics.* Miami, Fl.: Summy-Birchard, Inc. (Distributed by Warner Bros. Publications, Miami, Fl.)

Helmuth, L. (2001) 'Dyslexia: Same Brains, Different Languages.' *Science 291,* 5511, 2064–2065.

Jacques-Dalcroze, E. (1921) *Rhythm, Music and Education.* New York & London: G.P. Putnam & Sons, The Knickerbocker Press.

Jacques-Dalcroze, E. (1930) *Eurhythmics, Art and Education.* London, UK: Chatto & Windus.

Jourdain, R. (1997) *Music, the Brain and Ecstacy: How Music Captures Our Imagination.* New York: William Morrow and Co., Inc.

Margoliash, D. (2001) 'The Song Does Not Remain the Same.' *Science 291,* 5513, 2559–2561.

Martin, R. (1994) *Out of Silence: A Journey into Language.* New York: Henry Hold and Co.

Maurice, C. (1993) *Let Me Hear Your Voice: A Family's Triumph over Autism.* New York: Alfred A. Knopf.

Paulesu, E., Demonet, J.F., Fazio, F., McCrory, E., Chanoine, V., Brunswick, N., Cappa, S.F., Cossu, G., Habib, M., Frith, C.D. and Frith, U. (2001) 'Dyslexia: Cultural Diversity and Biological Unity.' *Science 291,* 5511, 2165–2167.

Sessions, R. (1950) *The Musical Experience of Composer, Performer, Listener.* Princeton, NJ: Princeton University Press.

Stehli, A. (1991) *The Sound of a Miracle.* New York: Avon Books.

Stryker, M.P. (2001) 'Drums Keep Pounding a Rhythm in the Brain.' *Science 291,* 5508, 1506–1507.

Szonyi, E. (1973) *Kodaly's Principles in Practice: An Approach to Music Education through the Kodaly Method.* New York: Boosey & Hawkes.

Tchernichovsky, O., Mitra, P.P., Lints, T. and Nottebohm, F. (2001) 'Dynamics of the Vocal Imitation Process: How a Zebra Finch Learns its Song.' *Science 291,* 5513, 2564–2569.

Tomatis, A.A. (1991) *The Conscious Ear: My Life of Transformation through Listening.* Barrytown, NY: Station Hill Press.

Wheeler, L. and Raebeck, L. (1972) *Orff and Kodaly Adapted for the Elementary School.* Dunbuque, Io.: Wm. C. Brown Co., Publishers.

Wickelgren, I. (2001) 'Working Memory Helps the Mind Focus.' *Science 291,* 5509, 1684–1685.

Williams, D. (1996) *Autism: An Inside-Out Approach.* London: Jessica Kingsley Publishers.

CHAPTER 8

Elements of Music for Sensory Adaptation

The most important tools at the music therapist's disposal in addressing issues of sensory needs in autistic populations are the six basic elements of music. These are: *rhythm, melody, harmony, dynamics, timbre,* and *form;* and there are variations within each element. Whether used individually or grouped, when these tools are thoughtfully applied towards adaptive goals they are unsurpassed in their ability to address sensory integration issues.

Rhythm

Rhythm is everywhere, and it is one of the first elements human beings instinctively detect when experiencing music. The universe consists of rhythmically paced functions: from pulsing lights and sound frequencies to the orbiting of planets; from the cycles of seasons and weather to phenomenal cosmic forces.

Plants rhythmically adapt to seasonal changes. Animal survival depends upon physiologic rhythms, including rhythmic neuronal firings in the brain, heartbeats, sleep cycles, breath pacing. Food is chewed in rhythm; language involves rhythmical labyrinths of punctuated sounds and silences; walking is a rhythmic fall and rebound; birthing contractions depend on rhythm; general daily conduct evolves in rhythmic patterns.

The drum is one of the oldest instruments devised by human beings, and is found in every culture in the world. Even certain species of birds use twigs to beat rhythms on hollow branches. Rhythm is a physiologic organizer. It is also a social unifier, requiring no particular "training" in order for it to be experienced and enjoyed in a group.

Research is showing that the auditory cortex and the motor cortex are closely involved in stimulating rhythmic movement. Rhythm as a musculotropic stimulus, it has been observed, can be useful in helping to induce a phenomenon known as *entrainment*. This is the alignment of a body's rhythmic pulse to the rhythm of a persistent, externally imposed, rhythmic beat. Ongoing rhythmic stimulation, it has been observed, can bring about system pacing, paced reflexive physical movement responses, modification of body tempi, and many aspects of physiologic operations that impact upon functional adaptation.

Alonzo, an eight-year-old autistic non-verbal boy, ran around the music therapy classroom aimlessly while the piano played and I sang a song describing and reflecting his behavior back to him. Alonzo remained at the far end of the large school classroom and did not approach the piano. Occasionally, he would stop and cast glances across the room toward the piano, but his physical behavior remained chaotic, distant, out of control.

Abandoning the piano and song, I opted instead for the simplicity of pure rhythm played on the congo drum. No singing; no melody; nothing but rhythm. In an instant, Alonzo's running halted, his body and mind frozen in a state of attention. He looked across the room at me and the drum. As suddenly as he had stopped, he began moving in an organized, rhythmic, stepping demeanor, toward the sound. His steps accented the pulse of the congo's beat as he neared the drum.

Alonzo sat himself near me and indicated a desire to play the congo. I positioned the instrument before him and took a bongo for myself. The remainder of the session consisted only of rhythmic, patterned drumming between us, on these two instruments. Anyone entering the room would never suspect this child was autistic and given to extremely erratic behaviors! Rhythm reorganized him completely. When extraneous auditory information (piano, voice, words, etc.) had been eliminated, the strict rhythmic pulse and patterns took charge of Alonzo's brain and body.

It is overwhelming how this single element of rhythm completely changed Alonzo's behavior within this large, echoing classroom. I recommended to his teachers that when they sensed Alonzo to be out of control, they might employ some hand-clapping and small hand drums to help him organize himself. Apparently the recommendation was acted upon because Alonzo, when hearing rhythmic hand-clapping or when playing on his tambourine drum, was able to subdue chaotic impulses, becoming less inclined to flee the scene. One teacher actually used pulsed hand-clapping to call her entire class of children to order!

Rhythm internalization, a key goal in music therapy for sensory integration, is a process in which the application of external persistent rhythmic stimuli can eventually help repattern and regulate instinctive rhythmic alignment in the internal physiologic environment (pulse, muscle contractions, heartbeat, blood pressure, breathing, etc.). The rhythmic regulation of internal processes, including cognition and language, is influenced, altered and paced in relation to persistent external rhythmic input (continuous disturbance!)

Music activities that include strong rhythmic components can impact upon adaptive motor planning, sensory organization, cognitive processes and general physiologic pacing. The nervous system can be influenced either to slow down or speed up the flow of information. It is not accidental that slow music slows and calms the system (inhibitory neurotransmitters are released) while spirited, jazzy music animates behaviors (excitatory neurotransmitters at work).

It has been observed that individuals in whom rhythmic internalization has taken hold tend to develop better focus and attentive behaviors, with more functionally organized body movements, upper-lower body coordination, visual and auditory focus and adaptive motor planning. When the body is rhythmically organized, it appears that other physiologic responses become more manageable.

Components of rhythm

It is not enough simply to say "rhythm". What is rhythm? There are four basic attributes of rhythm that can interact with human physiology and can contribute to rhythm's usefulness. I refer to three of the four attributes as *The Three Ps – Pulse, Pattern, Perseveration* (repetition). The fourth is *Tempo* (speed), which is actually an attribute of pulse, but is discussed separately for its role in clinical music interventions.

1. Pulse

The first important rhythmic attribute is pulse. Pulse, although often subsumed under the generic term rhythm, is actually the time-keeper controlling most of what transpires in a piece of music. It is the ticking-clock segment of rhythm underlying and unifying all that develops within a composition. It is music's pacemaker. Commonly called the "beat", pulse is the pacing of **strong**–*weak*–**strong**–*weak*, fall-rebound sound-motion in a consistent, evenly spaced manner. It usually involves the strong (fall) "beat", followed by a weaker (rebound) "beat".

Thus, a march pulse, comprised of four beats evenly spaced and strictly maintained, pulses as: **One** – *two* – **Three** – *four* – **One** – *two* – **Three** – *four* – and so on. A waltz beat, in three pulses, becomes **One** – *two* – *three* – **One** – *two* – *three*…The speed (tempo) of the pulse depends on the intent of the composer and/or the nature of an activity.

Pulse represents the constant underlying contractions over which all else takes place. When physiologic pulse is erratic, as we know from physical problems, the unsteadiness of the beat will cause other events to falter in a domino effect. In the heart muscle, for instance, if just one cell fires off-beat, it can cause ventricular fibrillation of the entire heart muscle, whose inner clock has suddenly become confused by the off-beat emission of one of its cells. This will obviously implicate all other life-sustaining functions.

More than likely, the phenomenon of rhythmic entrainment and musculotropic stimulation actually denotes a compliance and adjustment of motor impulses to the pulsations of rhythm stimulus. The speed of a pulse, i.e. how quickly or slowly the next "beat" happens, is of vital importance in addressing particular motor issues and many language development problems. Rhythmic speech, for instance, paces the brain's intake of cognitive information. When syllables are broken down into their rhythmic patterns, words become simpler to hear, repeat, and remember. The faster and more erratic the speech pulse, the more difficult it is for the brain to "catch" or understand everything. Remember that the brain likes things presented and stored in patterns.

Music therapists concerned with developing functional motor planning and rhythmic internalization carefully design activities to rhythmic pulsation according to goal results being sought. Allied therapies, especially speech and occupation therapy, benefit from applying rhythmic pulse and carefully selected speed of pulsation to achieve successful results.

2. Pattern

A pulse alone is no more interesting than a beating clock or a metronome. Besides, once the brain is attuned to a pulse and determines the information to be non-threatening, it often simply "tunes out" and stops further listening. Fortunately, rhythmic pulse is never alone in music. It is driven by something much more interesting: *rhythmic patterns*. Rhythmic patterns (which the brain loves!) "fill in the blanks" and keep the brain continually alert and curious about the variety of ever-changing musical information.

A pulse is *not* a pattern. A pattern consists of a variety of rhythmic inter-jections often teasing a pulse, organized in such ways as to bring about anticipation and changes of input over a paced beat. Off-beats in jazz are perfect examples of patterns teasing the strictness of a pulse. In the broader perspective, rhythm is a perfect integration of pulse plus patterned lengths of sounds flowing above, between, against or parallel to the beat. Pulse must remain steady. Pattern can be freer, erratic, always changing, with stops, starts, fast, slow, combined to add depth and dimension to the simple, constant, faithful pulse.

In language, the presence of pattern is very evident, especially in poetry. Every word, when divided into its syllabic rhythm, displays its pattern: *Sa-tur-day, Su–zie, we will come to play*… When this sentence is clapped over a four-count pulse – (1) Sa-tur-day (2) Su-zie (3) we will come to (4) play… the pattern becomes *three quick claps*, followed by *two slower claps*, followed by *four quick claps* completed by a *longer held clap*. Pulse paces, drives and causes an anticipation of pattern. Pattern embellishes, teases, drives and causes the anticipation of the next beat. Rhythmic pattern is one of the most important elements in pacing the learning of spoken language. It has been my experience that non-verbal children for whom language is broken down into rhythmically patterned syllables, spoken, clapped, and/or sung are more attentive and motivated to imitate and learn word sounds. This may be one reason why learning vocabulary in sung format can contribute to more efficient memory of lyrics, poems, even foreign languages (the brain loves patterns!)

In foreign language learning (though we may not realize it) one tends to learn by rhythmic and tonal patterning of words and phrases. (Often one remembers the word but its meaning may be elusive.) If language is spoken too quickly and arhythmically, the brain could have difficulty tracking and retaining patterned information.

Often clinicians, educators, caregivers and others tend to speak much too fast, especially to children or adults with learning and sensory deficits. In fact, many children's TV programs and CDs present information much too fast for absorption by any child, let alone one with sensory deficits. (I almost never recommend the children's CDs or tapes, having found most of them to be just too fast in speech and pulse, not to mention intrusive in instrumentations!)

For the brain, information paced by rhythmic pulse and pattern is non-threatening. As soon as information becomes structured and organized within rhythm and pitch patterns, which the brain prefers to process rather than random items, fear disappears and the brain allows the opening of passages to higher channels of cognition. Music is, after all, an experience enjoyed by the whole brain. The music of rappers is a perfect example of pulse and pattern interacting to drive home the verbal message.

3. Repetition (Perseveration)

The most effective aspect of rhythmic pulsation and pattern is its constancy and repetitive nature. Earlier chapters discussed physiologic continuous disturbance as a necessary catalyst to adaptation. The continuity and perseverative nature of rhythm provides the very repetitive continuous disturbance element that ultimately forces the brain to take notice of it. Tapping the foot, fingers tapping a table, mallets beating a drum – the brain attends to the repetitive nature of pulse interacting with rhythmic pattern.

While verbal repetition is often quickly tuned out and dismissed, if a simple verbal phrase is repeated to rhythmic hand-clapping (not even sung in pitches), the brain will sustain its attention and interest. Rhythmic repetition seems to drive the brain and system to attention, as I noticed with Alonzo. Soldiers march great distances to rhythmic phrases. Popular music's major rhythmic aspect is its repetitive nature. Often, just one word is rhythmically repeated (perseverated) over and over and over. Were it not for the rhythm (pulse plus pattern), the brain would tune out with the second repetition!

Rhythmic repetition, or perseveration as I call it, is the power behind the beat, and the driving force that ultimately beguiles the human body to pay attention, stay tuned, and eventually "give in" (adapt). The brain tolerates this repetition for as long as it takes to obtain the message. Since rhythmic messages are ever-changing processes of musical evolution, the brain stays with them.

4. Tempo

Tempo – speed – is subsumed in the pulse element, but a word about this particular aspect of pulse is warranted. The *speed* of a pulse often determines the effectiveness of a piece of music in eliciting certain psycho-emotional as well as physiologic sensory responses from a musical encounter. Whether one is listening to music or participating as a player, the speed in which music elements are ensconced plays a role in how attuned the brain will be and remain, relative to the material.

Very slow tempi often have the effect of inducing such calmness that the brain wants to tune out and sleep. Often it is difficult to remain focused and on task when tempi are very slow. This, however, could be exactly what a therapist is trying to discover, i.e. the extent to which a patient can attend. How long a patient can "stay with" the music – hold on to a piece of music information in memory until the next piece of information is presented and make links over large spans of musical input – provides important information about that person's internal rhythms and pacing. The use of very slow tempi can reveal much about auditory memory and cognitive processing.

Using extremely slow pulses with participants on the autistic spectrum can also reveal a great deal about neurologic function. Does the person become uncontrollably restless? Does the body move faster or slower than the tempo being presented? Many other questions arise with the use of very slow tempos. Most important is whether or not a continuous disturbance by imposed slow tempos will ultimately cause the system to adapt into a faster or slower body pacing to allow efficient motor planning.

It has been suggested that the speed of language could impact upon the understanding and imitation of speech. Therefore, could more functional expressive and receptive language be developed if songs were presented much more slowly in order to give the brain a chance to absorb the information efficiently? Music therapy can investigate this.

The other side of tempo is music which animates by being quite brisk, with pattern configurations that seem to enhance the speed of the pulse even further. Brisk, fast music animates the system, and can be applied quite effectively when a therapy goal is to speed up think-and-do responses, motor planning for task execution, and low muscle tone.

Tempo is not incidental in the work of music therapy. It is an aspect that, when conscientiously used for specific reasons, can alter physical and emotional responses. It also addresses issues of auditory tracking and discrimination, and others. It is has been observed that certain tempi equal to the speed of a normal beating heart can actually slow a fast heartbeat down to that "normal" speed; and that fast tempi can cause increased pulse and heart-rates. Tempo is a very important contributor to the overall story of rhythm, especially to theories of entrainment.

The above *Three Ps* and *Tempo* components of rhythm are the underlying foundations of music therapy interventions for achieving physiologic adaptation and cognitive learning.

Melody

Humans are first and foremost emotional animals. They also have an affinity for linking and tracking tones and pitches. Terrence Deacon, in his definitive book *The Symbolic Species* (1997) reminds us that millennia before speech as we know it evolved, extended vocalization was (and continues to be) the uniquely human form of social communication and symbolic expression of feelings and needs. Oddly enough, of all animals, the human being is the most limited in number of vocal "calls" characterizing needs and feelings. (A good reason for creating musical expression!) These human calls include primarily *laughter* and *sobbing*. Motorically, laughter involves a rhythmic *exhalation* of breath and vocal sound, while sobbing is the rhythmic *inhalation* of sounds. Deacon suggests these to be like two sides of one coin. Music is, conceivably, the symbolic extension of the expressions of joy in laugher, and sobbing in sorrow.

Along with laughter and sobbing, calls specifically human are *screaming* with fright, *groaning*, *sighing*, and *crying* with pain. These six basic human calls, and variations thereof, are exclusively available to all human animals. Dysfunctions of any kind seem not to thwart use of these symbolic calls. It is odd that, given the largeness of the human brain, so few calls are available in the human communication repertoire.

Deacon (1997) further conjectures that language development may ultimately have circumvented the need for more human calls, since humans could now articulate verbally what a call would symbolize. The more the neo-cortex expanded for cognition, the less the need for instinctive communication. Is Donna Williams (1998) correct when she posits that the autistic system which can sense things without dismissing anything is actually more able to make sense of the planet because instinct and intuition have not been lost? And that integrated sensing can actually limit human intuition and instinct?

While human calls remain limited to six basic forms with variations, certain vocalizations are still used to give emotional meaning to words. There is reason to suspect that speech *prosody* is a relative of ancestral call functions that indicated procreative and fear behaviors. Speech prosody (inflection) is virtually a method of communication, providing parallel channels to verbalization. Even foreign languages which others may not understand emit emotional content through inflective incantations. Intensities change, pitches rise and fall, attitudes permeate, regardless of word recognition.

Apparently, prosody is instinctive, although each culture delineates its own particular intonations. According to Deacon (1997, p.418): "Though tonal shifts [in prosodic emissions] can be used as phonemes, the changes in tonality, volume, and phrasing that constitute prosodic features are most often produced without conscious intention." Thus, given that human calls developed as symbolic communicators of feelings, it is more than likely that melody – especially instinctive vocal emissions of linked tones – preceded language in symbolically transmitting states of mind and emotions. And, coupled with rhythmic drive, the phenomenon of extended vocal emissions could have been the symbolic emotional language of human communities before "formal" language. This could be why it is often thought that humans are, in essence, "pre-programmed" to process "music" as symbolic of human experience. In fact, music speaks pure emotion. Vocal calls could have evolved into instrumental calls. Recently, a 50,000-year-old bone flute was discovered!

Melody, then, which may have evolved from human calls, is music's linear contour (peaks, valleys and flow) of tones linked horizontally, akin to *prosody* (inflection) in speech. As such, melody is the direct instinctive communication of a human emotional state – a human call (or calls) – the impact of which is immediately recognizable *without need of cognitive processing*. The same may be said of verbal inflections and vocal registers of speech. Before an infant cognitively understands the word "NO!", the inflection, vocal register and percussive rhythm used in expressing this negative concept are immediately understood. Fright follows (often leading to involuntary tears), induced by the sound, tone and volume of the voice.

Melodic contours (the shape of the melody's ups and downs) can either calm a system, or excite it. Regardless of response, however, it is a fact that the brain will remain in a state of attention to melodic flow in anticipation of forthcoming tones. It is not an accident that newborns immediately attend to lullabies. The combination of melodic flow, slow tempo and parental vocalization maintains attention as well as allows the brain to sense a level of safety which, in abating fight-fright-flight responses, will ultimately lull a child to sleep (or an adult, for that matter).

Melodic contours, such as wide sweeps and leaps from low to high pitches ("Twinkle, Twinkle, Little Star" leaps the interval of five tones before embarking on a tone-by-tone descending motion), or scale-wise melodies ("Mary Had a Little Lamb") will create different physiologic and psychologic states of anticipation. Melodic songs can stimulate speech centers and bring about the desire to intone the prosodic tunes of letters or words, eventually leading to speech imitation.

Melodies which imitate prosodic speech inflections will tend to evoke emotional responses similar to those evoked by spoken communication. Erratic melodies (such as in some modern music) can create a restlessness in the brain, which generally prefers orderly patterns. Staccato tunes will often induce a sort of laughter and joy. Laughter is a highly contagious human call, usually bringing a level of cohesion to a group. My lowest-functioning disabled child still attempts to imitate my giggles.

"Laughing music" in the form of staccato melodies and quick, short rhythms often induces similar responses of laughter, or at the very least, joy and happy smiles.

Often, when I play staccato or brisk melodies and ask what the music feels like, the comment is that "it sounds happy." Although it is tempting to ascertain a cultural orientation to certain musical attributes and responses, the fact that this type of melodic approach is found in many cultures would likely be more supportive of Deacon's idea that laughter, even as displayed musically, is not only contagious, but is a universal element adding cohesion to a group anywhere on the planet.

Melody, as a resource for music therapy, is invaluable in helping to determine auditory tracking, pitch discrimination and auditory memory skills. Much can be assessed when presenting a melodic line containing simple rhythm and little or no harmony. The ability accurately to track auditory information, as we learned in the last two chapters, is of vital importance in learning speech and speech affect. Many persons on the autistic spectrum are quite devoid of speech affect. Melody plays an important part in attaining emotional self-expression. The use of melody to induce prosodic vocal self-expression, and as a means of injecting emotional content and attitude into word meanings, is a dynamic music therapy intervention.

Harmony

It took many evolutionary millennia before the structures of "harmony" came to be included in musical form. Still today, there are many cultures that do not employ "harmony" as we have come to understand it in Western civilization. Religious chanting is harmonic by implication, since monks chant in strict unison (without the use of harmonizing voices). The element of harmony as our society understands it calls upon aspects of dimensional hearing and auditory scanning discussed earlier. Harmony provides emphasis to the emotional context of melody, again contributing implied dimensional/spatial references to audition.

Harmony is usually constructed around certain expected scale structures and resolutions. Communities throughout the world have devised culturally specific systems for harmonic tonal development and resolution.

Some systems use as few as four tones, others as many as 48 or more (including ¼ tones).

Without encumbering ourselves with the entire theory of music, let us say that at its simplest, harmony could be just one melodic voice suggesting certain harmonic possibilities. Or, harmony could be evoked by two concurrent melodic voices employing different pitches one from the other, moving simultaneously in linear (horizontal) fashion. In more complex forms, harmonic clusters of sound patterns can be the support beneath a melodic line, providing accompanying chord progressions (notes stacked vertically one over another, played simultaneously).

Harmony can entail multiple independent but interrelated voices superimposed one upon another, vertically, all moving in linear (horizontal) manner simultaneously (a virtual brick wall of tones moving in time and space). At times, the entire cluster of notes can become the "melodic" line. Regardless of the manner of harmonic input, harmony provides dimension to the emotional content of melody and rhythm. It adds *color* and *mood* to the expression of feeling within the melodic contour. Harmonic components also provide *depth* and sonic *texture* to the overall musical composition.

Harmony can add mystery to a fantasy or comic relief to a story, and can help induce guided mental imagery. It is very effective as a resource for dramatic enhancement to familiar fairytales and improvised stories when therapy intervention goals involve stimulation of facial and bodily affect, recognition and expression of feeling states and moods.

The element of harmony is used carefully in music therapy interventions, since it provides multiple auditory input that could be difficult to process if sensory issues are present. Used efficiently, harmony has the ability to stimulate auditory depth perception (upper or lower; closer or further) and can be employed in exercises aimed at strengthening auditory focus and figure-ground abilities. It is especially effective when melodic lines and sundry musical cues are presented over harmonic structures and a person is asked to detect one element from the other. Harmonic formations can also elicit mood changes and abstract imagery.

Timbre

Timbre is an ever-present factor in music and in life. It is the music element which is most often misunderstood by the listener. Timbre is the defining quality and texture of a sound. It is timbre that differentiates a drill from a drum, a flute from a trumpet, a male from a female voice, a soprano from an alto. It is this textural quality of the sound fabric-scape that the auditory system discriminates, identifies, interprets and codes for future use. Appropriately functional auditory discrimination of timbre and pitch is crucial for survival, and for development of verbal communication.

Composers and orchestrators use timbre to elicit particular emotional reactions from music. "Romantic strings" or "heavenly harp" are often used to lull a listener into quietude. Musical ebbs and flow (melodic contour, harmony and lethargic rhythmic pulse and patterns) would not necessarily achieve quieting results were the music played on instruments other than violins, cellos, harp. Music is orchestrated for these instruments precisely because of their soothing timbres. The same music played on tubas and trombones, for instance, would not necessarily have the same "soothing" impact (no offense intended!) We cringe at the sound of nails scraping a blackboard because our brains do not enjoy the timbre of that sound!

Timbre was one of the factors that contributed to our gong-child Jason's negative reaction to the piano, and to his tolerance of the recorder, violin, flute, and even the gong. Some vocal timbres could also be problematic for persons with auditory-integration deficits. The integration of frequencies that contribute to the quality of a tone could be deficient in many sensory-inadequate systems, rendering the sounds offensive to the ear.

Parents of several children with whom I work indicate that their child shuts down at the sound of certain voices – a teacher, mom or dad, a sibling, a caregiver. Although timbre is often not considered as a deterrent to listening skills, it can actually play a major role in shutting down attention, listening and cognitive processes. It can also induce behavioral problems (fight-fright-flight). The timbre of someone's voice can be agitating or soothing. Media broadcasters appeal to listeners when the timbre of their voices is soothing. Many children on the autistic spectrum have difficulty processing the variety of vocal and instrumental timbres approaching their ears.

Music therapy capitalizes on the element of timbre by selecting certain instruments especially for their timbrel qualities. Since timbrel frequencies could elucidate auditory processing and discrimination issues, the music therapist can quickly detect these through therapy interventions. Timbrel discrimination problems often parallel discrimination problems in speech and language processes. The ability or inability to discriminate differences between the timbre of a pitch played on a handbell and the same pitch on a xylophone key presented in a different timbre can be important information for both music therapists and speech pathologists working with auditory issues.

Dynamics

Music manipulates energy, resonance and sensory stimulation through the variance of volume (loud, soft, etc.). Musical dynamics – louds, softs, and gradual increases and decreases of volume – add one more auditory element to the drama of musical expression. The prosody and dynamics (intensity) of speech indicate the urgency and level of emotional state. The same is true of music dynamics. Why and when is music loud or soft? Obviously there is emotional content within the amount of energy used to present a musical comment. Dynamics dramatize melodic, harmonic and timbrel structures.

A listener is immediately engaged by dynamic nuances. Dynamics indicate states of mind and emotion. Notice that much of today's popular music does not involve dynamic nuances. Instead, there is a constant assault of overly amplified, excessively loud music screaming into the ear with desperate urgency. There is little dynamic graduation. It is all loud, or it does not exist. It wants to be heard. Is there a message here?

Music dynamics parallel human dynamics – moods, levels of excitability, and physical (muscular) and psychological states. With autistic spectrum populations, it is not unusual to find either very little dynamics in the playing of instruments, or predominantly loud monodynamic pounding as if out of rage or fear. In contrast, some musical expression by autistic spectrum persons displays erratic dynamic sounds, such as all soft except for a sudden loud attack. These displays are possibly due, in part, to inefficient physical muscular control. Implicated also is inefficient auditory-physical coordination – a motor plan unable to produce what is heard in one's head.

Persons lacking motor planning, whose physicality consists of low muscle tone, difficulty with upper-lower body coordination and general lethargy of movements are very well served by the element of music dynamics. Teaching a system to move with certain dynamic modulations supported by music dynamics is a goal of music therapy for sensory integration and motor planning. It takes certain energy and planning to beat a drum loudly, and to release tensions in order suddenly to play quietly. It takes different muscular energy and planning to walk and stomp the feet louder than the music of the piano, or suddenly to tip-toe to the quietness of the music, or clap loud while walking on tip-toes.

Music dynamics speak for themselves. Therefore very little verbal explanation is required in interventions that use dynamics to communicate information and elicit certain physical responses. There are unlimited possibilities for using music dynamics in therapy interventions. Soft music quiets the mind and body; loud music animates; crescendos (gradual increases in volume) and decrescendos (gradual decreases) instigate attention states, mood changes, excitement, contemplation, and more.

Loud vocalization can induce prosodic vocal expressions (shrieks, yodels). It can also assist with breath control, especially extended exhalation. Blowing hard to produce loud sounds on the recorder will exercise the diaphragm. Such interventions target discreet physiologic issues by using music dynamics as a resource for changes and adaptation. Dynamics also play a key role in emotional self-expression and recognition of feeling states. One *is* in what and how one is playing. One *is* one's sound – loud, soft, insecure, inflexible, low self-esteem.

The issue of flexibility and body dynamics can be addressed through variations in music and movement dynamics undertaken by both patient and therapist. Besides body dynamics, the auditory system is once again put to the test with dynamics. How loud is loud to one's ear? How soft is soft? What is the tolerance level for dynamics and timbre? Auditory perception of sound quantity is investigated through a variety of interventions involving music dynamics. Therapists devise interventions using music dynamics according to investigative assessment goals.

Form

The sixth and possibly the key element of music as therapy is form. As already stated, music is temporal and evolutionary by nature. But it does not continue ad infinitum. Music has shape. It begins…evolves and peaks… and then resolves. This aspect is pertinent to the development of task creation, task organization, and task completion. It is one of the most important contributing factors aiding the development of "attention" span.

"Attention" is actually a state of "anticipation". The brain waits and attends to information by remaining in a holding pattern until some resolution allows the processing to conclude. This could be as briefly as a nanosecond, in terms of physiologic transduction of information, or long enough for cognition to take hold and make sense of the information.

Music's *form* ultimately insists upon the act of waiting in anticipation (antecedent to the state of "attention") of closure. Since music form ultimately reaches conclusion, a participant in music therapy learns to bring an improvisation to some sort of conclusion rather than abandoning the task mid-sentence, so to speak. Waiting for a tune to end stretches the ability of a participant to "wait" until the end. It might be that initially, the child will wait through only one completion. This could be increased to two repetitions, then three and more, stretching attention and "wait" time.

Through sampling and imitating existing and familiar music, or by constructing lyrics that are then put to tunes, the advent of form evolves. Form invokes the cognitive process for planning and organizing. How a tune begins, where it goes next, how it can conclude, how long it should continue, how many repetitions would be enough, and similar considerations help the mind organize musical form. Eventually, the concept of structuring musical form takes hold without verbal prompting.

Musical form becomes a problem-solving, task-organization and completion event. Interventions using form to induce attention and the ability to wait confront issues of patience, delayed gratification, and other behaviors. Like waiting for the candy or cookie reward at the end of a task, musical form takes on an automatic "behavior modification" modality without being formalized as such!

Review

The six elements of music – *rhythm, melody, harmony, timbre, dynamics, form* – are important to understand when using music as a clinical intervention for sensory issues. As described, each component, whether applied individually or in relation to another, presents specific clinical advantages in addressing issues in autism and sensory integration.

It is not enough simply to refer to an event as *rhythm* without understanding the components of *pulse, pattern, repetition, tempo,* and how these combine to affect human behavior. In melody, we have emotion and remnants of human calls in extended linked and contoured flow. It requires careful temporal tracking of the relationship between one pitch event and another in order for it to be recognizable as a familiar tune, or to make sense as a tune altogether.

Harmony provides depth, texture, mood, feelings, amplification of melodic statements. It reinforces melody, insinuates tonal resolution according to culturally-specific harmonic treatises, and adds the need to employ "dimensional hearing" skills, as discussed in the previous chapter. Timbre is the quality of sound emitted from a particular instrument or voice, testing astute auditory discrimination and aspects of auditory tolerance. It is the difference between a bird call and a human whistle.

Dynamics is akin to the energy level of music. It is volume, expanding and decreasing to induce particular inhibitory or excitatory emotional responses. It is emphasis or de-emphasis of a musical idea, and has great implications in the work of music therapy in relation to physical dynamics, muscle tone, motor planning, vocal affect and breath control.

And finally, form, that most important element which defines a system of beginning-middle-conclusion, places a person at attention by creating a state of "anticipation" until the information is completed. It is one of the inherent behavior-modification aspects of a musical interaction, testing the ability of a participant to stay on task until the end.

In addition to the basic elements of music, there are the many instruments upon which these elements are presented. The types of instruments used with designated musical interventions increase the likelihood that successful adaptation and reorganization of a system in need will take place. The music therapist, working from the physiologic perspective of sensory adaptation, ultimately determines which element(s) on what instruments, for what sorts of activities and how often, will be prescribed in the form of interventions. These are based on careful physiologic assessment of need.

References

Deacon, T.W. (1997) *The Symbolic Species: The Co-evolution of Language and the Brain.* New York: W. W. Norton and Co.

Williams, D. (1998) *Autism and Sensing: The Unlost Instinct.* London: Jessica Kingsley Publishers.

Recommended reading

Gossard, T. (1997) 'Structures for Listening.' In D.J. Schneck and J.K. Schneck (eds) *Music in Human Adaptation,* 215–217. Blacksburg, Va.: Virginia Tech Press.

Gray, P.M., Krause, B., Atema, J., Payne, R., Krumhansl, C. and Baptista, L. (2001) 'The Music of Nature and the Nature of Music.' *Science 291,* 5501, 52–54.

Hero, B. (1997) 'Some Effects of Whole Number Ratio Intervals in Music.' In D.J. Schneck and J.K. Schneck (eds) *Music in Human Adaptation,* 107–132. Blacksburg, Va.: Virginia Tech Press.

Hero, B. and Foulkrod, R.M. (1999) 'The Lambdoma Matrix and Harmonic Intervals.' *IEEE Engineering in Medicine and Biology 18,* 2, 61–73.

Jourdain, R. (1997) *Music, the Brain and Ecstasy: How Music Captures Our Imagination.* New York: William Morrow and Co., Inc.

Kivy, P. (1990) *Music Alone: Philosophical Reflections on the Purely Musical Experience.* Ithaca, NY: Cornell University Press.

Meyer, L.B. (1956) *Emotion and Meaning in Music.* Chicago, Ill.: The University of Chicago Press.

Pinker, S. (1994) *The Language Instinct: How the Mind Creates Language.* New York: Harper Perennial.

Schatz, H.B. (1997) 'The Chord of Nature and the Evolution of Music Theory.' In D.J. Schneck and J.K. Schneck (eds) *Music in Human Adaptation,* 423–436. Blacksburg, Va.: Virginia Tech Press.

Slawson, W. (1985) *Sound Color.* Berkeley, Calif.: The University of California Press.

Storr, A. (1992) *Music and the Mind.* New York: The Tree Press/MacMillan, Inc.

Thaut, M., Miller, R.A. and Schauer, M.L. (1997) 'Rhythm in Human Motor Control: Adaptive Mechanisms in Movement Synchronization.' In D.J. Schneck and J.K. Schneck (eds) *Music in Human Adaptation,* 191–198. Blacksburg, Va.: Virginia Tech Press.

Thaut, M. (1997) 'Rhythmic Auditory Stimulation in Rehabilitation of Movement Disorders: A Review of Current Research.' In D.J. Schneck and J.K. Schneck (eds) *Music in Human Adaptation,* 223–229. Blacksburg, Va.: Virginia Tech Press.

Thaut, M., Kenyon, G.P., Schauer, M.L. and McIntosh, G.C. (1999) 'The Connection between Rhythmicity and Brain Function.' *IEEE Engineering in Medicine and Biology 18,* 2, 101–108.

Valentinuzzi, M.E. and Arias, N.E. (1999) 'Human Psychophysiological Perception of Musical Scales and Nontraditional Music.' *IEEE Engineering in Medicine and Biology 18,* 2, 54–60.

CHAPTER 9

Music Therapy in the Realm of Sensory Integration

The existence of music as an emotional form of self-expression may not be incidental to human function. Given the brain's efficiency in condensing superfluous information toward a more economic use of incoming information, it would seem highly unlikely that music would exist only for the sheer "pleasure principle", as some prominent authors would have us believe. (Is sitting for two hours on a hard chair in a concert hall "pleasure"? Why do we do this?)

More than likely, music, as part and parcel of human behavior, exists precisely for the purpose of emotional expression, and to assist in the adaptation process of human beings to their surroundings. In short, our brains conceived music because we need it to redirect tensions, to organize behavior and to express emotion.

No other experience is able to duplicate the abstraction of emotion in quite the same way as music. Would the human brain have created something totally irrelevant to its existence and survival? In fact, one theory my colleagues and I have contemplated is that the human brain, since it likes to compress information in short forms, might actually have taken extended prosodic (melodic) incantations (music of a sort) and contracted these sounds into what evolved into "verbalization", i.e. speech and language. We know, of course, that music immediately describes an emotion that it would take several verbal sentences to illuminate.

Music does not, it has been stated, particularly require neo-cortex processing. Language absolutely does. Music proceeds directly through the limbic system (amygdala, thalamus, hypothalamus, hippocampus, cerebellum, etc.), needing no further explanation from cortical lobes. Of course, the neo-cortex can play a convenient role in interpreting music, but this is not a requirement. Configuration of sounds will be responded to with or without "intellectual" processing. An infant understands music expression at the intuitive, sub-cortical level, without as yet having any developed "intellect". (Perhaps the neo-cortex needs music to interpret and understand "emotion" psychologically. Or perhaps the neo-cortex is just a file-cabinet where music information is stored, and the work is actually done at the primal level? At present we do not know.)

To the music therapist, the understanding of terms such as *vestibular* and *proprioception* might seem unessential. Why would a music therapist need to be concerned with whether the child's brain receives proper messages from joints and muscles? Standard music therapy goals for autistic children, as already stated, are usually directed towards addressing issues of cognition, "connectedness" (the opposite of "autism"), self-esteem, awareness and feeling good. It might seem irrelevant whether or not a child plays in rhythm, or uses varied dynamics, or plays with heavier mallets, as long as he or she plays *with* the therapist, others in a group and the music being presented.

However, approaching music therapy purely from the standpoint of "connection" and "warm fuzzies" is to omit an entire realm of physiologic clinical responsibility implied by the word *therapy*. As stated at the beginning of this book, *cenesthesia* – a system's sense of well-being – *must first be operative* before the gates of the paleoencephalon can open to higher level, cognitive (cortical) learning. When a system experiences sensory interpretation that may be stressful rather than comfortably functional ("normal") in the day-to-day world, the brain will be too busy dealing with the distress to allow "intellectual" activities to take hold. A body under constant siege needs to be stabilized first, before anything else can take place.

Does it matter whether a child plays or walks rhythmically as long as he or she is having fun? Yes, indeed it *does* matter whether a child walks or plays rhythmically, can discriminate pitch and timbre variables, recognize a familiar melody and organize movement with rhythm. Music for "connection" is only the tip of the iceberg. It is in the process of doing something *purposefully*, *accurately* and *in a variety of manners* that the intervention ultimately leads to the brain developing the capacity to repattern and retain new sensory information perpetuating functional adaptation.

The requirement of repetition, accuracy and exercises aimed at sensory/*physiologic* processes focuses attention on details, demands repetitive precision, incorporates a wide scope of sensory integration issues, and forces and reinforces new adaptive responses of the sensory systems. Ultimately, "good feelings" emerge from accomplishment, and from the system assuming a state of cenesthesia, when all the senses are coordinated and the system is comfortable with the information.

Integrating physiologic knowledge with therapy approaches

Essentially the music therapist, using the elements of music (Chapter 8) that are the tools of the profession, provides the "continuous disturbance" to coax the brain into dealing with new, alternative conditions (because the stimulus is not going away!) Ultimately changes in the feedback control system culminate in the development of new homeostatic reference points that supplant old ones. Once the brain's amygdala, thalamus and hypothalamus change their opinions about the body's state of siege, adaptive functional behaviors can take hold.

Several chapters have demonstrated how music therapy interventions can be used for sensory issues, on both reflexive and permanent functional accommodation levels. We have pondered Randy's humming, Jason's gong, Fanny's letter *F*, Ethan's perfect pitch, Marty's need to shut down one system in order to process another, and Alonzo's need for rhythm to organize chaotic movement. Many instances have suggested how music therapy treatment activities could improve physiologic function when particular sensory deficits exist.

Evaluating physiology for adaptive goals

In terms of sensory integration and one's ultimate mental well-being, we have learned that unless the RAS and *thring* (Chapters 3 and 4) feel "safe" and satisfied, higher learning (cognition) will be limited, if not impossible. Therefore expecting the behavior of someone on the autistic spectrum to "conform" on command is naive and unrealistic. Every human being, on whatever "spectrum" they happen to appear, is first and foremost emotional, not intellectual! So, instinctive (emotional) behavior must first be altered at the paleoencephalon (old brain) level, before intellect (the neo-cortex, or new brain) and cognition can be addressed.

Confronting the well-being (psychologic) aspect of autism means first tackling sensory physiologic issues. For the music therapist, that begins with the auditory system. Sound coming at us, or sent out, is a message of an emotional state. What can one person learn about another by observing the other's reactions to music? The primary question for music therapy to confront and resolve is: what kind of music will quiet a system in order for other work to take place?

Careful observation, coupled with knowledge of potential sensory and physiologic problems, will inform the therapist of existing conditions. This means intervening in a manner that results first in establishing certain physiologic "comfort" levels. Understanding adaptation, the brain and sensory systems along with theories of sensory integration make this possibility viable for the music therapist.

The following sensory aspects can often be observed within the first six weeks of music therapy:

Reactions to sound: since it cannot be "assumed" that sound is being perceived as transmitted, nor how it is being perceived altogether, and since the auditory system's processes cannot be seen, the therapist must note physical and facial affect in relation to sound presentation. Anything from a smile to a frown, to shrieking, satelliting (erratic movement around a room), to holding the ears shut, is logged for consideration as a possible "reaction" to sound. Is there recognition (by smile or similar response) of a familiar tune? Is rhythm altering body movement? Is fear present? Many other indicators become observable to the therapist aware of auditory components. A compilation of these notes will lead the therapist to an informed consideration of possible auditory issues.

Body attributes: observation of visible physical behaviors in the manner in which a person walks, runs (or not), moves arms and legs (or not), stands, needs to sit, reaches for or holds onto objects etc., leads to information about muscle tone and proprioceptive function. For instance, in the day-to-day world, it is often easy to observe if a (non-diagnosed) person carries tension by observing the shoulders and general rhythms of body movements. The "Type A" personality – highly competitive, impatient, quite ambitious, stressed, aggressive and needing always to control every situation – can often be detected by his or her overall tense physicality and body mannerisms, even before verbal contact is initiated. A 'Type A' personality generally tends to speak faster, be fidgety with darting eye glances, use excessive arm and body movements, pace about anxiously, and so on.

In the diagnosed populations, physicality is more than likely related to sensory issues. Tensions could indicate vestibular insecurities; is the brain sure where the arms are and what they're doing (proprioception)? Or the legs? Are the eyes confirming spatial information? Is the head being held upright and steady? Are eyes continuously scanning, or can they rest firmly on an object? Are heavy objects difficult to hold? Do objects tend to fall out of the hand? Are certain items repelling to the touch?

Movement: is a solid sense of balance observed? Can the person control the body to stop and start exactly on cue? Is facing in different directions (i.e. doing a movement in one direction, then turning to perform the same action in an opposite direction) disorienting their spatial concepts? Is there favoring of one side or the other? Has left or right-handedness been declared (this indicates whether mid-line orientation is intact)? Is there crossing of mid-line to reach the opposite side of the body (touching left knee with right hand, for instance)? Can the upper body undertake one activity while the lower body (legs) is doing something else? What is the level of muscle tone?

Do body movements tend to be slow, quick, unpaced, rigid? Is there comfortable flexion and extension of limbs? Does the body move within the rhythm of the music? Can the arms coordinate bilaterally, playing a drum with alternate arm movements as easily as with parallel arm movements? Can pulse be sustained in drumming? Marching? Is there upper-lower body coordination? Marching while drumming? (These are indicators of motor-planning issues.)

These and other questions indicate vestibular, proprioceptive and tactile issues impacting on motor planning, balance and sense of center, that could be present and need to be addressed through music therapy interventions. Can quick movements be immediately changed to slow movements (vestibular and motor-planning issues) when music changes? Is there facile imitation of the therapist's movements? Is there left/right confusion?

Affect and psycho-physiologic behaviors: are there specific elements of music that contribute to averse emotional reactions: Timbre? Volume? Pitch? Is fear demeanor possibly a result of the sound being considered threatening by the brain? Are there smiles, frowns, obvious signs of tune recognition? Is there animation with certain rhythms? Passivity with certain types of music? Can the body become calm? Is reaction to the music influenced by whether the child is standing, moving, sitting, lying? Do behaviors change if music activity precedes, follows or is simultaneous with physical activity?

Assessments and determinations in this area are important to the learning demeanor needed in school. Often the music therapist can detect whether a person functions better in one or another position in order to alleviate sensory/physical issues so that the brain is allowed to concentrate on learning. The occupation therapist can confirm the findings of the music therapist, and vice versa, so that they can collaborate on goals leading towards adequate function in the school setting.

Additional emotional factors related to sensory issues: entering the brain through the auditory system, music stimulates the limbic system, triggering emotional factors which induce motivation and willingness to make choices and undertake new sensory patterns. Since music is basically a whole-brain, two-brain (old and new) activity, music therapy also provides an opportunity to induce left-brain cognition by using the right brain to stimulate the left so the hemispheres can work cooperatively.

One informed "assumption" here (using the term carefully!) would be that music, given the right format employing appropriate elements and instrumentation, can be stimulating and enjoyable long enough to help a system calm down and relax (reducing the flow of cortisol and inducing the flow of dopamine). Repetition of similar interventions over several sessions might reinforce the sense of "trust" for the music environment (non-threatening), after which further sensory issues could be explored.

What is being suggested by the above observations is that "connection" or "relationship" is really only the first step on the road to determining goals and interventions which can induce permanent functional adaptations that will pervade in all areas of human function for the autistic child.

Aspects of music therapy treatment

Now the work begins. In order to move, play an instrument, sing or beat a precise rhythm on a drum or tambourine while simultaneously marching, skipping, or running, the brain must know where the body is in relation to gravity (vestibular orientation), and where its arms, legs and torso are in space (through proprioceptive messages from muscles and joints).

Among its chores, as we now understand, the auditory system must correctly confirm that what it hears requires a particular response. The visual system supports action by providing spatial references to guide limbs. All this requires automatic coordination in central processing. With repetition, patterns become internalized – automated – and can be generalized to other activities that require motor planning and pacing.

The premise of occupation therapy's sensory integration treatment is that the brain can be induced, on the sub-cortical level through specific sensory-motor tasks, to develop functional (adaptive) responses to the environment.

The premise of music therapy treatment for sensory integration is that it can develop both the cognitive and intuitive/emotional adaptive responses on both the sub-cortical and the cortical levels. Music therapy works with what is there (not what's missing), building upon that which is already functioning by providing new input which the brain can use to help expand its knowledge on all levels. Whatever the child presents, whoever the child *is*, provides material upon which to expand.

Exactly how the brain does what it does is the subject of speculation. Neuroscientists observe cerebral "light shows" through advances in imaging technology. But exactly what happens beyond the light show, and how and why it happens, is still as much a mystery as the creation of the universe. Observations cause us to make assumptions. These, as we are seeing, can at times be inapplicable if incorrect. The work of music therapy is to use music for enjoyment, to be sure, but especially to apply it in ways that will teach the "old" brain new tricks in a very non-threatening, non-intrusive manner.

Looking at the whole child from the vantage point of sensory perception and functional adaptation, the music therapist can develop short- and long-term goals and activities pertinent to both the specific treatment goals and to overall goals supporting sensory-integrative issues as outlined in previous chapters. The ultimate goals, of course, are to make positive impact upon functional adaptation through repatterning and reorganization of sensory precepts, and to foster that sense of well-being – that state of cenesthesia. *This takes many interventions over extended periods.*

Since music is a multisensory intervention, the music therapist often has the advantage of being able to reach multiple sensory systems – vestibular, tactile, proprioceptive, auditory and visual – all at once. Beating a standing drum by using heavy weighted mallets, which involves organizing bilateral parallel and alternating arm movements while maintaining the rhythmic pulse and pattern of the music, surely constitutes a multisensory activity! Motor planning, auditory processing, proprioceptive input, visual verification and tactile sensations combine to execute such a task.

Since the brain enjoys processing patterns, it often "forgets" what it cannot do, and suddenly the body is doing things it never knew it could do, in an organized manner, with visual contact, auditory concentration, muscular pacing, and more! The sheer *motivation* factor, and the driving "continuous disturbance" of repetitive pulse and pattern, produce new feedforward and feedback information never before available to, nor sought by, that brain. Continuation of these types of activities could ulti mately lead to the establishment of new homeostatic reference points and adaptive future responses.

Instruments for sensory adaptation goals

Music therapy treatments for autism and many other diagnoses, when based on physiologic information, address: motor planning, vestibular and proprioceptive deficits, tactile defensiveness, auditory function, audio-visual coordination, physical coordination, communication and language. Incorporated into and often resulting from adaptation in these areas are: creativity, self-initiative, social interaction, sense of self and others, body pacing and self-organization, task organization, and general functional adaptation to environment.

Therapy approaches for sensory dysfunction are always "child-centered" because a particular child at a particular time is being addressed by the treatment. Any preferences and moods displayed by the child at that moment can be shaped and redirected toward specific sensory adaptation goals, because any observable behaviors provide the therapist with further information about physiologic function *at that particular moment*.

Music is, after all, a reflection of mood and emotion, and of how the brain and body are attending to moment-by-moment physical and emotional circumstances. The key is for a therapist continually to integrate the psycho-emotional with the physiologic aspects of the problem, in order to evolve a truly holistic therapy intervention. Concerns for behavior and cognition must temporarily be placed second to physiologic well-being.

Objectives for reaching goals dealing with adaptation are approached through music and movement, with occasional use of occupation therapy items such as a *trampoline* for centering and rhythmic jumping, *teeter-totters* and small step platforms for vestibular exercises and games done to music and large *therapy balls* to bounce upon (which acts as speech stimulation) for vestibular and rhythmic internalization purposes.

Treatment plans, goals and tasks are designed to address identified, prioritized sensory deficits, formulated from the music therapy assessment period, observation, and sensory dysfunction information. Auditory and other sensory problems are presumed to exist. Sound is introduced with extreme alertness to acute tonal, timbrel and volume sensitivity, as previously mentioned. Exercises and sundry improvisational musical activities can be designed by the therapist to shape each session effectively according to goals that address sensory and later, cognitive issues.

Keyboards

Clinical treatments that employ keyboard improvisation and a variety of instruments of diverse timbres are very effective in inducing adaptive changes. The element of musical spontaneity provides the flexibility needed to alter moods, patterns, pulse, dynamics, pacing, tonalities and movement cues. Improvisation is used either to arouse or quell movement – an essential component of a treatment plan.

The *acoustic piano*, which is able to emit a wealth of sound vibrations that stimulate multiple sensations beyond the auditory, impacts especially upon the tactile and proprioceptive senses. A therapist can even place a child in a sitting position directly on top of a piano to allow vibrations to come directly in contact with the body for further tactile and proprioceptive stimulation. The acoustic piano's emission of vibrational overtones, often reverberating and inducing overtones from surrounding instruments in the therapy environment, is a direct stimulation of inner auditory processes.

Electric keyboards are effective in reducing the amount of vibrations permeating a room, and are useful when major hyperacusis or other auditory sensitivities exist, as was exemplified by Jason. Many electric keyboards provide opportunities to explore timbres and auditory discrimination elements that might otherwise be unavailable. Beyond these advantages, however, it has been my personal belief that electric keyboards seem rather less effective than acoustic vibrations (which are natural rather than digitized sounds) in inducing accurate discrimination processing.

Sometimes the use of *pre-taped music* and *electronic rhythm simulators* can free a therapist to prompt a child physically, but this, too, appears to be less effective than spontaneous music-making which is able quickly to change tempi, patterns and sounds as needed in the moment. Recall that a predictable, continuously similar stimulus can cause the brain eventually to "tune out", which is the exact opposite of music therapy treatment goals for adaptation. The point is to keep the brain *tuned in*, so that new reactions can be developed.

Stringed instruments

Stringed instruments (guitar, violin, cello) are excellent to use for tactile bilateral motor-planning issues, and for developing and understanding mid-line activities. The *violin* and *cello* are especially useful for centering, at mid-line, the central visual focus of the eyes. Central visual use (as opposed to peripheral) is further supported by the manner in which two arms embrace and play the instrument(s) at mid-line.

In order to extract a sound from a violin or cello, the bow must be centered between the bridge and the fingerboard, and drawn across the strings. Bilateral non-parallel upper body movements are employed; one arm holds the fiddle and fingers the strings, while the other bows. The eyes must guide the actions or a good sound will be difficult to obtain. (Only the experienced string musician can play with eyes closed!)

In addition to physical and visual coordination, upper body dynamics come into play. How light or heavy the arms are when holding the instrument or drawing the bow will determine how pleasing the sounds are. When I suggest to my patient that drawing the bow on a violin string is like petting a kitten, I notice an instinctive release of tension and grip. The bowing arm's dynamic posture changes. Proprioceptive information for motor planning often becomes more reliable with repetition, until a wider range of upper body dynamics is made available. This later transfers into the manner of holding a pen or pencil in school.

The *guitar*, played by therapist or child, can be beneficial especially for tactile input, mid-line orientation and non-parallel bilateral arm coordination. The sound of the guitar accompanying a song, or simply strumming restful sounds, is a system-relaxer apparently enjoyable to all children. Allowing the child to strum while the therapist fingers the chords provides tactile stimulation, but caution must be used. This strumming action could sometimes be an uncomfortable sensation to a tactile-defensive child.

Learning actually to play chords on the guitar is extremely complicated for someone lacking tactile discrimination, since much depends on finger sensing for the location of various strings. It requires good motor planning and the ability to *see-sense-hear* correct chord changes. It may be a frustrating experience, ineffective if tactile sensory issues exist.

Aside from two hands being required to do two completely different things on a guitar, the manner of holding the instrument across mid-line, and insufficient auditory processing (or theoretical knowldge) related to chord changes could create more problems than resolutions. Unless a child displays unique talent and instinct for guitar playing, it would not be recommended for those with proprioceptive, tactile and auditory problems. Other instruments could better serve those purposes and allow for more successful interaction.

Percussion

Hand percussions (afuche cabasa, vibraslap, heavy hand cymbals, claves, maracas) provide vibrational, tactile and proprioception stimuli. As well as developing upper body muscular tone, the use of heavier instruments will submit substantial proprioceptive information to the brain, indicating where the arms are, how far they are bent and how much force and energy are needed to negotiate playing the instrument(s) successfully.

The *afuche cabasa* is especially useful in providing tactile input. Occupation therapy prescribes a system of "brushing" as part of a "sensory diet" to stimulate proprioception and alleviate tactile defensiveness. The cabasa can play a similar role to the brushing techniques of occupation therapy. Since drawing a sound from the cabasa requires the rotation of the B–B chains wrapped about its carriage, it provides tactile input to the palms of the hands. When rhythm is present, and the brain relaxes to the music, tactile sensitivity gives way to fun and games. The cabasa can also be "brushed" along legs, arms, and other parts of the body in rhythm, providing tactile and proprioceptive input to other parts of the body. A standard size cabasa is quite heavy. To play the instrument, the arms bend at the elbows and one hand grips it while the other rotates the beads. Motor planning, muscle tone of the arms and coordination are involved in the action.

Claves can also be heavy, and require mid-line parallel organization of both hands in order to clap the beat. Someone with mid-line orientation and upper-body motor-planning problems will be observed having difficulties beating two sticks together efficiently, with eyes rarely centering on the task.

Unique opportunities for auditory/visual tracking and integration are provided through use of larger, heavier *hand bells*, which are struck and moved about so the eyes and ears can coordinate in pursuit of sound. Changing bell tones means first finding the correct bell by looking for it, reaching to obtain it, and clanging it on time. This involves coordination of auditory, visual, proprioceptive and tactile systems, plus muscle tone and motor planning.

Along with heavy hand bells, larger and heavier *maracas* contribute to motor planning for the arm and sustaining of task. The bending of the elbows and the grip required to hold onto instrument in order to shake maracas contributes to proprioceptive input, notifying the brain about where and how the arms and hands are doing things in accordance with what is required.

An array of *drums*, including bongos, snare, bass and alto drums, and a variety of *Orff-type instruments* (xylophones, tone bars, chimes, etc.) support rhythmic activities involving upper-body motor planning and bilateral arm movements coupled with auditory discrimination, rhythmic internalization, sequencing, cognition, and especially eye-hand coordination objectives. These instruments are also invaluable in developing rhythm internalization and structured, physically and mentally coordinated musical interaction.

For proprioceptive input, it is recommended that heavier mallets are used, with thick grips for holding the mallets securely yet comfortably without having completely to close the fist in order to keep them in hand. Many mallets with thin grips are efficient at providing accurate proprioceptive feedback about arm positions, muscular force and other physical requirements needed to execute drum playing without frequently dropping the sticks.

A drumming task is an attempt to teach the brain about physiologic elements it needs to know. This means sending more exaggerated information to the brain at first, before adjustment to "normal" can be made. Mallets that are too long besides being too lightweight and thin present more problems than remedies for upper-body motor-planning issues. How far to extend the arms in order to reach the drum can be as much a part of the information required as how much to bend the elbow, how high to raise the arm in order to strike the drum, or how much force is adequate for the task. Mallets are instruments in themselves and need to be considered carefully in treatment so that successful drumming goals can be attained.

Xylophones, tone bells, metallophones

The playing of designated tones on the *metallophone* or *xylophone* requires visual attention and eye-hand coordination. It therefore contributes important visual and physical feedforward and feedback planning information to the brain. Eventually the "habit" of visual tracking, and the coordination of arm movements with visual tracking, takes hold in efficiently resolving a task. If a child is asked to strike only the D and A pitches on a xylophone, without touching any other, then the eyes and motor planning must be put into operation in compliance with the task!

Sometimes it takes many sessions before accurate aim and positive changes begin to take hold, but when they do, the sense of fulfillment on the part of the child is extraordinary! Meanwhile, the brain obtains the rhythm and spacing of arm movements – just enough horizontal movement to reach each tone, just enough pressure to strike the tone, and continuous visual tracking and confirmation of movements. The task becomes more and more successful as both single-arm and bilateral arm use increase the likelihood of adaptive changes. This can, of course, be progressed into playing additionally specified tones, familiar tunes, different tones and/or rhythms per hand, and more.

Blowing instruments...

Many autistic children display oral-motor deficits hindering food consumption and speech production. Recorders, harmonicas, kazoos and wind instruments assist with centering eyes and body at mid-line, and organizing tongue action and breath (diaphragm) control, impacting on speech and language oral-motor planning. These instruments also provide tongue and diaphragmatic movements that stimulate internal proprioceptive transducers.

The *recorder*, because it is placed inside the mouth and has a mouthpiece large enough for the lips to enfold comfortably, is especially beneficial. The recorder is played with head erect and arms comfortably hanging from the shoulders to the elbows, bending at the elbows. Therefore, a most natural body position is assumed. The playing of recorder brings everything to mid-line: eyes, hands, mouth, tongue, auditory focus, tactile sense. Often children with autism find it difficult to sustain holding onto the recorder with both hands. This provides the therapist with some clues about mid-line orientation and bilateral arm capabilities. The better the child learns to hold the recorder with both hands, the stronger the mid-line orientation becomes.

The *harmonica* produces sounds on both the inhale and the exhale. Thus it is a wonderful instrument with which to pace breathing. The *kazoo* requires the player to hum a tone into the instrument. The timbre of the hum is altered by the vibrating flap inside the kazoo. Just blowing into a kazoo does not produce a sound. When humming into a kazoo, the vibration ("buzzing") to the lips, tongue and inner front portions of the mouth provides a great deal of stimulation and feedback to the oral-motor system. Since talking means producing audible sound on the exhale, the kazoo can play an important role in developing extensive vocalization without "fear".

Instruments that require placement *inside* the mouth would be preferable for addressing oral-motor, tongue and lip issues of language and eating disorders. Instruments pressed *onto* the lips could be beneficial for vibrational sensations to the lips. Breath control intricacies will differ between instruments placed inside the mouth and instruments pressed onto the lips. Other blowing instruments employed by some therapists for discreet goals include *reed horns* and similar items.

An important consideration in the selection of blown instruments is their ability to produce sound *effortlessly*, thereby alleviating potential impediments to a blowing task that could compound sensory and oral motor problems.

...and vocalization

Vocal activities in song, and the production of nonsense sounds and imitation of sounds tend to organize language articulation, breath control and auditory acuity. As stated above, kazoos and recorders have worked wonders in stimulating additional vocalization and humming in non-verbal populations. This has extended into vocal affect, instilling inflections and prosody in persons with autism and Down Syndrome, who tend toward mono-tonal speech. In stimulating the exhalation of tones, the brain can learn how to exhale sounds that are later shaped into letter sounds and words.

Vocalizing familiar songs using only *la-la* and similar non-verbal vocalizations (based predominantly on vowel sounds), instead of singing actual words, tends to have more influence on *vocal imitation*. Words are often difficult to "hear" and imitate, and the cognitive need to define words can deter motivation. Furthermore, as stated in previous chapters, assumptions about verbal processing and comprehension cannot be accurately made. A therapist, educator, or parent may not always know for sure that words are "getting through" and being understood instead of being processed as purely random sounds. If words are being processed as random sounds, these sounds may be much more difficult to imitate than vowel sounds with limited consonants.

The encouragement of vocal sound imitation is strongly recommended. The inclusion of words to a song is at the discretion of the therapist, who has made an assessment of abilities.

Additional instruments

Many other instruments can aid in sensory adaptation, auditory discrimination and visual acuity. To play a *triangle*, for instance, much visual-motor planning is involved, lest the mallet strike the side of the triangle inappropriate to the obtainment of a sound (a triangle keeps moving around as it is being held).

An array of African *rattles, talking drums*, primitive noise-makers, *clackers* and instruments adapted to physically handicapped populations are also beneficial when applied for specific sensory issues. *Slit drums* and similar instruments provide opportunity for auditory attention and discrimination of subtler, at times less audible, clear pitch frequencies.

Gongs are exceptionally useful for auditory attention, especially when the child remains attentive until the sound dissipates. Vibrations of a gong also can provide proprioceptive feedback, giving someone an experience of sensing the body due to external vibratory input. Other resonant instruments, such as sundry *chimes* that can be played by the therapist and moved around the head of the child, will induce auditory tracking and attention.

Small *maracas* in the shape of eggs, fruit and vegetables, even tiny maracas called *chiquitas*, when embraced in the palms of the hands provide proprioceptive and tactile feedback from the hands, elbows and arms to the brain.

It is at the discretion of the therapist which instruments and therapy approaches will provide the most appropriate stimulus for addressing specific sensory goals. Instruments requiring mallets; those struck by hands or shaken or rattled; those requiring individual fingers or vocal input; each provide the brain with an opportunity to use muscles and motor planning in unique ways. Age-appropriateness of instruments may also be a consideration, along with timbre, pitch and volume tolerance, physical abilities, goals and preferences of the child.

Instruction as therapy

Instrumental instruction and training as part of treatment can have important impact on many physiologic, psycho-emotional and cognitive elements discussed throughout this book. Any undertaking, on any instrument, qualifies as a potential treatment device. Interest, motivation and discipline to "learn" an instrument bespeaks that brain's ability to become organized. This can be capitalized upon quite effectively, especially in developing cognitive goals along with physiologic and emotional adaptation. What's more, many children being treated often display musical talents that could develop into something more substantial in the future.

Keyboard instruction and training is especially invaluable in developing eye-hand coordination. Since both arms and hands participate in the same manner when playing a keyboard instrument – i.e. individual finger digits must strike individual tones (or chords), arms move horizontally back and forth on a keyboard and eyes look at notation, while motor-planning practice places hands and finger on the correct tones –thus many physiologic issues are addressed extremely well through this task. No other instrumental participation develops fine-motor (finger) abilities quite like the piano does, and so helps the hands and fingers to get ready for school use.

Of course not all children have interests in organized piano playing, but many do. Marty, (Chapter 7) who turns away from the sound to shut down one sense in order to use another, has learned to play piano. He is autistic, completely non-verbal, with many sensory issues, but also seems to have some sort of absolute pitch, can sing anything in key, and provide the correct "next tone" in a fill-in song; he lights up when he sits at the piano. He is eight years old, and has learned to identify abstract symbols designating piano pitches (from middle C both up and down!)

The idea of his playing the piano was instigated by Marty. Now, he points to the notation with his left hand, while finding the tones (he now knows where the tones are on the piano) of the tune with his right. And vice versa. When both hands are required, and no one is pointing, he has learned visually to track the information by himself. (Computer games at home have also helped.) And *voila!* He plays "Old MacDonald" and grins from ear to ear.

Marty's playing of the piano enabled the visual, auditory and tactile senses to operate simultaneously. Previously, as we recall, Marty tended to shut down one sense, either visual or tactile (or both) in order to focus his "hearing". Now, in order to play the piano, he must look, do, hear at once. In addition, he also sings the tune while playing, actually pronouncing most of the words accurately! This ability has rippled into his school activities, so that he can look at a shape and copy it while continuing to look at it. This is the precursor to learning to write.

Marty's auditory tracking and pitch discrimination skills are so keen that they guide his hands into finding the correct next pitch without prompting. He accomplishes this purely by "touch" and auditory collaboration! Also, his internal visualization skills have improved as a result of his external visual attention and tracking of notes on the piano. Overall, the residual effects of Marty's learning to play piano continue to increase in any number of ways.

Carl, a teenage boy with Asperger Syndrome, has become so proficient and advanced on the piano that he has recently won a scholarship to a summer music program. This has placed him at the center of notoriety among his high school classmates, much to his surprise, not to mention all the other physiologic and concentration benefits his brain now enjoys! Carl also plays the violin and has the social opportunity to take part in his school's orchestral program.

Eleanor, a five-year-old Down Syndrome child with some autistic-type behaviors, often has great difficulty remaining "on task" for more than a fleeting moment. During one of our sessions she was introduced to the violin. Eleanor, never having held this instrument in her life, immediately knew how to hold the bow and what to do with it! When the violin was placed under her chin with her right arm extended to embrace the instrument at its shoulder, and her left arm was guided over the strings for the first time, Eleanor took off! At no time did her eyes leave the task (which is at mid-line).

Eleanor's bowing arm moved effortlessly, back and forth over each string, with the bow always remaining centered between, and parallel to, the bridge and the black fingerboard. Eleanor played and played as if the violin and bow were part of her limbs. As long as the piano played, she played. Eleanor could remain on this task for the entire 45-minute session, if she were permitted to do so. Her bowing arm's physical dynamics instinctively responded to loud and soft sounds from the piano. Her playing never screeched!

The violin is who Eleanor is – undiagnosed! Parents have procured a tiny violin for her, that she permits no one at home to touch. It is Eleanor's property and identity. She has begun "formal" instruction for 15 minutes of our therapy session. Currently, Eleanor delights in playing the open E (highest pitch) and G (lowest pitch) strings. And Eleanor sings her favorite songs (with lyrics) all the while she is playing the violin. The message to me, her therapist, is that her brain not only *can* organize and remain on task with motivation, but *wants* to!

This child is definitely talented for the violin. The activity has already influenced Eleanor's ability to stick to something for prolonged periods, impacting on other areas of her behavior. Visual focus and mid-line visual focus have improved, as have eye-hand coordination, visual attention and tracking, vestibular comfort (she stands on a small step when she plays, to induce adaptive balance correction), bilateral arm coordination, and any number of other things. Eleanor has been recommended to receive formal violin instruction from a close associate who often consults with me on special needs children. This will not replace therapy, but will be in addition.

A music therapist can discover hidden talents usually dismissed or referred to by lay persons as "splinter skills" (whatever that means). In fact, a skill is a skill. All skills are "splinter skills"! *Any skill that organizes the brain into functional behavior is valid and important, not "incidental".* Skills instinctive to the system are perhaps even more valid than "learned cognition", because as we have learned, it is first instinct, not cognition, that aids survival. And instructive music therapy can bring about startling instinctive as well as cognitive achievements.

Music instruction as therapy, vocal or instrumental, can become part of the brain's training process for a multitude of issues. In addition to mere cognitive development, instruction encompasses:

- staying on task
- auditory tracking
- visual tracking
- eye-hand coordination
- extended visual and mental attention
- bilateral arm and finger coordination
- sequential memory and recall
- abstract information processing
- anticipating and planning ahead
- rhythmic internalization
- self-discipline
- accomplishment and self-esteem
- many other valuable skills.

Keyboard instruction is especially beneficial in bilateral fine-motor development. Aspects of *see-think-do* relative to information-processing time can also be improved with piano and other instrumental instruction. Although instruction can serve therapy purposes, it is important that a music therapist is the provider of instruction for a diagnosed child. This is because the trained music therapist has knowledge of human function other than just musical – information not readily available to the local instrumental or vocal teacher.

The manner of assessing a diagnosed child's physiologic and cognitive needs in a learning environment, the approach to handling the child, the adaptation of training materials, the expectations of the therapist/teacher, and the knowledge of how much is enough, lie within the realm of the music therapist. Parents and caregivers need to understand the difference between a *teacher* and a *therapist*, in order to seek the best possible approach to musical training for a diagnosed child that will ensure beneficial and ancillary development.

Summary

Music therapy treatment for sensory integration fosters a child-centered approach. Structures and directives aiding the learning of new instincts enable efficient functional adaptation. Activities and use of certain instruments are guided by child-initiated interests at a particular time, and/or therapist-organized suggestions.

The child's personality and presenting behaviors *in the moment* provide a therapist with the opportunity to view and assess specific physiologic and holistic needs leading to successful treatment. Choice, task initiation, decision-making, and individuality are prime elements in activating the child's motivation to reorganize and undertake unfamiliar things. Music elements play a role in influencing responses and behaviors. They can relax the system from physiologic or psycho-emotional stressors, opening the gates to cognitive centers.

The primary concern of music therapy for sensory integration is the well-being of the system. Once stressors are addressed and systematically dispensed with, other developmental issues fall in line. *Physiologic comfort   psycho-emotional stability   cognitive ability* – in that order. Improvement of skills in music therapy undertakings indicates that sensory information is becoming better organized and interpreted by the brain, and functional physiologic accommodation is becoming a new homeostatic norm *for that system.* Within this physiologic framework learning can take place.

The most important idea to keep in mind in relation to physiology and learning, for any individual, is that *any new experience provided to the brain begins a process of adaptation and learning by that brain.* And, when an experience is applied as a "continuous disturbance", the brain, an organ that instinctively likes to "perfect" and organize what it knows, will ultimately learn to call for adaptive new responses.

The application of music, instrumental playing and vocalization for sensory-integration problems provides opportunities often unavailable through other means for a brain to organize the body. Sitting at a drum for three minutes may be three minutes more than that brain has ever experienced or learned before!

Any opportunity the brain is given to experience a functional behavior will result in something being learned, retained and used in other situations. The continuity of treatment and application of well-planned stimulus input will eventually achieve learned positive results. "Connection" and "self-esteem" are automatic by-products of physiologic comfort.

Recommended reading

Begley, S. (2000) 'Music on the Mind.' *Newsweek* 24 July, 50–52.

Blood, A.J., Zatorre, R.J., Bermudez, P. and Evans, A.C. (1999) 'Emotional Responses to Pleasant and Unpleasant Music Correlate with Activity in Paralimbic Brain Regions.' *Nature Neuroscience 2*, 4, 382–387.

Brewer, C.B. (1997) 'Learning Progress through the Use of Music in the Creative Process and in Critical Thinking Skills.' In J.D. Schneck and J.K. Schneck (eds) *Music in Human Adaptation*, 317–318. Blacksburg, Va.: Virginia Tech Press.

Dess, N.K. (2000) 'Music on the Mind.' *Psychology Today*, September/October, 28.

Kartha, D.K.M. (1997) 'Magic of Hand Drumming: Hand Drumming as an Activity Promoting Human Adaptation through Enhancement of Skills.' In J.D. Schneck and J.K. Schneck (eds), *Music in Human Adaptation*, 199–202. Blacksburg, Va.: Virginia Tech Press.

Kaye, M. (1997) 'Music of the Spheres: Mystic Probability Becomes Implemental Reality.' In J D Schneck and J K Schneck (eds) *Music in Human Adaptation*, 291–299. Blacksburg, Va.: Virginia Tech Press.

Legge, M.F. (1997) 'Hypnocise – A Rehabilitative Modality Using Pentatonic Scales and Octotonic Modes.' In J.D. Schneck and J.K. Schneck (eds) *Music in Human Adaptation*, 379–394. Blacksburg, Va.: Virginia Tech Press.

Legge, M.F. (1999) 'Music for Health: The Five Elements Tonal System.' *IEEE: Engineering in Medicine and Biology 18*, 2, 80–88.

Nakkach, S. (1997) 'Into the Core of Music Healing.' In J.D. Schneck and J.K. Schneck (eds) *Music in Human Adaptation*, 441–458. Blacksburg, Va.: Virginia Tech Press.

Patrick, G. (1999) 'The Effects of Vibroacoustic Music on Symptom Reduction.' *IEEE: Engineering in Medicine and Biology 18*, 2, 97–100.

Thompson, B.M. and Andrews S.R. (1999) 'The Emerging Field of Sound Training.' *IEEE: Engineering in Medicine and Biology 18*, 2, 89–96.

Weiss, C. (1997) 'Thought Forms and Music.' In J.D. Schneck and J.K. Schneck (eds) *Music in Human Adaptation*, 277–288. Blacksburg, Va.: Virginia Tech Press.

CHAPTER 10

Formulating Music Therapy Treatment for Sensory Adaptation Goals

Music therapy, we are reminded often throughout this book, is a *clinical treatment*. Yet it is "entertaining" and "fun". That is *precisely* why music works so well. (Cherry-flavored medicine is still medicine!) Once the physiologic stress systems relax, new messages are allowed up from the paleoencephalon to the neo-cortex for high-level cognitive processing and retention. In effect, music acts to reduce stress in the paleoencephalon so that instinctive and cognitive learning can take place in new ways. Therefore music is perhaps the single, *most direct* and powerful catalyst in helping to reorganize autistic and other atypically stressed systems. Previous chapters discussed brain function, adaptation, sensory systems, audition, music elements, and interaction of these with the work of music therapy.

There is at least one further consideration that needs to be made clear: *"Adaptation" does not imply "cure"*! *Adaptation* means the setting of new homeostatic reference points – new standards – by which the brain and nervous systems check physiologic information, comfort levels and well-being, causing the body and mind to react more beneficially to stimuli.

Adaptation implies *adjustment* to another alternative. *Cure* implies removing a disease altogether. It would be an ideal world if "adaptation" and "cure" were synonymous, but this is not the case. Unfortunately, care-givers, teachers, even therapists, would like to look upon "therapy" as a "cure". This issue is being raised at this point because in order fully to comprehend and integrate the information presented thus far into the work of music therapy, a positive mind-set is helpful, but *realistic expectations* are critical. *No therapy can promise to cure.* It can only promise to do its best to "alter" for the better.

A diabetic receiving music therapy treatment will not be "cured" of a disease that will always require the supply of insulin. The adaptation of this body is its system's acceptance and absorption of externally supplied insulin, and the psycho-emotional adaptation to an altered lifestyle – one in which the awareness, acceptance and requirement to eat or eliminate certain foods become adaptive and comfortable. Neither music therapy nor any other therapy will "cure" diabetes. They will only attempt to suppress certain resulting symptoms.

Music therapy will not "cure" autism. However, certain aspects of autism's physiologic discomforts can be contained or permanently altered. More functionally adaptive behaviors can develop that better comply with social and educational expectations. As the system balances itself physiologically and moves toward comfortable cenesthetic "function" (sensory integration), psychological and cognitive behaviors can become more suitable to environmental and social conditions.

It is also important to understand that because music therapy is a *treatment* aimed at changing instinctive mechanisms, the attainment of functional adaptation is directly related to the amount of application of the treatment. As with the above example of a diabetic who requires life-long application of insulin, the autistic spectrum system may require and will certainly benefit from life-long, ongoing music therapy treatment.

There are no formulas outlining how much, and how long, would be adequate to make an adaptive difference. Observation confirms that changes do take place. Unfortunately, observations also confirm that regression takes place if stimulus is removed too soon, or discontinued permanently.

In several instances, children for whom schools contracted private music therapy services began to display more functionally adaptive behaviors and performed appropriate cognitive function in school settings. As soon as behaviors and performance improved, however, schools opted to discontinue music therapy interventions, or replace music therapy with benign music recreation. This was done on the basis that lack of funds and "improved performance" no longer warranted the intervention. In all these

cases, there was observable reversion to pre-therapy behaviors and physiologic function.

Recreational music activities are not the same as music therapy interventions. Recreational music might be enjoyable in the short term, but does
not usually effect long-term changes. The detriment to progress when
music therapy is discontinued too soon is akin to discontinuing an
important medication just as it begins to take effect.

Parents and caregivers often do not advocate continuation of music
therapy treatment, preferring instead to "barter" this in exchange for other
services. It therefore becomes the responsibility of the music therapist to
interface music therapy with allied interventions in presenting a case for
continued treatment. Accurate evaluation of a patient, a complete analysis
of physiologic and psychologic function, and the issuing of a comprehensive report outlining precisely *how* music therapy addresses the findings
will demonstrate how important this intervention is.

A report must also indicate *how much* weekly music therapy would be a
minimum, and if possible, *what period of time* would be feasible for adaptation to become observable. Different ages, different functions on the
autistic spectrum, the extent of ancillary therapies, and other variables play
roles in these considerations. A *therapy maintenance* program may also be
proposed to ensure that changes become supported with ongoing
treatment.

Music therapy interventions are unique within their modality, and the
treatment establishes its own goals. Although treatment may parallel or
support the goals of other interventions, music therapy goals do not need to
copy or "read" like goals of other clinical treatments. Music can illuminate
issues that other interventions do not, and can go well beyond many other
interventions in achieving adaptive behaviors. In fact, other treatment
modalities might actually adopt some goals from music therapy, rather than
vice versa.

In addition, a music therapist does not have to feel compelled to
function like a speech pathologist or an occupation therapist. I have often
been asked to provide consultation time to teams of therapists working
with a child, recommending ways in which they could expand upon the
learning that takes place within the music therapy environment. As a
member of a treatment team, the music therapist is often in a position to

teach practitioners of other health professions quite a bit about how music interacts to achieve physiologic results, language, organized movement, rhythmic balance, attention, motivation to learn, and so on.

Below are some areas of deficits resulting from sensory issues that are successfully addressed and altered with music therapy. Music therapists who approach their work with sensory issues in mind often identify these areas in school and institutional objectives and rehabilitative goals. It may be helpful to include some of them here in order to illustrate the connection between individual educational plans (IEPs), institutional rehabilitative goals and the objectives of music therapy.

Progress in these areas becomes generalized as a new manner of functioning, reaching well beyond the music therapy environment into cognitive learning, social skills, connectedness, and more. Interventions designed to incorporate sensory and behavioral factors are developed by music therapists individually, according to the developmental level of the child being treated, presenting needs relative to goals being addressed, available equipment, and the unique creative intuitions of each therapist.

Rhythm internalization

Physiologic pacing is a predecessor to comfortable physiologic function. A non-paced system, as discussed in earlier chapters, causes physical stress, anxiety, inefficient task execution, lack of coordination and many more problems deterring comfortable behavior. Therefore one of music therapy's major contributions to sensory integration is the opportunity to aid the system into rhythmically organized responses.

Any rhythmic music task that incorporates *physical participation* can aid rhythm internalization. A predominance of drumming and rhythmic movement is highly recommended.

Some tasks can include:

- rhythmic jumping on the trampoline while holding a pair of maracas (for auditory feedback while jumping) or while beating a drum
- "marching" while sitting in a chair (stabilizing the torso to relieve vestibular problems temporarily)

- drumming with bilateral arm movements and heavy mallets (paced proprioceptive feedback), standing and sitting at the drum(s) and cymbal(s)

- dropping a ball onto a tambourine, on a strong beat (requires waiting, anticipation, motor planning, listening, impulse control, visual focus and more); same activity while moving

- jumping over sticks or other items, in time to music (e.g. "Jack be Nimble" and others).

Adaptive responses to environment of auditory and visual stimuli

The myriad of musical instruments, their timbres, shapes, sizes, colors, spatial locations, means for extracting sounds, how to arrange in order to play, all combine to address common IEP (individual education plan) and/or institutional issues of:

- task organization and implementation

- ability to stay on task

- modulation from one task to another

- acceptance and making of a variety of choices and sounds

- acceptance of changing order and routine

- willingness to explore environment: move or be still, play or listen, combine instruments for new sounds, etc.

- communicate desires and needs

- body in relation to space and sound.

Auditory integration and discrimination

This area, crucial to language development, refers to adaptive responses to sound and the ability to discriminate, identify, internalize and reproduce accurately sounds being presented or requested:

- imitation and/or repetition of sounds, beats, pitch
- rhythmic pulsing: "following the beat"
- auditory tracking: note-for-note; up, down; interval, same/different rhythm, pitch, timbre
- short phrase, long phrase, pitch, inflection, contour
- identifying specific instrumental timbres
- locating sound sources
- matching sounds to instruments and instruments to sounds.

Auditory-physical integration, motor planning, vestibular actions, body coordination in space

Music therapy interventions that address these issues include activities and exercises involving:

- jumping on the trampoline while holding maracas or beating a hand drum
- rhythmic movement coordinated with hand-drumming (march and beat drum)
- movement and rhythmic manipulation of various props (balls, ribbons, sticks, bells, other)
- use of spatial dimensions; vertical and horizontal levels
- changing of speeds (tempi), pulse and rhythmic patterns
- physical responses to specific musical cues (stop, start, sit, stand, change direction, tip-toe, run, walk, skip, fast, slow, patterns, other).

Auditory-visual integration: see-hear sound

This complicated area of sensory integration uses music activities designed to address issues of:

- eye-hand coordination (motor planning)
- ears guiding eyes which then guide arms to achieve a task (teacher dictates and writes on board, you hear, see and copy)
- visual-auditory tracking and short-term memory (seeing and hearing simultaneously, accurately, sequentially)
- spatial auditory-visual sound location
- keyboard training
- visual identification of "picture" (musical notation) of rhythm being played (walking notes, running notes, skipping, etc.).

Auditory-mental-physical coordination

Typical populations (we, the undiagnosed) take for granted the element of *hear-think-do*. But in systems devoid of adequate sensory integration, there is a lag in processing time whereby what is heard is not registered quickly enough to call for a coordinated physical response. This is very evident in autistic (especially lower functioning) and learning-delayed behaviors and body movements. The *think and do* element is virtually non-existent and it is often mistaken for "inattentiveness", or other behavioral acts.

The music therapist addressing this issue can create many exercises specifically aimed at the "think and do" adaptive process, some of which have already been mentioned above and throughout the book. Sample activities include:

- internalizing (automating) rhythm, changing three steps to four steps if meter changes, etc.
- fall-rebound awareness: shift of accents (e.g. walk four steps, but beat drum only on first; then repeat, beating drum on second; then third, etc.)
- three tunes – three drums (tune no. 1, play drum no. 1, etc.; tunes are not played to end, but shift mid-phrase in order to ensure that listener "hears" change and shifts to correct drum designated for that tune, etc.)
- movement-sound coordination; sensing of body parts, etc.

- directive songs requiring quick and exact body actions

- some music notation and instrumental-skills learning as part of the therapy

- drum speak: beating while speaking a sentence; conversation held while beating syllables of words.

Pacing of body movement, breath

Through rhythmic internalization and motor-planning activities involving blowing a recorder while marching, for instance, or playing instruments which are strewn about the room, and activities geared toward altering body dynamics (walking heavy, jumping light, etc.), the body becomes paced, and breathing is coordinated with body movements, becoming more efficient. Pacing of body movements and breath are crucial in influencing the development of language, along with deficits involving:

- attention, anticipation, waiting

- attention to details; accuracy in movement execution

- self-organization and impulse control

- visual mid-line focus

- speaking on the exhale.

Sequencing

Developing, retaining and sustaining logical processing orders is required of cognitive learning. Music, as we know, is automatically sequential. One tone links and relates to another and another. Soon, a melody becomes recognizable. When lyrics are used, multiple sequencing takes place, as well as sequence and cognition of "meaning" (which music alone does not require). This multifaceted sequencing experience provided by music therapy interventions not only paces and regulates motor planning (see above), but also contributes to the ability of the brain to organize information for functionally adaptive uses.

The more the stimulus input for sequential learning, the more neural networks apparently develop. There are brain studies indicating that sequential muscular information (through, say, keyboard learning) influences growth in right-brain cortex. Music activities abound for developing sequencing skills, in addition to those already mentioned above. The creative music therapist will devise activities related to IEP sequencing goals, and issues related to the findings of occupation therapists, speech pathologists, other clinicians and educators.

Sequencing involves well-functioning short-term memory. Therefore musical memory games, tune recognition, picking tunes out "by ear", connecting graphic images to tunes, and other tasks contribute to sequential learning. Sequencing also aids the music therapist in assessing whether there is accuracy in auditory tracking, or whether the visual or auditory sense is somehow impeding sequential memory or sequential retrieval.

Limit-setting and behavioral redirection

This is the most employed restriction in school environments. Without accounting for physiologic problems that could be causing certain behaviors (see Chapter 1), the modification of what is deemed "inappropriate" has become an absolute obsession for most educators and caregivers alike. Infinite "methods" and programs exist for "behavior modification" (cookie rewards and all!) These are neither discussed nor subscribed to in the music therapy approach presented in this book. Unfortunately, IEP goals that discuss *behavior redirection* (without treats as reward) instead of behavior "modification" (treats and all), is usually considered (by either school or parent) to be less "legitimate" or "important". Therefore a music therapist, although involved with "child-centered" treatment, is often asked to address behavior modification.

In many ways, music therapy can be looked upon as a behavior modification tool, but not in the manner of traditional applied behavioral analysis, nor of traditional "behavior modification" programs. *Music, itself, is the modifier.* It asks the system to "wait until done", play on cue, wait to insert the correct word, stop playing when the tune is done, sustain a rhythm whilst a tune is playing, remain on task until all draws to a close, listen, look, and enjoy playing a favorite instrument or hearing a favorite song.

Music requests a level of compliance from the listener and from the participant. And even the most severely dysfunctional person seems to know to "wait till it's over". Thus the music therapist is in a prime position to use music as a method for redirecting atypical and non-productive behavior. *Music, itself, is the reward!*

Children learn to develop *compliance intelligence* through sessions paced and balanced with the alternations of "routines" and "freedoms". This involves active responses to givens, compromise, turn-taking, learning to contend with needs and wishes of others versus self, being awarded self-choices, and so on. *Expectations* are understated or non-existent. There are no "right" and "wrong" ways of playing an instrument, as long as neither the instrument nor a person is physically jeopardized or endangered by the behavior.

Music therapy is involved in *redirecting* a presented behavior toward an activity addressing a predetermined goal. Thus screaming and agitation can result in a "screaming contest" to see who can scream louder and longer (exhale and diaphragm exercise). Or screaming can turn into an operatic-type "aria" (vocalization). Running can become paced by the playing of music that contrasts the running with "marching" rhythms and songs; disorganizing a room (displacing instruments, etc.) can be diverted into "let's play these instruments now that they're all on the floor," and so on.

Most importantly, the music therapist, in converting (redirecting) behavior into something functional, is (a) not delineating a "wrongdoing" but rather converting a negative into a positive; and (b) not escalating the situation with expression of anger or command. Sudden cessation of the music stimulus often serves immediately to redirect a behavior.

Ignoring a behavior frustrates the child's need to obtain, for whatever reasons, attention through negativity. The therapist who "tunes out" or "turns off" by simply turning away from the behavior will generally find that the behavior ultimately reorganizes itself into something else: perhaps sitting in a quiet corner, or some repetitive manipulation of an item, or something similar.

As exercises confronting behavior issues are created and presented continually by the music therapist, adaptation ultimately takes place and transfers to other, non-musical areas of function. Once the brain learns, through experience, how to respond to a given, it is less likely to "forget" it, and tends to generalize the information into other areas of function. All this, however, is contingent upon continued diligence in addressing physiologic reasons for behaviors.

Creativity, self-initiative and task organization

Music therapy interventions play a major role in stimulating adaptive and instinctive intelligence that touches upon emotional/ psychological issues such as elements of self-exploration, self-expression and an awareness of self. In certain cases of autism, the elements of curiosity and creative play seem lacking, or are limited by sensory dysfunction (see Chapter 2). However, within the music environment, especially with adequate prompting, instruments making sounds become playthings, and defenses (especially tactile) are set aside for the moment. And, as we learned, the accumulation of "moments" results in functional adaptation. The more music interaction there is with a therapist, the more play, opening up the way to creative expression/imagination, organization of random non-structures (when therapy is non-directive or solely directed by the participant), and an element of "allowing-ness". The music becomes the organizing factor and the most persuasive aspect of task organization, setting aside, for the moment, certain sensory issues. Ultimately, the issues may be displaced permanently.

Speech and language

Autism, as well as other diagnoses, often brings with it severe language deficits. Oral-motor stimulation, breath and tongue control, auditory integration, as well as auditory-visual coordination, must be available and functioning in order for speech to develop. Visual attention to how words are formed by others is important for enabling "imitation" by the learner. Auditory-visual integration enables babies to copy language from parents. Thus repeated exercises involving auditory-visual coordination, plus the playing of wind instruments (kazoos, recorders, harmonicas) will eventually assist in expanding vocalization, and even word formation in aphasic autistic persons. Fill-in songs, drum-speak (beating the rhythm of words on a drum while speaking them), sound stories and similar tasks address these issues.

Music therapy support for cognitive and allied therapies goals

Music therapy, compared to other therapies, is still in its infant stages of development. It is only recently that the training of music therapists has become unified academically and philosophically. As a result there are still many areas of the profession that require development. Among these is the area of assessment and evaluation for music therapy goals. At the time of writing, there are no standardized testing tools for music therapy that look at the whole person from the physiologic, psycho-emotional, cognitive and musical perspective. Various attempts have been made to "assess" a child for music therapy. However, most have involved parodying speech pathology and educational IEP goals.

It is up to the individual music therapist to understand physiologic information well enough to assess the whole child, from all perspectives, and present the case for this treatment as being the highly unique, holistic intervention that can address the findings. Because music is "joyful" and eases stress, it enables other things to happen. As stated earlier in this chapter, music therapy is its own intervention, and not a step-child of occupation therapy, speech pathology or academic educational goals. The goals of music therapy are *systemic* – physiologic, psychologic, cognitive, emotional.

Music therapy supports other interventions by the very fact that it can go beyond them in uniting both sub-cortical and cortical activities of the brain toward a holistic adaptation. It supports the rhythmic needs of OT by supplying rhythm. It supports oral-motor and cognitive requirements of speech by supplying instruments and tasks that support language activities and cognition. It supports educational (academic) goals by preparing the mind and body to handle the act of learning.

Music therapy works to prepare and lead the system toward functional adaptation. This generalizes and pervades other areas of behaviors. Music therapy is therefore unique in its tools and approaches. When presented in this manner, it is accepted as a viable, important treatment for the betterment of an autistic or otherwise diagnosed system.

Parents, teachers, caregivers and therapists understand the value of music therapy when clinical language is used to describe the intervention.

Everyone enjoys music. How well one understands the extent of its influence on human adaptation is another matter. It is that understanding that will determine how accepting of music therapy treatment parents, educators, healthcare professionals and therapists will be; and how successful the treatment will be.

How much therapy is enough?

Chapter 4 discusses adaptation as being newly learned instinctive commands based on repetition of stimuli. The "continuous disturbance" presented by a stimulus will alter a homeostatic reference because "something's gotta give!" Chapter 4 also informs us that, in the case of physiologic adjustment to high altitudes, it takes the better part of a full year of continual, daily exposure before long-term changes take effect.

Based on what is known about physiologic and cognitive adaptation, the amount of music therapy prescribed must be viewed as part of successful treatment. How much is enough? Would we expect a child – any child – to become a well-educated adult by being sent to school for an hour just once or twice a week? It is well established that skills and cognitive training require continual repetition in order to "take hold". A tennis player going onto the court one or two hours a week would be unlikely to qualify for a Davis Cup competition! An ice-skater practicing an hour or two a week would probably not do quadruple turns easily!

The amount of music therapy treatment time is as important in teaching the body new skills as is the time invested in teaching any other skill. It is the education of the paleoencephalon and cortex that is being sought, and, like skills training, it takes time. There is therefore no such thing as "too much" exposure. There can be, as we saw, "not enough". In assessing and planning recommendations for treatment with music therapy, the therapist needs to consider what minimum input will adequately begin the re-education process. The maximum is unlimited.

I generally recommend a minimum of two to two-and-a-half hours per week, depending on the case, continuing throughout a child's formative years. It is preferable to have that time spread between several therapy contacts distributed over the week. Three or four 30-minute or 45-minute sessions can provide consistent treatment continually reinforced by ongoing patient–therapist interaction.

Frequent shorter sessions work better than fewer long ones because the brain and body tend to "shut down" when tired or receiving too much input over long periods of time. The best learning tends to take place in small increments over shorter periods of time. If frequent shorter sessions are not possible, then longer sessions with several breaks in between activities are recommended, to replenish energy and concentration. (The same activity, repeated many times in one session, is not recommended. The brain prefers variety!)

The point at which the process of adaptation becomes evident is precisely the point when continuation of music therapy is most vital. Stopping treatment can mean regression. As stated before, the more the treatment (training) reinforces the newly learned behaviors, the more the long-term adaptation is assured. Clinicians presenting evaluations and treatment recommendations on these terms are most successful in prevailing upon schools, parents and health professionals to include or continue music therapy for autism behaviors and sensory integration. It is quite cost-effective!

CHAPTER 11

Conclusion

We are emotional animals

David is 13. He has been diagnosed with Asperger Syndrome and allied cognitive difficulties. He is handsome, extremely verbal, well developed for his age, with an abundance of high energy. David is curious, displays the usual physiologic disorganization involving his vestibular and motor-planning systems, and is in constant motion.

David's behaviors are erratic, non-conventional, demanding, bordering on Oppositional Defiance Disorder (ODD). He opposes most directives, argues constantly, avoids any activity that requires cognitive "thought", shouts contradicting commands and parodies the behavior and comments of others. David has been on and off cocktails of medications including psychotropic drugs, tranquilizers, "uppers," "downers," and others.

David personifies pure *fear*. That is the basic core emotion to which his system has adapted and for which it is attempting to compensate. All of his behaviors point to his visceral fear responses. David is in continuous survival mode. He displays attention deficit disorders, peripheral vision, ambient hearing. His eyes dart back and forth around the room, influencing his movements in the directions his visual system takes him.

David is easily distracted, unable to "stay on task" for any length of time beyond 30 seconds. He wants to play every instrument, but cannot seem to "organize" and stay with the task before darting off into some other request. He wants to write a song but cannot seem to sequence words and thoughts well enough. His system has much to learn.

David's case summarizes all the information and theories presented in this book. Except for the fact that he has fluent expressive and receptive

166

language skills, his reading skills are on fourth grade level (if that), his math less than that, his "appropriateness" (whatever that means) completely inconsistent.

All the information gathered in this book combines to clarify David's fear responses and suggest how to approach treatment. Logic and psychological "lectures" will not change David's physiologic behaviors. He cannot be "talked into" feeling better, feeling unafraid. David hardly understands what he is feeling and why he behaves the way he does, let alone what it is like to feel "safe" and "comfortable" within his body. He has spent most of his 13 years being told: "stop," "don't," "behave," "do this ... that ...," "behave and receive a star," "be quiet or receive no reward," and heaven only knows what else.

What options does David have to "comfortably control" his environment? It is not surprising that he resorts to shouting commands, probably not unlike those he has heard all his life. He calls attention to himself through negative actions; he does not understand the rules and requirements; and he spends much of his time apologizing, even when it is unwarranted. These behaviors are *his system's adaptations,* based on how his brain receives and processes sensory information.

It may take another 13 years of interventions to allay David's fear responses. After all, they have been inbred since birth. Had I less physiologic knowledge, I would be at a loss in approaching treatment of this young boy. My understanding of basic adaptation and sensory systems led me to the conviction that, before anything else, *I must help this child slow down his body rhythm.* Unless his brain learns to slow the body down before installing a response to stimulus, David's erratic behaviors will never cease. New sensory interpretations are necessary.

We begin every session with the lights turned down, sitting on the floor, blowing into our recorders, with pure American Indian flute music in the background. David found this to be excruciatingly difficult for the first few times. (It is not surprising that he prefers fast, loud rock and roll!) Not only did he fidget, but he refused to blow into the recorder, and interrupted the activity with constant caustic remarks and questions. "I don't want to do this," "I don't like that music," "I don't want to sit on the floor," and more. His brain desperately resisted making changes.

Although I basically subscribe to child-centered approaches, I also believe that a child, or system, may not always recognize "functionally adaptive' choices that will teach the brain new things it desperately needs in order to encourage changes. What's more, I, the therapist, also have needs and choices that others must consider. This, too, is a learning process. And with David, my system needed quieting as much as his. My response to David's queries was non-verbal. I simply continued to play. He eventually became quiet and, although he did not blow into the recorder, he did become less restless. In each session, any conversation and activity that follows the preliminary quieting time is usually executed with better-paced thoughts and movement.

Other activities, of his choosing, are shaped to address slower-paced motor planning, visual tracking (which is very poor), physical coordination, sequencing, auditory discrimination and memory (also poor), task organization, and undertakings similar to some mentioned in earlier chapters of this book. But always first and foremost is my interest in slowing down his system's response time. Usually the slower processing and calming of his system lasts for several hours beyond our sessions, as his parents confirm.

We have been working together for over a year, only one hour per week, but exciting adaptations are already evident. His "fear" still predominates his actions, but he is often less fearful with directives, and has less of a need to "control". He is beginning to trust his body.

Mind and emotion

Current neuroscientific research continues to confirm that we are first and foremost animals of *emotion*. Before "reason" ever enters the picture to explain, psychologically, what was experienced as *fear*, the experience has already happened and passed. What remains in the mind is an allusion, sometimes even an illusion, to what has happened in the paleoencephalon.

What are we mostly "afraid" of? Danger and harm to our existence and perpetuation of the species. This is instinctive. We basically have no control over these responses. They are genetically inscribed as part of humans' inscriptive accommodation and adaptation to the planet. The sense of danger is real, even if the source of the danger is imagined! As long as the brain instinctively *thinks* it is in danger, it will put the body into survival mode.

Every case in this book exemplifies some form of "fear" and "danger" in which the brain thinks the body is. Ensuing behaviors quite naturally, instinctively, incorporate fright-fight-flight responses. Any body – diagnosed or undiagnosed – can find itself in a "fear" and "danger" mode, for infinite reasons. A musician about to go on stage feels "fear" butterflies in the stomach (a fight-or-flight sign that the digestive system is being shut down so that extra blood and oxygen can go to the brain); a shadow in the dark woods impels the heart to pump harder so that enough blood and oxygen can help the flight to safety.

Autistic physiologic function is nearly always in survival, flight-or-fight mode. Senses are interpreting benign information as threatening. Sometimes potentially threatening information is sensed as benign! Whatever the brain knows accumulates from what the brain receives and interprets. The "mind" is not involved until the amygdala, hypothalamus, thalamus and other areas of the limbic system decide to allow it in. "Fear" responses cannot be "reasoned" away.

David is a perfect example. If he could "reason" away his fears, he would do so, because the brain does not like to do what it does not *have* to do. Man behaves in ways the brain thinks the body needs to, for whatever reasons. These behaviors cannot be willed away. They must *systemically*, and systematically, be altered. This is where the work of music, and music therapy begins.

Music in human adaptation

Music exists for a reason. It probably preceded language as an emotional communicator, perhaps expanding upon the human repertoire of calls associated with fear, procreation, discomfort and distress. The animal brain, especially the human animal, is an amazing organ. It enjoys patterns, compiles and condenses information, orders the behavior of physiologic systems, monitors survival, seeks perpetual calm and does not do anything it does not have to do. Humans created music. It is everywhere in the world. It must have a role in human adaptation, or why would the brain bother to develop this form of expression?

The role of music in pacifying human emotions is documented, as is its role in lifting spirits and inducing movement. No society is devoid of some form of musical activity. The four basic human needs – survival of the self, survival of the species, self-determination and spirituality – are addressed by music in every way.

Music is the instant communicator of emotion, directly interpreted by the amygdala and hypothalamus in the limbic system. When these two major players decide that the incoming sound of music is safe, the entire system relaxes, and the gates to the upper learning centers (neo-cortex) are opened. If humans could manage without music, it would not exist.

Music therapy is a treatment that uses elements of music to help a system learn to handle new ways of responding to sensory input. Music therapy helps a system allay "fear", reduce stressors and enjoy functional adaptation to requirements of our planet and our society. Not only is music therapy its own profession, but one that can address a multiple of sensory and cognitive issues in ways often not entirely understood by the world at large.

It is not enough simply to say that "music makes you feel good" or that it "changes you", without fully understanding or discussing why it does what it does, and how it can be applied to do exactly those things. In developing goals and treatment for children on the autistic spectrum, the music therapist has an ominous responsibility of applying his or her comprehensive knowledge of physiology, adaptation, brain function, audition, elements of music, instrumental and vocal skills toward the application of music in the interest of functional sensory adaptation.

The music therapist must also be able to know what he or she is looking at when observing behaviors deemed typical of the autistic spectrum. Some questions a music therapist must ask are *why* a behavior is happening, *what* this behavior indicates; *how* music treatment can impact upon what is being observed; *what kind* of intervention will be effective and *how much*.

Music therapy, like play, occupation, behavior therapies, and the rest, does not lend itself readily to rigorous scientific explanation. The brain seems always to be one step ahead of researchers! Findings are anecdotal at best, and based on observations, insights and informed assumptions. It is important to understand that music therapy does not replace other interventions, nor does it need to copy the goals of other therapies in order to be effective.

This intervention is not merely a form of "musical OT," or "musical learning to read or do math," or "musical speech pathology." Although it can affect all those areas of function, music therapy is a discreet, well-focused application of musical elements for attaining clinical goals. It is what it is, in and of itself. The intervention is unsurpassed in its ability to address sensory integration goals in autism.

Sensory integration deficiencies play a prominent role in autistic processing and resultant behaviors. Other diagnosed populations share this problem as well. When the system is not properly interpreting information from the environment, it *cannot* adapt satisfactorily. Adequate sensory information processing is important for functional adaptation. And functional adaptation is crucial for survival. Music therapy, dependent on auditory processing in conjunction with overall sensory function, must concern itself with the impact of these dysfunctions if goals for healing and betterment are to be successfully achieved.

The way a music therapist observes behavior is important in determining what is happening before his or her eyes. What the behaviors indicate about the functioning and adaptive responses the autistic system has adopted in dealing with its environment, and how to best approach the issues, are contingent upon how the therapist interprets what is seen.

Armed with an awareness of sensory integration and physiologic information processing relevant to adaptation, the music therapist is in a position to design goals, objectives and strategies for treatment. With continuous repetition of treatment stimuli, the altering and repatterning of brain processes for accommodating new, more functional responses and behaviors can result.

Adaptation is individual. Autistic behaviors are adaptive responses. This is one reason why autism is considered to be on a *spectrum* of deficient function. Each physiologic system responds according to its own interpretation of sensory information. Responses to interpretation of sensory information result in "survival" behaviors not often understood by the general population. The aims of therapy are to help each system repattern to adopt new and different interpretations of incoming sensory information.

It seems logical, therefore, for music therapists, educators, caregivers, and health professionals to understand functional adaptation and issues of sensory malfunction in autism (and other atypical systems), as these are addressed by the rich and multisensory resources of music and instrumental playing. Sensory integration and comfortable physiologic function are ultimately affected by the ability to make music. In the end, connection with others, communication, learning, attention, compliance and self-esteem emerge.

Self-esteem will not yield sensory integration, but sensory integration can yield self-esteem.

A word about group therapy

Music therapy in children's group settings does not pre-empt consideration of physiologic and sensory integration issues. In all probability, most of the children in a homogeneous group will display similar sensory needs, varying only in intensity and amount. Determination of an autistic child's "group readiness" depends upon whether the music therapist believes the group experience will be more beneficial than a one-on-one treatment process. It may also depend upon the particular setting of the group (school, private, home, etc.), and on whether or not aides are available to assist with certain activities.

Many of the clinical experiences described throughout this book have been successfully adapted to group encounters. Additional goals for group music therapy generally include social skills, communication with peers, turn-taking, choice, handling disappointment, delayed gratification and general interaction requirements in social situations. *However, sensory integration and physiologic goals need always to be kept close at hand.*

Inability to delay gratification or await one's turn, when seen from the physiologic point of view, is not necessarily a "behavioral problem." It could indicate neurologic disorders such as Attention Deficit, among the many other issues explained earlier in this book. These may need to be addressed more carefully in separate individual interventions.

All children in a group setting should be assessed for auditory and visual physiological processing to ensure that treatment in a group can comfortably address the various functioning levels and physical problems that could arise as a result of group encounters (music too loud, too much visual input, panic and fear, etc.). The ideal situation, for autistic children who are "group ready", is a combination of individual and group treatment. This ensures that treatment of any and all deficits will be equally addressed, some within "real" circumstances.

Finally...

The information presented in this book supports the clinical approach to music therapy from a *multidimensional physiologic perspective*. In so doing, it addresses the integration of the senses for the holistic – cenesthetic – betterment of the autistic and special needs child. This yields functional adaptation and interaction in negotiating a very demanding, difficult world. This book is not intended as a compendium of tasks, but rather as an introduction to physiologic information and perspectives that can help the music therapist assess more astutely the behaviors and presenting problems of an atypically functioning patient.

The music therapist has a distinct advantage in addressing sensory integration issues: music can focus on many deficiencies simultaneously, tap the limbic system for emotional support, balance cognitive and intuitive brain processes (right and left cortical hemispheres), and provide interventions that are fun, creative, transferable to other areas of learning, familiar and functional to physiologic repatterning. The creating of musical exercises for interventions with autistic and otherwise diagnosed populations is not difficult, once the patients' physiology and sensory deficits are adequately understood.

It is hoped that the information given here can assist the therapist, and anyone associated with special needs populations, in determining what and why certain problems exist, and which sensory and physiologic systems might be implicated, in order to develop objectives, goals and interventions directly addressing targeted physiologic and emotional issues.

The most appealing advantage of music therapy from a physiologic perspective is that the therapist can actively participate with the child in the process – an opportunity not available to other sensory integration therapists, who basically function as observers to a task. This ingredient alone takes the work of music therapy to a higher level, where connectedness and rehabilitation are attainable.

This is how the ultimate state of "cenesthesia" is reached.

Recommended reading

Altenmuller, E.O. (2001) 'How Many Music Centers are in the Brain?' In J.R. Zatorre and I. Peretz (eds) *Biological Foundations of Music*. New York: Annals of the New York Academy of Sciences, Vol.930, pp.273–280.

Ayotte, J. and Peretz, I. (2001) 'Case Study of Dysmusia: As a Developmental Disorder of Pitch Perceptions.' In J.R. Zatorre and I. Peretz (eds) *Biological Foundations of Music*. New York: Annals of the New York Academy of Sciences, Vol.930, pp.436–438.

Balter, M. (2001) 'Language, Brain, and Cognitive Development Meeting: What Makes the Mind Dance and Count.' *Science 292*, 5522, 1636–1637.

Bharucha, J.J., Tillmann, B. and Janata, P. (2000) 'Cultural Adaptation of the Brain to Music and Speech: An FMRI Study of Listening to Indian and Western Music, Hindi and English.' *Abstracts, Biological Foundations of Music Conference* 20–22 May 2000. NY Academy of Sciences.

Brust, J.C.M. (2001) 'Music and the Neurologist: An Historical Perspective.' In J.R. Zatorre and I. Peretz (eds) *Biological Foundations of Music*. New York: Annals of the New York Academy of Sciences, Vol.930, pp.143–152.

Cross, I. (2001) 'Music, Cognition, Culture and Evolution.' In J.R. Zatorre and I. Peretz (eds) *Biological Foundations of Music*. New York: Annals of the New York Academy of Sciences, Vol.930, pp.28–42.

Drake, C. (2001) 'Universals of Temporal Processing.' In J.R. Zatorre and I. Peretz (eds) *Biological Foundations of Music*. New York: Annals of the New York Academy of Sciences, Vol.930, pp.17–27.

Drayna, D., Manichaikul, A., deLange, M., Sneider, H. and Spector, T. (2001) 'Genetic Correlates of Musical Pitch Recognition in Humans.' *Science 291*, 5510, 1969–1972.

Fukui, H. (2001) 'Music and Testosterone – A Hypothesis for the Biological Foundations and Origin of Music.' In J.R. Zatorre and I. Peretz (eds) *Biological Foundations of Music*. New York: Annals of the New York Academy of Sciences, Vol.930, pp.448–451.

Halpern, A.R. (2001) 'Cerebral Substrates of Musical Imagery.' In J.R. Zatorre and I. Peretz (eds) *Biological Foundations of Music*. New York: Annals of the New York Academy of Sciences, Vol.930, pp.179–192.

Huron, D. (2001) 'Is Music an Evolutionary Adaptation?' *Proceedings of Biological Foundations of Music Conference* 20–22 May 2000. NY Academy of Sciences.

Hyde, K., Peretz, I., Ayotte, J. and Clement, J. (2000) 'Determination of Pitch and Temporal Discrimination Thresholds in the Adult Dysmusic.' *Abstracts, Biological Foundations of Music Conference* 20–22 May 2000. NY Academy of Sciences.

Krumhansl, C.L. and Toiviainen, P. (2001) 'Tonal Cognition.' In J.R. Zatorre and I. Peretz (eds) *Biological Foundations of Music*. New York: Annals of the New York Academy of Sciences, Vol.930, pp.77–91.

Parsons, L.M. (2001) 'Functional Neuroanatomy of Music Listening, Discrimination, and Performance.' In J.R. Zatorre and I. Peretz (eds) *Biological Foundations of Music*. New York: Annals of the New York Academy of Sciences, Vol.930, pp.211–231.

Peretz, I. (2000) 'Autonomy and Fractionation of Musical Processes.' *Abstracts, Biological Foundations of Music Conference* 20–22 May 2000. NY Academy of Sciences.

Repp, B.H. (2001) 'Effects of Music Perception and Imagery on Sensorimotor Synchronization with Complex Timing Patterns.' In J.R. Zatorre and I. Peretz (eds) *Biological Foundations of Music*. New York: Annals of the New York Academy of Sciences, Vol.930, pp.409–411.

Samson, S. (2001) 'Cerebral Substrates for Musical Temporal Processes.' In J.R. Zatorre and I. Peretz (eds) *Biological Foundations of Music*. New York: Annals of the New York Academy of Sciences, Vol.930, pp.166–178.

Schlaug, G. and Chen, D. (2001) 'The Brain of Musicians: A Model for Functional and Structural Adaptation.' In J.R. Zatorre and I. Peretz (eds) *Biological Foundations of Music*. New York: Annals of the New York Academy of Sciences, Vol.930, pp.281–299.

Sternberg, E.M. (2001) 'Piecing Together a Puzzling World' (review of the film *Memento*, Christopher Nolan, Dir., on the subject of short-term memory loss). *Science 292*, 5522, 1661–1662.

Trainor, L.J., McDonald, K.L. and Alain, C. (2001) 'Electrical Brain Activity Associated with Automatic and Controlled Processing of Melodic Contour and Interval.' In J.R. Zatorre and I. Peretz (eds) *Biological Foundations of Music*. New York: Annals of the New York Academy of Sciences, Vol.930, pp.429–432.

Tramo, M.J. (2001) 'Neurobiological Foundations for the Theory of Harmony in Western Tonal Music.' In J.R. Zatorre and I. Peretz (eds) *Biological Foundations of Music*. New York: Annals of the New York Academy of Sciences, Vol.930.

Trehub, S.E. (2001) 'Musical Predispositions in Infancy.' In J.R. Zatorre and I. Peretz (eds) *Biological Foundations of Music*. New York: Annals of the New York Academy of Sciences, Vol.930, pp.1–16.

Zatorre, R.J. (2001) 'Neural Specializations for Tonal Processing.' In J.R. Zatorre and I. Peretz (eds) *Biological Foundations of Music*. New York: Annals of the New York Academy of Sciences, Vol.930, pp.193–210.

Appendix A

The Role of Music in Physiologic Accommodation

Its Ability to Elicit Reflexive, Adaptive, and Inscriptive Responses

Daniel J. Schneck, Virginia Polytechnic Institute and State University
and Dorita S. Berger, Board-Certified Music Therapist,
Norwalk, Connecticut

Literally, the word "accommodate" means "to" (ac- or ad-) + "measure" (-modus) + "with" (-com-), or "to fit." Thus, in a general sense, *physiological accommodation* refers to the ability that a whole organism—or part thereof, such as an organ or tissue—has to acclimate itself either to a new, different, modified, possibly threatening, or otherwise special situation—or to a change, variation, permutation, or other diversification in its intended use. Moreover, depending on the time-scale associated with both the onset and the persistence of the acclimation process, accommodation may be described as being short-term, medium-term, or long-term. That is to say, accommodation may be one of the following:

- Immediate (or at worst, minimally delayed), but relatively short-lived (on the order of minutes or less); i.e., instantaneous, temporary and transient—examples of which include instinctively reflexive "fight or flight" responses to life-threatening disturbances, sensory facilitation that results from persistent stimulation, and neural accommodation that follows continuous excitation.

- Significantly delayed, but lasting longer (perhaps up to an entire single life-span); i.e., phase-shifted from the perturbing stimulus, but sustained in a steady-state sense. In the latter case the responses become conditioned reflexes (in the "Pavlov's dogs" sense), "tenured adaptive responses" (in the sense of bone remodeling under stress, and other examples of *functional adaptation*), and/or behavioral modifications (such as the geographic relocation of whole populations).

- Permanent, long-term (lasting generations) adjustments that are actually inscribed into genetic changes that get carried forward into future progeny. Examples include our shift from walking on four legs to walking on two, or from being herbivorous creatures to being omnivores, or the evolutionary loss of our tails.

For purposes of discussion, then, one may speak of (i) reflexive, (ii) adaptive, or (iii) inscriptive (genetic) accommodation.

Going one step further, it is convenient to define physiological accommodation in an *engineering* sense by fitting the process into a standard feedback-control diagram, such as is given in Fig. 1. The rationale for this diagram, and a more complete description of how it relates to physiological function, can be found elsewhere [1-3]. Suffice it to say here, that from the model portrayed in Fig. 1, one can develop a mathematical formulation that can be used to quantify short-, medium-, or long-term physiological accommodation. This article describes how such a formulation can be derived, and it includes a discussion of how the specific elements inherent to *music* uniquely synergize with basic physiological function to elicit specific responses that play a significant role in the accommodation process.

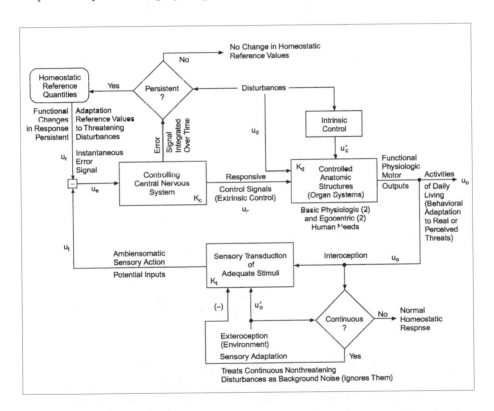

Figure 1 Standard canonical representation of a typical feedback control system, modified to include "floating" set points or accommodation (adaptive) response mechanisms (see references [1–3]).

Mathematical Description of Physiological Accommodation

Let u_o represent any of the functional physiological outputs that result from the activity of various *controlled* anatomical structures—structures that collectively comprise the entire human organism. Suppose that these anatomic organ systems experience disturbances u_d that drive u_o away from desirable homeostatic reference quantities u_r to which u_o attempts to conform [1]. The quantities u_r are established "set-points" that reflect the organism's *instinct* to satisfy two basic *physiologic* needs and its *desire* to satisfy two acquired egocentric needs [3]. Physiological needs include: (i) the maintenance of one's *own* life (i.e., survival of the "self") and (ii) the perpetuation of the *species* (sometimes referred to as the drive towards "sexual fulfillment"). Egocentric needs include: (i) control of one's own destiny (what the Constitution of the United States calls the "right" to life, liberty, and the pursuit of happiness—and which often accompanies one's quest for status and power; i.e., control over *others*) and (ii) the compulsion to make some "sense" out of why we are here, and to give meaning and purpose to life (sometimes referred to as the drive toward "spiritual fulfillment"). Thus, u_r represents both homeostatic variables critical to *life*, and humanistic variables critical to *lifestyle*; and, as a set, they represent target values for u_o—target values that may or may not change in the accommodation process, as discussed further below and elsewhere [1-3].

Whatever u_r happens to be at any given time, the corresponding value of u_o is maintained within an acceptable narrow window around u_r by *controlling signals* u_c and u'_c, which "correct" u_o as necessary. One distinguishes between two types of physiological control; i.e., (i) *intrinsic control* u'_c that results from response characteristics that are inherent to the very properties or nature of the organs or tissues, themselves—such as *Starling's Law of the Heart* (which intrinsically governs cardiac output by relying on the innate length-tension properties of cardiac muscle to compensate for increased venous return to the heart by pumping more blood out with each stroke [4]); and, (ii) *extrinsic* control u_c wherein *target organs or tissues* respond to hormones or neurotransmitters that originate from another anatomical region of the body—such as the autonomic hormones or the nervous or endocrine systems [2-4]. In turn, the ability of *either* u_d (which, too, may be *internal*—derived from the consequences of metabolic processes—or *external*—due to environmental "insults") or control signals u_c and u'_c to affect the controlled element of the feedback control system depends on the *response characteristics* (i.e., input/output properties) of said element. The latter are often defined in terms of a complex, nonlinear *transfer function*, the magnitude of which measures the "gain" of the element, and the phase angle of which measures the extent to which there is a "delay" between an input to the element, and its response (output) to that input. The transfer function for the controlled elements in Fig. 1 shall be written generically as K_d—which, like the various "u_r's" (life and lifestyle), "u_c's" (intrinsic and extrinsic), "u_d's" (internal and external), and "u_o's" (activities of daily living), may or may *not* remain constant in the accommodation process. Indeed, the three time-scales defined at the start of this article will determine whether or not the u_r's will change or the K's will change, or whether nothing will change or *everything* will change!

Recognizing that, in the most general sense, u_o may depend not only on u_c, u'_c, u_c and K_d in a direct (proportional) sense, but that u_o may also depend on the time-history (integrals) of these variables, their rate-of-change (derivatives), nonlinear interactions, and complex (phase-shifted) relationships, one may write, generically, for the *controlled elements* in Fig. 1:

$$u_o = u_o(u_c, u'_c, u_d, K_d, \dot{u}_c,$$
$$\dot{u}'_c, \dot{u}_d, \dot{K}_d, \bar{u}_c, \bar{u}'_c, \bar{u}_d, \bar{K}_d, ...)$$

(1)

where the dot over a variable is a short-hand notation for rate-of-change, the bar over a variable denotes some form of integral (history), and the remaining dots imply nonlinear and higher-order terms. From Eq. (1), one may write:

$$du_o = \frac{\partial u_o}{\partial u_c} du_c + \frac{\partial u_o}{\partial u'_c} du'_c + \frac{\partial u_o}{\partial u_d} du_d$$
$$+ \frac{\partial u_o}{\partial K_d} dK_d + \frac{\partial u_o}{\partial \dot{u}_c} d\dot{u}_c + ...$$

(2)

$$= K_1 du_c + K_2 du'_c + K_3 du_d$$
$$+ K_4 dK_d + K_5 d\dot{u}_c + ...$$

(3)

where $\partial u_o / \partial u_c = K_1$ defines how the output signal u_o is affected by *changes* du_c of the extrinsic control signal u_c and similarly, for K_2, K_3, K_4, K_5,.., relative to, respectively, *changes* in the intrinsic properties of the organs or tissues involved (du'_c), the disturbances u_o, the transfer function characteristics of these controlled elements (dK_d), and so on.

If, and to what extent, u_o may need adjustment is determined by interoceptive (corporeal) and exteroceptive (ambient) sensory transducers, each of which monitors and is responsive to a specific *adequate stimulus*—such as light (eyes), sound (ears), chemical agents (taste, smell), external forces (taction), anatomical orientation of body parts (proprioceptors), and temperature (thermistors). The bias and sensitivity of these transducers is such, however, that unless the corresponding *receptor potential* generated by adequate stimulus excitation is of sufficient *threshold intensity*, and unless such excitation is persistent in a *threatening* way, the sense organs or tissues eventually treat the disturbance as "background noise" and ignore it—a form of accommodation known as *sensory adaptation* [2, 3].

An adequate stimulus of sufficient threshold intensity that is *not* continuous in a benign fashion will be converted by a sense organ into a corresponding *action potential* u_t (transduced signal), which is sent up-the-line for further processing and evaluation by the central nervous system (brain plus spinal cord), the main *controlling elements* of the entire physiologic feedback control network. Note, then, that the eyes do not "see," nor do the ears "hear." The former merely converts the visible light portion of the electromagnetic spectrum (in a frequency range from some $4\text{-}7.5 \times 10^{14}$ Hz) into corresponding action potentials, as does the latter for sound energy in the frequency range of 20-20,000 Hz. Translation of these transduced signals u_t into an "image" or "words" or "music" is a *perceptual* interpretation that takes place in the central nervous system and is greatly influenced by the psychological state and experience of the "perceiver." The sensory conversion process takes place in accordance with the transfer-function characteristics of the particular organ or tissue involved, designated here as K_t. Thus, again, one may write, generically:

$$u_t = u_t(u_o, u'_o, K_t, \dot{u}_o, \dot{u}'_o, \dot{K}_t, \bar{u}_o, \bar{u}'_o, \bar{K}_t, \ldots)$$

(4)

where *interoception*, u_o, which monitors internal (corporeal or somatic) homeostatic variables critical to life—such as body core temperature, heart rate, blood pressure, respiration rate, "vital signs," and so on—is distinguished from *exteroception*, u'_o, which monitors the environment through, for example, the "special" senses of vision, audition, taction, olfaction and gustation; and, where neither u_o nor u'_o is presumed to be exciting the sense organs in a manner that would result in sensory adaptation, wherein $u_t \to 0$. From Eq. (4), one may write:

$$du_t = \frac{\partial u_t}{\partial u_o}\, du_o + \frac{\partial u_t}{\partial u'_o}\, du'_o + \frac{\partial u_t}{\partial K_t}\, dK_t$$

$$+ \frac{\partial u_t}{\partial \dot{u}_o}\, d\dot{u}_o + \frac{\partial u_t}{\partial \dot{u}'_o}\, d\dot{u}'_o + \ldots$$

(5)

$$= K_6 du_o + K_7 du'_o + K_8 dK_t$$

$$+ K_9 d\dot{u}_o + K_{10} d\dot{u}'_o + \ldots$$

(6)

where, again, $\partial u_t / \partial u_o = K_6$ defines how the transduced signal u_t is affected by *changes* du_o in the excitation signal (monitored adequate stimulus) u_o, generated by anatomical interoceptors; and similarly for K_7 relative to anatomical exteroceptors (organs of special sense), K_8 relative to alterations in the transfer function characteristics of the sense organs, and so on. Note that *sensory adaptation* to benign persistent stimulation is embedded mathematically into dK_o, i.e., changes in the transfer function characteristics of the sensory transducer elements, themselves. Such changes can also result from the aging process (such as loss of hearing), from disease (such as diabetic retinopathy), from accidents or physical trauma, from dietary deficiencies, and from psychological factors that may affect the physiological properties of sense organs.

Once converted into ambiensomatic action potentials u_o, output signals u_o monitored by the body's feedback control sensory transducers are compared with corresponding reference set-points u_r for these same output variables to determine if any corrective action is necessary. The difference, $|u_r - u_t|$, is called an *error signal* u_e. Moreover, here, too, the corrective action—in the form of a responsive control signal u_c (in the case of extrinsic control)—is proportional not only to the *magnitude* of the error signal u_e (which is called *proportional control*), but also to its time-rate-of-change $\dot{u}_e$ (called *derivative control*), its time-history $\bar{u}_e$ (called *integral control*), the transfer function characteristics K_c of the controlling elements of the feedback control system, higher-order nonlinearities, and phase-shifted complexities [2]. Thus, one may write, generically, for the *controlling elements* in Fig. 1:

$$u_c = u_c(u_e, \dot{u}_e, \overline{u}_e, K_c, \dot{K}_c, \overline{K}_c, \ldots) . \tag{7}$$

A similar expression for intrinsic control u'_c would have the latter be a function of u_o and the inherent properties of the controlled elements, themselves—which also could be affected by age, disease, accidents, physical trauma, diet, stress, proper rest, exercise, and psychological factors. All of this notwithstanding, however, intrinsic control through u'_c will not be addressed herein, because the emphasis in this work is mainly on extrinsic control through autonomic and endocrine pathways. Thus, from Eq. (7), one may again write:

$$du_c = \frac{\partial u_c}{\partial u_e} du_e + \frac{\partial u_c}{\partial \dot{u}_e} d\dot{u}_e + \frac{\partial u_c}{\partial \overline{u}_e} d\overline{u}_e$$

$$+ \frac{\partial u_c}{\partial K_c} dK_c + \frac{\partial u_c}{\partial \dot{K}_c} d\dot{K}_c + \frac{\partial u_c}{\partial \overline{K}_c} d\overline{K}_c + \ldots \tag{8}$$

$$= K_{11}du_e + K_{12}d\dot{u}_e + K_{13}d\overline{u}_e + K_{14}dK_c$$

$$+ K_{15}d\dot{K}_c + K_{16}d\overline{K}_c + \ldots \tag{9}$$

with the K's defined in a manner similar to those in Eqs. (3) and (6).

The set of Eqs. (3), (6), and (9), at least in principle, can be solved simultaneously for the dependent variables u_o, u_t, and u_c to arrive at a generic feedback-control system input/output relationship to describe the behavior of the model depicted in Fig. 1. Details will, of course, depend on the *functional form* of Eqs. (1), (4), and (7), on how many of the relevant transfer functions are actually known for any specific situation, on what variables are involved, and for how exact a solution one is looking. Usually, physiological feedback control systems may be modeled as nonlinear (or quasi-linear), second-order (or higher), critically or overdamped networks, with transfer functions that reflect the state-of-health of the system involved. That is to say, K_7, for example, in Eq. (6) can be "adjusted" to simulate a pathological exteroceptive condition such as blindness or deafness, as can K_6 be adjusted to simulate an internal disease such as muscular dystrophy or multiple sclerosis. Other examples and applications of the above formulation are discussed elsewhere [2, 4, 5]. Suffice it to say here that the engineering formulation serves as a convenient *phenomenologic model* that can be used to define the three types of physiologic accommodation introduced earlier and to discuss the role played by music in affecting the accommodation process.

Immediate, Short-Term, Instinctive Reflexive Responses

The significance of this type of response is the fact that immediate, short-term, instinctive reflexive activity is characteristic of the innate inherent *natural* (inborn) ways that the body reacts *first* to *all* forms of intero- and exteroception [3]. That is to say, the human organism is, in essence, a creature of *emotion first*, and reason second (in *series*, not in parallel) as it seeks to satisfy its human and humanistic needs, and as it reacts to real or *perceived* threats to these needs [3, 7, 8]. The anatomical verification of this instinctive emotional response is found in the hierarchy of information-processing channels that u_r goes through as the controlling central nervous system decides what to do with it. That is, the fact that the *first* sequence of neural pathways carries u_r through the 500-million-year-old *paleoencephalon*—the "old" brain (which includes all of the brain *except* the cerebral cortex, or 5-million-year-old *neocortex* [3, 7, 8])—confirms the notion that instinctive human responses are, first and foremost, *emotional*. The "new" brain only receives information if the old brain says it's OK, in a series neural configuration, and, even then, the old brain delivers to the new brain only whatever information it chooses to "pass on"—a privilege that comes with seniority!

As you read this article, your paleoencephalon is processing visual stimuli (words) and is deciding whether or not the stimuli represent corporeal danger, and, if so, how best to respond. If the raw information is perceived to be immediately threatening—for instance, if what looks like a dot on this page is thought to be (or is, *actually*) a flea—the paleoencephalon's "fear" or "danger" lights will come on, ordering the body into a "fight-or-flight" mode—its primary line of defense against imminent danger. In this mode, all information-processing channels to the neocortex shut down completely, in favor of the "911" networks that cause muscles to flex, breathing and heart rates to increase, blood flow to the gastrointestinal system to be re-routed, and other reflexive responses to be activated, allowing the body to "brace" for action that may bring the fate of the flea into question. If, on the other hand, the spot on the page is, in fact, just a dot, and there is no perceived "clear-and-present-danger" that requires an immediate "fight- or-flight" protective response, your paleoencephalon switches from the latter mode into a more rational, but still instinctive behavioral mode. Behavioral adaptation in the more benign short-term is represented by reflexes (so-called "paw-to-jaw" responses) that cause us to eat when we feel hungry, drink when we get thirsty, put on a sweater when we get cold, or fall asleep when we tire. Note that these paw-to-jaw reflexes are still of a "911" nature, but they are not associated with the same sense of urgency as are those that characterize fight-or-flight responses.

Only if and when the paleoencephalon decides that u_r is not of a nature that threatens any of the four physiologic and egocentric needs defined above, will it open the gate and allow sensory inputs to go up to the neocortex—the new brain— for further cognitive processing that enables us to learn something new, which may require medium- or long-term accommodation, as necessary. Studies of cerebral processing of *musical* inputs suggest that, very early in the evolutionary process, the paleoencephalon developed a synergetic relationship with the elements of music, which elements get processed in a very meaningful way through the older, more instinctive cerebral pathways that course through the brain. In other words, there may be a natural music-paleoencephalon "understanding"—a synergy that may explain why music has such a profound effect in eliciting specific types of behavioral responses [7, 8]. Moreover, this synergy: (i) allows music processed through the paleoencephalon to gain *access* to regions of the brain otherwise restricted or "sheltered" from intrusion [7, 8, 13]; (ii) lets music thus *uniquely* affect the psychological state of the "perceiver"—hence directly influencing the *interpretation* of $u_t(u_o)$, or the *response*(u_c) to $u_d(u_c)$; and/or (iii) gives music the ability to profoundly bias the very *establishment* of u_r —both in terms of the physiologic homeostatic variables critical to life, and the psychological egocentric variables essential to lifestyle.

There is also reason to believe that in terms of the model depicted in Fig. 1, and the formulation developed from it, none of the activities associated with short-lived *sensory adaptation* to benign persistent sensory excitation, or with *fight-or-flight reactions* to perceived life-threatening disturbances, or behavioral responses to less-urgent indispositions, results in an adaptive physiological accommodation that produces significant changes either in the reference set-points u_r or in any of the system transfer functions K. That is, the immediate adaptive response may call for momentary *perturbations* around the set-points u_r (for which the phrase "floating physiologic set-points" has been coined [1, 2]) and/or around the established transfer functions K_i $(i = c, d, t, 1, 2, ...)$. But in a more permanent sense, the *mean* values around which such short-lived perturbations may take place remain essentially unchanged. Hence, one may say that in a *homeostatic sense*, immediate short-term instinctive reflexive responses take place in accordance with the requirement that, relative to the mean, $du_r = d\dot{u}_r = d\bar{u}_r = 0$ and $dK_d = d\dot{K}_d = dK_d = dK_t = dK_t = d\bar{K}_t = dK_c = d\dot{K}_c = dK_c = 0$. The latter is not so for medium- and long-term accommodation.

Delayed, Medium-Term, Conditioned Adaptive Responses

The significance of this type of response is the fact that delayed, medium-term, conditioned adaptive activity is characteristic of the body's ability to *change* u_r in a more lasting sense when it is appropriate to accommodate a persistent u_d. Thus, for example, a hematocrit of 45% may suffice to meet the body's need for oxygen at sea level, and there may be no need to change this value on a permanent basis if you go to Mile-High Stadium in Denver, Colorado, for just one day to see a football game. But, a hematocrit of 45% will simply not do if you *move* to Denver permanently and your body is asked to tolerate a mile-high decrease in oxygen concentration (u_d = anoxia) for a sustained period of time, and it will *certainly* not do if subsequent generations of your family settle in Denver forevermore! Enter *functional adaptation*—the body's ability to *change* u_r (*adapt*) in accordance with a sustained u_d that alters its functional expectations.

The reference set-points that drive the body's homeostatic regulators are determined by its desire to satisfy the human and humanistic needs introduced above; and the extent to which those needs are being met is embedded in the associated physiologic concept of *cenesthesia* (or, *physiological consonance*, to borrow a musical term). Derived from the Greek "koinos," meaning "common" (cen-), and the suffix "-aisthesis," which means "sensation" (esthesia), *cenesthesia* refers to the generalized, abstract "feeling" of normal functioning of the body as a whole —a "common feeling" that gives one a sense of well-being, a sense that all tissues and organs are working in a synchronized resonance to provide for the proper functioning of the *whole* body, acting as *one* symbiotic unit. Whether conscious or subconscious, whether based purely on anatomic physiological "scientific" criteria or on cultural influences, whether real or perceived ("programmed" images of yourself), whether inherited (genetic) or the result of functional adaptation—regardless of the source, values of u_r with which your body attempts to comply are manifestations of its ultimate quest for cenesthesia. Once established, these values of u_r can ultimately be encoded into the human genome (inscription) and passed on from generation to generation, and they remain in force so long as subsequent disturbances u_d are presumed to be acute, short-term, and temporary (you go to Mile-High Stadium for just one day to see a football game, returning back to sea level, say, within a week or less). But, as soon as the disturbances become chronic and persistent—potentially threatening to the organism's human and humanistic needs—functional adaptation kicks in to alter u_r. In other words, the body decides that u_d is something that needs to be contended with on a more permanent basis, and, so long as a change in u_r will not adversely affect the well-being of the organism as a whole (or, in some cases—such as a high-grade fever—even if it *will*) u_r is, indeed, changed to accommodate u_d more effectively.

Thus, under prolonged anoxia (you do, in fact, *move* to Denver), within a few months a blood test would reveal that your hematocrit has now been "reset" to around 50-55%, that the mean corpuscular hemoglobin content of your red blood cells is some 1.67% higher than it was at sea level, and that even your total blood volume has gone up nearly 20%—all designed to allow your blood to carry as much oxygen as it did at sea level, in the wake of the decreased supply that it experiences at 5200 feet above sea level. Once adaptation has been accomplished, your heart can slow down again and you no longer have to breathe more deeply, nor do you find yourself having to stop and rest often during long walks—some of the body's "fight-or-flight" responses that adequately served to meet your needs during one week in Denver have now given way to functional adaptation responses that will meet your needs more effectively for the rest of your life in Denver. And if all else fails, you can always move back down to sea level; i.e., *behavioral responses* can again come into play in the medium-term if functional adaptation fails to get the job done.

Studies seem to confirm that early on in the human evolutionary process, the elements of music played (and still do, even today) a significant role in meeting the body's quest for cenesthesia. In other words, not only is music processed in unique ways by the older more instinctive cerebral pathways of the paleoen- cephalon, but the latter, in an *adaptive* sense, apparently discovered cenesthetic qualities in music—qualities that affected the establishment of set-points u_r and control signals u_c in accordance with the cenesthetic needs of the organism [3, 7, 8]. Thus, (i) the human system not only seeks but, in fact, *requires* music to effectively impact upon many areas of basic adaptive function and development; (ii) the ultimate quest for cenesthesia may explain, at least in part, why music originated and evolved to play the major role that it does in satisfying the most basic of human needs; and (iii) the physiological basis for the profound effect that music has on the human's quest for cenesthesia derives from its ability (again) to affect *both* u_c (i.e., to provide a euphoric "alpha state" and elicit the release of calming hormones and neuropeptides) *and* u_d (i.e., to enhance immune responses and ameliorate the disposal of biochemical toxins). The latter point will be addressed in somewhat more detail below, but what happens if not only *you* move to Denver permanently, but your entire family remains in Denver for generations to come?

Permanent, Long-Term, Genetically Encoded Responses

Viewed in terms of the feedback-control model illustrated in Fig. 1, the hierarchy of events that trace the body's response to disturbances u_d may be described, then, as a time-dependent five-step sequence that proceeds from (i) immediate, instinctive reactions involving momentarily "floating" target values for homeostatic regulators—with no essential *change* in system parameters u_r or K_i—to (ii) facilitated accommodation (momentary "floating" but not permanent changes in K) to more persistent, but benign disturbances [2,5]—to (iii) conditioned reflexes involving the development of newly programmed neural information networks—to (iv) delayed functional adaptation with changes in u_r but not in the transfer functions K_i—and, ultimately, to (v) genetically encoded, long-term, permanent changes that involve *both* u_r *and* K_i. That is to say, in the long-term sense, your subsequent generations of Denver natives will all have higher values of u_r—for hematocrit, mean corpuscular hemoglobin, total blood volume, and so on—but, their bodies will operate around these reference values using control signals u_c that will have reverted *back* to their original sea-level values.

This increased effectiveness, wherein less of a control signal, u_c, is required to produce the same, or better, results, is due to the fact that genetic changes in the anatomy and physiology of the tissues and organs that respond to u_c—such as the bone marrow, which produces red blood cells, or the kidneys, which regulate total blood volume—have allowed these structures to become more *receptive* and sensitive (biased) to the control signals (such as hormones and enzymes) to which they respond. In the context of feedback control, "more receptive" means that the transfer functions for the target organs and tissues involved have also been modified in the long term, along with u_r. Thus, for example, if bone marrow at sea level has a certain number of receptor sites for the substance erythropoietin (which stimulates it to produce red blood cells), over the course of time the bone marrow of Denver natives will be genetically coded to possess a greater number of these erythropoietin-receptor-sites. Thus, "Denver" bone marrow will be more responsive to erythropoietin, allowing less of this control substance to elicit a correspondingly greater effect.

There is, of course, an upper limit to physiological accommodation—bone marrow can only tolerate so many receptor sites for erythropoietin, and the body can only manufacture so much erythropoietin, u_c. As the organism approaches the point of saturation, *no* amount of further stimulation can elicit a further response; and, as saturation levels are approached, it takes progressively stronger and stronger stimuli to generate an adaptation response. The process is anatomically and physiologically self-limiting, but music, in particular, has been observed to have a powerful influence in affecting such variables as: (i) the *rate* at which the accommodation process approaches saturation; (ii) *which* of the accommodation variables (e.g., u_r, K_i) reaches a saturation level before any of the others do; and, to a certain extent, (iii) *what* those saturation levels actually *are*. Furthermore, music can (iv) *temper* the body's response to persistent u_d—which may explain its effectiveness in healing; (v) *influence* one's perception of u_d as being threatening or nonthreatening— which may explain its effectiveness in expanding and enhancing both the creative and cognitive processing of cerebral information; (vi) *affect* what type of control signal u_c will result from what type of disturbance u_d—which may explain its ability to elicit specific types of behavioral responses; and (vii) moderate the long-term genetic changes that ultimately alter K_i —which may explain its effectiveness as a long-term therapeutic modality.

Indeed, investigators are beginning to show direct correlation between the musical scale as we know it and base-pair sequencing patterns in genetic material [9]. The base-pair sequences can be translated into musical patterns by exposing the bases of DNA to infrared light, measuring which wavelengths each base absorbs, converting those wavelengths into corresponding frequencies, and dropping those frequencies down about 35 octaves to bring them into the audible spectrum, thus converting the natural resonances of DNA into the register of the human ear. Results to date have been astounding [9], and the implications of *this* role of music in human adaptation are quite dramatic! Imagine, the elements of music as the very determinants of DNA base-pair sequencing in certain situations! There is much work yet to be done, but the potential is limitless. So, too, is the potential for approaching the study of science through music [10,11]. For instance, 1997 Scholastic Aptitude Test results recently released by the Educational Testing Service in the United States revealed that students with music coursework or experience scored 37-to-62 points higher on their SATs than did students with no course work or experience in music. And, one cannot overlook the potential for using the body's natural affinity for music as a means to effectively manage hospitalized patients [12]. But why music? What exactly is it about the elements of music that causes them to synergize so effectively with natural physiologic processes? Not all of the evidence is in yet, but certain aspects of the role of music in human adaptation deserve further investigation, as elaborated upon below.

All God's Creations Got Rhythm

Perhaps *the* most fundamental axiom of physics is that energy (in whatever form) is *cyclic* in its regular manifestations to some observer (frame-of-reference). That is, the phenomena of reality follow a distinct periodicity, with time and length scales of varying magnitude, which are defined according to the observer's range of measurement (scale-of-perception). Thus, for example, we receive time cues from the natural periodicities of our universe (daily (circadian) day-night cycles, yearly (circannual) seasonal cycles, lunar cycles, and so on), from our awareness of the biorhythms associated with physiologic processes (such as cyclic beating of the heart (time-scale on the order of 1-to-2 seconds), respiration rate (time-scale on the order of 4-to-6 seconds), the 4-to-6 hour cravings for food (hunger cycles), the rhythm of our walking patterns (on the order of 80-or-so steps per minute), and our periodic need to sleep for about 8 hours out of every 24), and from our sensory perception of such forms of energy as sound (20-20,000 Hz of *mechanical* vibrational energy) and light (4-7.5x10^{14} Hz of *electromagnetic energy*).

The reason(s) that periodicity is so inherent to the nature of our universe has to do with both the matter of *limited resources* (imagine the size of a stomach that would be required to accumulate all at once, at the very instant of birth, *all* of the food one will ever need throughout his or her lifetime, to be dispensed as necessary to provide for the nutritional needs of the organism; not to mention what it would take to keep that food from spoiling for 100 years or so!) and to the matter of *inertial resistance* to perma-nent changes in equilibrated states (which resistance sets up restoring forces u_c to counteract disturbances u_d to such equilibrated states). Thus, we have a "gas tank" (stomach) that we *periodically* fill and empty several times a day, a "fuel pump" (heart) that *cyclically* fills and empties to keep the "river of life" (blood) flowing, an "exhaust system" (bladder) that *alternately* fills and empties so that we don't have to wear diapers (or a Foley catheter) continuously, and information-processing channels (neu-ral-networks) that "*unload*" (discharge, or fire) and "reload" (recharge, polarize) every time they transmit a message—Morse-code style. Throughout our universe, we find example after example after example of processes that, due to limited resources or to restoring forces, rely on getting only part way toward a goal, then reloading to do the same thing again, to advance a bit further, and then doing it still again, and again, and again...

Because our evolutionary heritage has caused us to adapt to internal and external environments that ebb and flow with different scales of periodicity, so, too, did the most fundamental element of music—*rhythm*—surface to reflect and express our *awareness* of those periodicities. That is, recognizing that (bio)rhythm is not only a fundamental *physiologic* process, but a fundamental process of all of nature, it seems obvious that rhythm should *capture* our attention. It is thus not surprising to learn that we *respond* to rhythm—that we all "tap our feet to the beat"; hum along with "The Lit-tle Drummer Boy's" mesmerizing "pa-rum- pum-pum-pum" (in Katherine Davis, Henry Onorati and Harry Simeones' traditional Christmas jingle); sway along with the late Frank Sinatra as he invites us to "Come Swing With Me" (in his 1961 Capitol Records album); waltz, tango, boogie, jive, rock-and-roll, hop, skip, jump, or other-wise "dance the night away." And we further conclude that it is only natural for the most basic element of music to *be* rhythm. In fact, among the most primitive of instru-ments were those in the percussion family—the drums—the medium through which we express our inherent internalized "beat." Conversely, we are also not surprised to learn that pulsed stimuli of various kinds can *resonate* with the "natural clocks" of the brain that ultimately control cyclic physiologic function, and that certain emotional states and various levels of consciousness are correlated with those resonances [8]. In-deed, it is quite likely that many of the therapeutic effects of music may be traced to the influence of exteroceptive rhythm on subcortical structures of the brain such as the limbic system, particularly as these structures relate to the perception of time, and to the associated concept of a "pleasing resonance" [2].

That is to say, the frequency range of musical sounds evolved in some sense to be "symbiotic" ("living together") with corresponding rates at which the brain processes information [7], such that there results from this synergy some form of "pleasing resonance" (cenesthesia or *physiologic consonance*). Acting in concert with the limbic system of the paleoencephalon, the musically induced synchronized resonance may act to produce a state of euphoria that is unlike one produced by any other means. This euphoric state is a synergized cerebral activity, akin to that which one derives from meditative states wherein cerebral energy expenditure is minimized, and the mind engages in imagery that bespeaks of calm receptiveness, insulated from the dangers of the outside world [2, 4]. Supporting the above hypothesis is the added observation that when individuals listen to a certain frequency of music, that frequency, quite specifically, shows up as identifiable "spikes" appearing in the subject's electroencephalogram (EEG)[7]. And, of course, the very word "music" derives from the Greek goddesses of the fine arts and sciences (Muses)—who were conceived to be beautiful, pleasing, and inspiring.

By contrast, the *opposite* of cenesthesia, or physiological *consonance*, is a dysfunctional state of *dysaesthesia* (deranged or impaired sensation), which one might term physiological *dissonance*. The discordant, asynchronous nature of the physiological state characterized by dysaesthesia is associated with a corresponding state of anxiety, emotional stress, poor health, energy dissipation, and other symptoms of a functional imbalance that results from *dissonant* "beats" in the biorhythms of life. Thus, health becomes synonymous with physiologic consonance, and disease becomes synonymous with physiologic dissonance—and various types of music can actually *drive* (physiological *resonance* or synesthesia) homeostatic regulators toward either extreme.

Melody: The Language of Emotion

As mentioned above, the human organism is first and foremost a paleoencephalon-driven creature of *emotion*, rather than a neocortex-driven creature of reason. Thus, along with its inherent sense of rhythm, the body seeks as well a means to express its emotional nature. A long time ago, then, we learned to use our anatomical broadcasting ability (voice) and signal-receiving faculty (hearing, tactile stimulation) to string together sounds (air vibrations), one-following-the-other (that is, in series, linearly, or *horizontally*)—into a consecutive sequence of pitches, which, taken collectively, added up to express a thought, an idea, a mood, or an emotion. Innate human vocalizations, in their most primitive forms, convey specific (or discrete) emotional survival needs and mating calls. These sound effects include screaming, crying, sobbing, laughing, groaning, sighing, and so on [14]. As language evolved through prosody (versification) and inflections, these calls were further refined into rhythmically interrupted repeated sequences and tonally linked incantations. In music, such a recognizable series of pitch arrangements is called *melody* (from an ancient Greek word that means "song"), which is the *second* most basic element of this art form.

Melody is a complete nonverbal statement, having a beginning, a middle, and an end. Indeed, melody developed as the adaptive *language* of moods and calls—communicated through a unique syntax that conveys the spectrum of human emotions —from one emotional extreme (pure dissonance, "dysaesthesia," "fight-or-flight," anxiety, fear, panic, anguish, rage) to another (pure consonance, "cenesthesia," relaxed, calm, tranquil, safe, euphoric). The sequencing pattern of musical pitches, especially as it relates to the spacing between successive intervals (small steps, medium or large leaps, and so on) also gives melody a characteristic contour—its own terrain or profile—within which are contained *inflections* that define the landscape of the emotion. Add to that (i) an associated sound *quality* (*timbre*, the *third* most basic element of music, derived from the Fourier-spectrum of sounds produced by less-than-perfect vibrating sources), (ii) sound *volume* (loudness, or intensity, known in musical terms as *dynamics*), and (iii) a certain rhythmic cadence and tempo (speed) at which the sequence of musical pitches is delivered, and the emotional meaning that is conveyed in melody becomes truly well-defined.

In an adaptive sense, one is *born* with the innate drive to attend to sound and melody, seeking some type of resolution that satisfies the basic human (life) and humanistic (lifestyle) needs discussed above. That is to say, one enters this world already endowed with an instinct for *auditory tracking* [15]—an inherent ability to respond immediately to melodic resonance and rhythm, to track it, to identify and interpret it, and to react to it, anticipating and waiting for *resolution*. The brain absorbs and sustains every sound it hears, it remembers each pitch in sequence until the next one arrives, and it stays tuned in to what follows until it is convinced that the emotion being conveyed has been successfully attended to and resolved. The physiological organism learned to do this "auditory tracking" early in its evolutionary adaptive heritage. It learned to satisfy its instinct for *personal* survival by vocalizing its calls and listening carefully to the sounds and melodies of nature—to the hisses of cats, the hoots of owls, the rattle of snakes, the animal calls in the hunt, tribal war chants—sounds and melodies that warned of environmental threats, assured a sense of safety, or introduced a responding call from a mate. In the mountains of Europe, farmers yodel to call their family or other farmers in their brood to gather. Each person's yodel has a slight variation that identifies who's doing the calling, the urgency of the call, and where the yodeler is located. Similarly, all animals produce melodic warning signals to alert their clan of impending danger.

Humans learned to satisfy their instinct for survival as a *species* by vocalizing mating calls, which existed as a means for communication long before verbal syntax did—and which still prevails even today. Humans learned that chanting, toning, and, more recently, "rapping," somehow helps to satisfy the need for self-expression and spiritual fulfillment. Indeed, for more than 1000 years, the "official" music of the Roman Catholic Church has been the Gregorian chant—monophonic melodies that set the mood for the rituals of spiritual enlightenment—and for even longer, Jewish cantors have chanted Hebrew prayers in synagogues around the world to inspire their congregations in worship.

As a nonverbal means for communication, melody serves as its *own* language, a *universal* language that is innate—able to elicit responses without "saying so." And we have learned to distinguish among sounds and melodies that alarm us, as opposed to sounds and melodies that pacify. In western culture, we are joyous when we listen to waltzes, polkas, marches, or Dixieland jazz; we are saddened by the blues, dirges, requiems, or "chansons tristes" (melancholy songs); lullabies calm and pacify us; fanfares stimulate and excite us. Melodies can make us angry, they can scare us, they can quiet us, they can arouse us. In short, melodies can elicit the entire spectrum of emotions associated with human behavior and the human experience. And all of these adaptive responses that are the result of musical stimulation can be directly traced to the effect that music has on provoking the organism to issue forth the control signals u_c that arouse it to action; namely, hormones and neuro- transmitters.

Hormonal and Neurotransmitter Control Signals

Hormones and neurotransmitters (neuropeptides) are the physiological chemicals of emotion. In particular, flight-or-fight reactions derive from the activity of adrenalin, norepinephrine, and an entire category of chemical substances called *catechol-amines*—which are released in response to stress and to a perception of danger (note that the danger need not necessarily be *real*, it need only be *perceived* to be real by the person experiencing it). On the other hand, feelings of ease and well-being derive from the relaxing activity of dopamine (an adrenal hormone), endorphin (a natural pain-killer manufactured in the brain), and an entire category of chemical substances called *enkephalins*—cerebral neurotransmitters that are released in response to pleasing inputs (or inputs *perceived* to be pleasing). Enkephalins may regulate mood by counteracting the activity of stress-inducing external stimuli that would otherwise lead to disappointment, anxiety, and depression (physiologic dissonance). Thus, these neurotransmitters create in the organism, a *natural* "high" state similar to the euphoria produced by morphine or other opiates.

Enkephalins are also released from nerve endings responding to stimulation that corresponds to the cerebral *alpha-state*. The alpha-state is characterized by 8-to-13 Hertz waves that appear in the EEG of an awake individual who experiences pleasant feelings of well-being (physiological consonance, cenesthesia) and tranquility, along with an increased *awareness* of emotions, relief from anxiety, and general complacency at the conscious level. One can be trained to identify and "generate" these alpha waves through biofeedback techniques (many of which rely on musical stimulation). It is these 8-13 Hz waves that conspicuously disappear from the EEG when the brain (mind) displays any type of excitable attention or alertness, or when it focuses on objects in the visual field (the eyes must be closed to elicit alpha-wave activity), or when it is otherwise distracted by environmental stimuli. But the relationship of musical stimulation to the elaboration and release of hormones and neurotransmitters addresses just one aspect in the biochemical realm. Another equally important component of the biochemical ensemble has to do with emotional states (and their mediation, amelioration, or exacerbation through exposure to music). Such states relate to the accumulation of biochemical *toxins* (lactic acid, nitrogenous and nonnitrogenous waste products, carbon dioxide, histamine, and others); *free radicals* (highly reactive groups of atoms containing an unpaired electron, which adversely "attack" healthy cells in order to reach a more stable compound state); and other *pharmacological agents* that are stress-induced. Persistent exposure to excessive quantities of these biochemical agents is physiologically dangerous, but some studies suggest that in those instances where music has the euphoric ability to ameliorate excitable emotional states, it does so by eliciting the release of chemical substances that counteract the adverse effects of toxins and free radicals. In other words, music acts as a stimulus for the body to write its own best prescriptions—producing "cleansing" *pharmacological purifiers* and "invigorating" *therapeutic tonics* that energize the organism towards a state of cenesthesia.

Harmonize the World

In an evolutionary sense, other musical elements—such as consonant and dissonant *harmonies* [16] (a *fourth* fundamental element of music that involves pitches strung together *vertically* and sounded simultaneously to produce chords and introduce the concept of *dimensional hearing*, the architecture of music [17]), various forms and styles, structure, and so on—are historically more recent. They represent adaptive physiologic responses to advances in technology, changing social patterns and customs, political influences, evolutionary and environmental alterations, and so on. Space does not permit us to address here in any great detail these other musical elements, but suffice it to say that it is time to recognize that music plays a major role in the physiological quest for cenesthesia. Studies are confirming that, in terms of the schematic depicted in Fig. 1, music has a significant influence on (i) the body's perception of and reaction to disturbing signals; (ii) the transduction of output signals into sensory action potentials; (iii) the establishment of reference signals and homeostatic operating set-points; (iv) the elaboration of control signals, hormones, and neurotransmitters; and (v) the transfer function input/output response characteristics of the various elements that comprise the organism's functional parts. Moreover, the mechanisms by which such influence becomes manifest include (i) ameliorating the adverse effects of biochemical toxins; (ii) stimulating the release of therapeutic hormones and neuropeptides; (iii) resonating in a symbiotic sense with natural physiological periodicities; (iv) charting neural networks to parts of the brain not otherwise accessible; and (v) causing new and improved codes to be inscribed into the human genome. Indeed, the elements of music uniquely synergize with basic physiological functions to play a significant role in the adaptive process. It is time to recognize this fact and no longer treat this art form as a "nice" but "unnecessary" part of the human experience—especially in the education of our children.

References

1. **Schneck DJ**: Feedback control and the concept of homeostasis, *Mathematical Modelling*, 9(12): 889-900, 1987.

2. **Schneck DJ**: *Engineering Principles of Physiologic Function.* New York: New York University Press, 1990.

3. **Schneck DJ**: A paradigm for the physiology of human adaptation, in *Music in Human Adaptation*, Schneck, D.J., and Schneck, J.K. (Eds.). St. Louis, MO: The Virginia Tech Press/MMB Music Inc., 1997, pp. 1-22.

4. **Schneck DJ**: *Mechanics of Muscle: Second Edition*, New York: New York University Press, 1992.

5. **Milsum JH**: *Biological Control Systems Analysis.* New York: McGraw-Hill, 1966.

6. **Schneck DJ**: A generic transport equation and the forces of nature, *Mathematical Modelling and Scientific Computing*, 1(6): 537-551, 1993.

7. **Schneck JK, Schneck DJ**: Sensory Integration and Differentiation of Auditory Information as it Relates to Music. Virginia Polytechnic Institute and State University, College of Engineering, Department of Engineering Science & Mechanics, Biomedical Engineering Program, *Technical Report # VPI-E-96-02*, March 4, 1996.

8. **Schneck DJ, Schneck JK, eds.**: *Music in Human Adaptation.* St. Louis, MO: The Virginia Tech Press/MMB Music, 1997.

9. **Alexjander S, Deamer D**: The infrared frequencies of DNA bases: Science and art, *IEEE Engineering In Medicine And Biology Magazine,* this issue, pp. 74-79.

10. **Schneck JK, Schneck DJ**: A physiological basis for recognizing the importance of the fine arts in public education, *VMEA "Notes,"* XLI (3): 16-19, November 1989.

11. **Frank M**: Music makes good scientists, in *Music in Human Adaptation*, Schneck, D.J., and Schneck, J.K. (Eds.). St. Louis, MO: The Virginia Tech Press/MMB Music Inc., 1997, pp. 203-208.

12. **Patrick G**: Effects of vibroacoustic music on symptom reduction in hospitalized patients, in *Music in Human Adaptation*, Schneck, D.J., and Schneck, J.K. (Eds.). St. Louis, MO: The Virginia Tech Press/MMB Music Inc., 1997, pp. 219-222.

13. **David W, Gfeller K, Thaut M**: *Introduction to Music Therapy: Theory and Practice.* St. Louis, MO: MMB Music, Inc., 1992.

14. **Deacon TW**: *The Symbolic Species.* New York: W.W. Norton, 1997.

15. **Berger DS**: Music therapy, sensory integration and the autistic child, in *Connections: Integrating Our Work and Play; Proceedings of the Annual Conference of the American Association for Music Therapy.* Silver Spring, MD: AMTA, June, 1994, pp. 97-118.

16. **Valentinuzzi ME, Arias NE**: Human psychophysiological perception of musical scales and nontraditional music, *IEEE Engineering In Medicine And Biology Magazine,* this issue, pp. 54-60.

17. **Berger DS**: Are you listening? A workshop exploring concepts of dimensional hearing, in *Music in Human Adaptation*, Schneck, D.J., and Schneck, J.K. (Eds.). St. Louis, MO: The Virginia Tech Press/MMB Music Inc., 1997, pp. 209-214.

Sample Music Therapy Evaluations, Treatment Reviews, Progress Briefs

Dorita S. Berger

1. Child A:	**Music Therapy Evaluation**
	Male, 5 years old. Multiple delays with some autistic characteristics. Suffered strokes in utero resulting in poor vision bordering on legally blind; expressive and receptive language delays; sensory integration issues.
2. Child B:	**Group Music Therapy Treatment Update**
	Autistic male, 15 years old; on psychotropic medications for perseverative behaviors, attention deficits and self-control. High functioning on the spectrum; good language and cognitive skills; excellent musician.
3. Child C:	**a) Overview of Treatment** **b) Progress Report, 9 months later**

Female, 3+ yrs old. Down/Autism. Referred to in Chapter IX as Eleanor (pseudonym); verbal delays, sensory issues, comprehension deficits.

4. Child D: **Overview of Treatment Objectives**

PDD/Asperger Syndrome, David (pseudonym), 13 and a half years old; described in Chapter XI, Conclusion. Review of treatment provided to the school and allied therapists.

The enclosed materials are actual reports of patients in music therapy treatment. In the interest of privacy, all names and pertinent personal information have been changed or omitted.

DORITA S. BERGER MA MT-BC

Board Certified Music Therapist   THE MUSIC THERAPY CLINIC

MUSIC THERAPY EVALUATION

CLIENT NAME: *(Child A)*   D/O/B: *6/21/96*
                Address   Diagnosis: *Unspecific: Multiple Delays,*
                Address   *Possible PDD*
Parents: Date of Report: *April 24, 2000*

(Child A) was referred for music therapy by psychologist (Dr. G) and has been involved in one-on-one music therapy sessions weekly, since January 20, 2000. The following evaluation and recommendations derive from eleven sessions to date, at 45 minutes per session, totaling 8.25 hours of treatment.

Introduction

Prior to reading this evaluation, it is important to understand what Music Therapy is, and how it differs from academic, skills-oriented training. As with other clinical interventions, Music Therapy seeks to provide a level of comfortable physiologic function that can ultimately induce functional adaptation to the environment, and to the ability of the brain to pattern, process, retain and recall cognitive and intuitive appropriate responses. Functional physiologic adaptation ultimately impacts all areas of learning. Thus, Music Therapy as a process-oriented intervention, based on the cumulative continuous application of specific stimuli, enables the brain and body to obtain organized information in ways that ultimately affect and redirect intellect and behaviors.

Resources of Music Therapy interventions include the six basic elements of music – rhythm, melody (tune), harmony, timbre (the unique quality of an instrument or voice that differentiates it from another), dynamics (louds/softs), and form (beginning-middle-end). Using these resources, both patient and therapist engage in the physical act of playing a variety of instrumentations, often including voice and movement, to help reinforce the repetition of stimuli targeted toward problematic issues in

order to alter and obtain specific results. As with any other therapy intervention, Music Therapy goals focus upon altering the functionality of the
system, applying goal-oriented music activity toward that end.

Music Therapy as a child-centered clinical intervention, affects sensory
integration issues, attention and extended eye contact, rhythm internalization for organizing body movements and muscular control, auditory
tracking, auditory integration and figure-ground focus, eye-tracking, information processing, behavior, independence, self-awareness and
self-knowledge, organization of self and environment, awareness of others,
and a variety of cognitive issues. It provides a "safe" environment for
obtaining new ways of interacting with another, and provides a key
element to learning – motivation! Individual music therapy services are
currently being contracted by several school districts throughout Fairfield
County. Schools across the country are providing music therapy services to
special needs populations. Further information and research studies on the
effectiveness of Music Therapy with special needs populations may be
researched through the web site of the American Music Therapy Association at www.musictherapy.org.

General Observations of Child A

Child A is a pleasant child age 3 years 10 months, of average height for his
age. His demeanor is very congenial, pleasant and completely connected to
the music environment. At each session Child A displays excitement,
enthusiasm and curiosity about the variety of instruments available
throughout the room. From the outset, it is quite clear that Child A has
severe visual problems and relies extensively upon his hearing and his sense
of touch. Similar to working with a blind child, Child A's demeanor, vestibular insecurity, deficient spatial awareness, sense of perspective, distance,
high and low, demonstrates severe impairment.

Upon entering the room for the very first time, Child A did not provide
direct eye-contact to therapist, but ran directly into room towards the
instruments of choice: specifically, the standing snare drum and other
smaller hand drums. He did not especially ask for nor seek mallets in order
to play the drums, but rather, relied on playing them with the tips of his
fingers, investigating the textures of the drum, and the sounds. As he played

each drum, he neared his ear to the drum (usually tilting his head toward the right ear).

His first several sessions were disorganized. Child A made his preferences clearly understood by using the third person "he" rather than first person "I" want to play... "He likes drums"; "He doesn't want the maracas", and so on. In addition, the first few sessions found him rather resistant to being organized, and he preferred to skitter about the room touching this, playing that, and trying everything available. However, it was very evident from the beginning, that rhythm is a physical organizer for Child A. His disorganized movements immediately became paced and pulsed to the beat of the music. His drumming was extremely organized and rhythmic, and he was able to maintain this rhythmic stance for the duration of the music. It made no difference whether the music was a recognizable "tune" or an improvisation within a very rhythmic beat.

Child A displayed limited facial and body affect of likes and dislikes, demonstrating delight by smiling occasionally as an indicator of enjoyment and/or recognition of a familiar song. He responded with a quiet stare when music stopped, as if waiting in anticipation for music to begin again, and immediately verbalized description of what he just became engaged with ("he played drum..."), and surveyed the possibility once again of playing another instrument. However, he was not particularly musically engaged or connected to the therapist. That is, he played because music was available, but he was completely into himself when he played, as if he went internal into his musical train of thought without ever looking at therapist during activity. However, auditorily, he was completely engaged, as demonstrated by his ability to stop and start each time the music stopped or started. At those points, he would look up to therapist in anticipation, often declaring "He's not finished playing drum...". Modulation is difficult for Child A, although in this short amount of time, he has come a very long way.

Child A was not particularly happy with physical prompting for playing instruments in a defined way. Overall, he sought to be extremely independent of therapist, basically resistant to prompting, remaining completely attached to the activity and the music-making for the duration of each 45-minute session. As the encounters accumulated, Child A became more and more organized and able to attend to task and therapist without much scampering about the room. In effect, the more familiar he became with the routines and what was available for music-making, the more in control of himself he became, and the more able to follow directives.

Physical Skills

Due to Child A's visual problems, his physical skills are somewhat underdeveloped. His visual issues contribute to his inability to accurately imitate the movements of others or to incorporate these by copying them into his own body actions. However, as stated earlier, rhythm appears to be a highly organizing and stabilizing factor for Child A. In the presence of rhythm, he is able to bring muscular activity to a stable and comfortable level of function. His gait in march-like pattern becomes less self-conscious and somewhat more balanced and secure. His ability to beat the drum while marching – i.e., upper/lower body coordination – is becoming more secure and fluent. And his physical whole-body activity when music is available, seeks to be coordinated with his visual and auditory processing, although this will require much more input in order for it to become completely comfortable and functional.

At this point, his vision in conjunction with motor activities is somewhat disparate. When he is active in upper body motions (playing drums, etc.) he tends to shut his vision down and devote auditory attention. Thus mid-line issues become present, and it is unclear where he determines his mid-line, both vertically and horizontally, to be. He attempts to avoid this issue as much as possible. Therefore, he has great difficulty playing drums with arms crossed, for instance. Or reaching across his body for a drum placed at the other side of him.

The trampoline presents major vestibular issues for Child A. He is completely insecure going up and down in vertical sequences, uncomfortable with his balance. He leans forward a great deal, and prefers not to jump if at all possible. In stepping onto the trampoline, or stepping down, he has difficulty gauging accurate distance between the trampoline height and the floor. He enjoys moving rhythmically to the music, once on the trampoline, but would like to avoid this activity completely! Holding a pair of heavy maracas while jumping demonstrates his upper/lower body coordination deficits, but he is becoming much more comfortable hearing the sound of his jumping (as the maracas make sounds while he jumps and holds them).

Although in the beginning Child A had difficulty being completely still, during the past several sessions, he has become much more able to stand and perform a task for extended time and repetitions, and has also shown the ability to modulate without anxiety, from one task to another. He has become much less distracted by items around the room, and can remain with one activity.

He is quite able to play drums bilaterally in parallel motion, although his right arm is always a touch slower than his left arm, as they come down together on a drum. The coordination of left and right requires some work. In bilateral alternate movements for playing the drum, Child A often requires prompting if he has not provided sufficient visual attention to "copying" what therapist is doing. Verbal prompting, as well as physical prompting are required in order to suggest to Child A's brain that it coordinate the rhythm of alternate arm movements in pulse to the music

In addition, if asked to play two arms parallel on a drum, switching between two drums (first two arms on one drum, then two arms on another), there is difficulty with motor planning, and he can sustain this activity only briefly.

Stopping, starting, running, marching, are activities presented to Child A, and he is trying to negotiate these to the best of his ability. However, visual constraints and his insecurity with spatial dimension are limiting his ability to free himself into the movements. He has progressed immensely in these activities since we first began working together, and he enjoys the excitement of these tasks, and is much more able to modulate from one to another.

In general, the presence of music has enabled Child A to make great physical strides in sustaining and pacing his energies. Motor planning issues will persist, but are increasingly organizing for more functional execution of musical tasks.

Sensory Function

Child A accepts auditory information very appropriately. Functioning as a blind person would, Child A's auditory attention is quite astute, and it appears that he is accepting general music flow quite well. However, his auditory processing of very high, or very low frequencies is still being explored, with focus on how he tends to integrate these frequencies. Language development depends on auditory processing and integration of linked pitches, and music therapy intervention is one of the most successful methods for the developing brain to learn accurate sound processing.

Child A follows the sound of an instrument and responds to loud vs. soft sounds, identifying these as loud and soft. He plays the snare drum in one manner, however, which indicates a motor planning issue of muscular control in using his muscles adequately to emit loud and soft sounds. This implicates body dynamics, and music therapy interventions continue to address the issue of "hear/do" to alter flexibility in motor control.

Child A's auditory focus and tracking, auditory figure-ground, auditory discrimination, although functioning initially at an "acceptable" level, requires much intervention to become clear. Tracking and focus is required in following teacher instructions, hearing information, and attending. Auditory figure-ground is the ability to focus on the foreground of sound, putting superfluous sounds in the background. He has the ability to do this, but requires much more work in order to secure this. Because his visual does not support his auditory processing, music therapy can address the strengthening of auditory figure-ground, as well as discrimination of sounds (what's a car screech from a human scream, for instance), because music processing does not necessarily require visual support. While his abilities here remain unclear – especially as far as frequencies of speech and prosody incantation are concerned – what or how, exactly, Child A perceives when he hears will directly impact the development of his receptive and expressive language skills. Music Therapy seems the most obvious intervention in aiding auditory adaptive function. In this brief evaluation period the exact processing by Child A of auditory information is difficult to gauge. Because it is unclear exactly what Child A is hearing, it will take some time to help Child A display his ability to discriminate differences in auditory information. Further investigation will yield insight into this area of auditory perception, which, as stated above, is crucial to receptive and/or expressive language development.

Child A is now able to sustain extended visual attention as long as music activity is present, whereas, when just language is being used he scans the room, loses eye-contact with therapist, and seems highly uninvolved. He is also now able to provide extended task and auditory figure ground attention, when the task of listening to the directive words of a song asking him to play this or the other instrument, is present. This is an amazing achievement from our first few sessions, when he was totally uninvolved with any directives. He attends visually to the instrument he is playing, visually following his arms and crossing mid-line. In addition, Child A has been able to hold the violin with one arm while bowing on the string with the other arm, and actually looking down his nose (literally) dead center, to follow as the bow crosses the string. This has greatly strengthened his eye-hand/auditory coordination. Auditory/visual/physical attention is becoming increasingly obvious and expanded as sessions accumulate. This points to the beginnings of self-awareness and knowledge that it is he – and his body – playing. A sense of organized independence encourages further learning. Eventually such tasks lead to upper-body motor planning, willful and purposeful use of hands and arms, and rhythmic self-control.

Visual Processing is the most acute issue thus far in sensory integration for Child A. This deficit impacts on Child A's motor planning, imitative capabilities, environmental evaluation and organization, vestibular insecurities, interactive communicative abilities, relationship to others, task organization and attention, and distractibility. Visual/auditory coordination will continue to be a crucial adaptive issue, if Child A is to succeed academically. Visual tracking (oculomotor planning), depth-perception, visual discrimination and figure-ground, and visual/auditory verification are issues which are currently being addressed in music therapy. As such, the use of specific instruments, such as the xylophone, which requires visual attention in order to play individual tones, playing of several instruments in sequence, and other activities, are being directly focused on visual issues. Picture association (find picture A, on chart B, and push that picture to hear the song we just sang) is a very difficult process for Child A, but his motivation to hear the tune we just sang (it's a song-playing book) drives him to try to find the correct picture. He is also giving visual attention to the pictures on the page which define the song.

In addition, playing the recorder (blowing instrument), brings visual to mid-line, as he holds the recorder with both hands and looks down the shaft to find where the sound is coming from. He blows this instrument, which also contributes to breath control issues and speech development, and provides much visual attention to both instrument and therapist. The kazoo is used to elicit vocal inflection, which is lacking and will require much work. Circles and Figure 8's using a scarf which he swirls across his body induces eye tracking to follow the scarf. He enjoys this activity, which is prompted by therapist or parent.

Visual/physical coordination is another issue being addressed, not only through instrumental playing, but movement and drumming as well. Imitation is a constant intervention. The floor drum is used here to help Child A try to imitate physically what therapist is doing. Auditorily, he imitates the rhythm, but visually he does not pick up on the exact manner in which the therapist is playing. Much more work is needed here.

Tactile information is highly stimulating and sought after by Child A. The cabasah instrument (a rhythm instrument with chains of BB's around a metal tube) is akin to OT's brushing stimulus and is thoroughly enjoyed and centering for Child A. He does not seem to display any tactile defensiveness, except when he is not quite trusting of why therapist is prompting his arms. He prefers not to be prompted, but this is most likely due to a need for willful independence, rather than tactile defensiveness. Child A uses his hands and fingers as a blind child would, touching and sensing the shape, size, and texture of items. He is quite secure learning about the environment in a tactile manner. Thus, music therapy intervention coordinates tactile need with auditory and visual input, in order to help the brain confirm that what is "felt" is in fact looking like, or sounding like "this". Eventually he will become secure with defining the environment without necessarily touching it to confirm what he thinks it is. (It is interesting to note that he does not bring things to his sense of smell, as other blind people do.)

Fine and Gross Motor Planning are areas in which Child A obviously needs work. Through rhythm and movement activities, with music to drive the system, these areas will be greatly impacted by music therapy intervention. Rhythm internalization for gross motor planning is a developmental area which can eventually result in efficient body propulsion through space. Rhythmic movement on the trampoline, done to rhythmic music, already has caused Child A's brain to "forget what it couldn't do" because of his desire to stay with, and move to the music. The Auditory Cortex is in very close proximity and directly related to the Motor Cortex, thus rhythmic music can greatly influence motor planning. (Research on Music Therapy with stroke victims confirms this).

Fine motor is difficult to assess at this time through music but seems to be age-appropriate at this point. However, with ample presentation of holding and playing of hand instruments, his ability to grab, hold onto, and play an instrument, or flatten his hands in order to make sounds on the piano or drum will strengthen his potential development of purposeful hand activities, individual finger movement, and writing. In addition, his eye-hand coordination abilities can develop appropriately.

In general, sensory issues, including auditory integration, auditory/visual/physical integration, body dynamics and motor planning proprioception and vestibular aspects, and language skills are areas which can uniquely be addressed through music therapy.

Cognitive Skills

Child A seems to understand much of the receptive language information presented at our sessions. He also seems quite able to ask appropriate questions, provide appropriate answers, request items of interest or needs, describe activities he has undertaken, and present a sense of logical sequential progression of information. He also seems able to "learn" quickly, and retains much of the information from one session to another. He recalls words to familiar songs, and fills these in when sung by therapist, although he is not especially interested in using incantation (i.e., doesn't actually *sing* sing). Also, his vocal projection is timid, and therapist is always requesting he speak up or sing louder.

He seems to know about the alphabet and about numbers. At this early stage of music therapy intervention, cognitive issues have remained in the background temporarily, in order to address the larger issues of physiologic function. Unless Child A's sensory system becomes better coordinated and regulated, cognitive processing will not be achieved in a comfortable manner. Thus, for the next several months, more attention will be paid to physiologic intervention. (Any knowledge can be attained and accumulated once the system is happy and functioning well!).

Therapist has found Child A to be personable and unfrightened by the introduction of cognitive information. Now that he is better able to "attend" and take "directives" in a congenial and cooperative manner, much information will have the opportunity to find its way to Child A's memory bank for retrieval. He is quite a teachable young man, enthusiastic and willing, as long as there's music around to calm and relax his struggling system. Since auditory influx of information is his safety factor, music – especially rhythmic music – will always be useful in programming information into Child A's brain!

My observation is that Child A is ready and willing to "learn" cognitive information and functions best when highly motivated and challenged to attend, and when rhythm and music is present. He seems able to "anticipate" what is being presented, and his gazing into my face and mouth seem to indicate an ability to remain still and attempt to absorb what is happening as long as music is somehow involved. Music creates an extended attention to task, and his eyes do not look away as long as I play and sing directly to him. It is clear by all indications, that cognitive training can be part of the music therapy treatment. Colors and shapes, letters, numbers, words (two bells, one triangle or "circle" drum, etc.) and writing can definitely be presented within the musical setting.

Investigation of cognitive skills requires more extensive evaluation. On a preliminary level, it appears that cognitive input through musical stimulus will be successful. This will ultimately transfer to other learning aspects in a variety of settings. Once the brain is patterned to absorb information in organized, rhythmic fashion, and is reinforced through ongoing cumulative interventions such as Music Therapy, a child of Child A's demeanor can surely develop cognition quite well.

Psycho-emotional and Social Cues

Child A obviously enjoys being in the presence of music; and there is emotional affect indicating contentment. Also present seems to be a sense of self and other, some understanding of common social cues (my smile, frown, shaking head for "no" or "yes", etc.) He does not imitate therapist facial expressions or affect but gazes attentively at them when possible. Child A seems to have some awareness of personal boundaries and enjoys proximity as well as distance from me. He definitely requires ample space and time to absorb and internalize a situation. He appears to be quite capable of doing so appropriately, as demonstrated by his relaxing to allow hand-over-hand maneuvering in order to play an instrument a particular way. When therapist comes near, he no longer withdraws, frowns, or seeks to distance himself in any manner spatially from therapist, and now allows closeness when being prompted for a task. Trust will always be an issue for Child A, since he is visually unable to confirm friend or foe! If he can't assess your smile, he can't determine your friendliness! And his vision issues will affect his picking up of social cues, so physical touch directives and auditory cues will be most essential.

Recommendations and Preliminary Music Therapy Goals

Music therapy is often one of the most appropriate and effective services for children with brain function issues. We know that the brain immediately attends to music. We know that information is processed, retained and recalled when provided through a musical format. We know that rhythm animates and organizes the system. We know that music stimulates language learning. We know that music can elicit emotion, interaction, and interdependence. Music Therapy has been playing a prominent role in helping Child A develop in all of the areas discussed above. As stated in the introduction, Music Therapy is a treatment intervention in which the elements of music are applied to address presenting issues and specific goals. These are integrated with goals of allied therapies, and school curricula.

   With enough exposure to this intervention, the positive results of music therapy application permeate throughout all areas of learning, both cognitive and intuitive. Both areas are essential for integrated learning. Creativity is the source of curiosity and the seeking of information by the brain. Therefore, the intervention of music therapy reaches well beyond standard therapies and education. It reaches into the inner child seeking to be discovered and taught! In Child A's specific case, records show that some brain damage may have occurred in the right brain areas. Although music is a whole-brain activity, the right brain areas are particularly active with music. Therefore, much brain rehabilitation can take place with the intervention of music, which will ultimately impact the whole brain's rehabilitation! The right brain is nearest to the amygdala, the emotional brain. Therefore, affect, recognition and expression of feeling states, are impacted through music. It is an essential area of integrative development of both intuitive function and cognitive function.

Because the brain "attends" to music, tracks sequential tones linked to one another (following a tune from one note to another), and orders the body to move rhythmically, music has the ability to:

- automatically stimulate rhythmic movement and physical coordination

- pacify or animate and coordinate sensory systems

- aid vestibular regulation through rhythmic motor planning and proprioceptive stimulation

- contribute proprioceptive feedback through muscle contractions when playing instruments (drums, etc.) and surrounding vibrational stimulation due to live instrumental playing

- aid in language and cognitive development

- provide rhythmic proprioceptive information to the brain for self-organization

- extend attention, absorption and retention of cognitive information, and much more.

Child A is a personable willing participant in a music activity, as demonstrated in all sessions thus far. He "attends", wants to be prompted into participation, enjoys moving rhythmically, and even contributes vocal input from time to time as if to join in the singing/playing activity. Because he is so attentive and organizable, Music Therapy can have a great impact on his betterment and development.

Without an organized, comfortable physiologic system, learning is impossible. It is only when the body no longer feels threatened by incoming sensory information, that the brain can relax and process information beyond the paleoencephalon (the survival old brain) into higher cognitive function. These are facts currently being substantiated by the great majority of brain research. Thus, a system in which there are so many physical issues, cannot be comfortable enough to learn math and reading.

Therefore, the first important interventions must deal with these primary issues, before any further cognitive learning can take place. Music Therapy is precisely such an intervention, which has been shown to reach a dysfunctional system on both the sub-cortical as well as the cortical levels of function.

Because of Child A's ability to provide consistent attention span, task attendance and cognition interest within the music environment, the non-threatening form of stimulus intervention that music provides can easily address several issues simultaneously, including sensory/physical, psycho-emotional and social, communication and social interaction, and elementary cognition. It is recommended that Child A receive a minimum of three 45-minute sessions per week of one-on-one music therapy. Child A displays a strong ability to sustain complete attention to music and musical tasks for at least one hour at a time. Three weekly 45-minute sessions will allow appropriate pacing of activities within each session, enabling Child A to take the time he seems to need in order to focus and process stimulus and information without haste, and to develop functionally adaptive patterns of movement and cognitive responses. Three (or more) contacts a week with therapist will provide needed repetition and recurrence required to ultimately reinforce consistent adaptive learning responses. The more contact, the more time, the sooner the progress. Because music therapy is a cumulative process, the more extensive the exposure, the better the effect on adaptation.

The following areas can be efficiently addressed through Music Therapy goals:

- **Auditory Integration issues:** location, auditory focus, tracking, figure-ground, discrimination.

- **Sensory/auditory/visual integrative issues:** specifically, extended auditory attention and integration; auditory/physical coordination; auditory/visual coordination; visual focus; attention; tracking.

- **Physical coordination**, bilateral integration of physical movements through rhythmic movement and activities providing appropriate proprioceptive and vestibular stimulus through music activities.

- **Breath control and language stimulation** through such activities as playing of recorder, vocalization tasks, fill-in songs, sound imitation; expressive language development; conversations.

- **Self-Regulation**, motivation, curiosity, appropriate use of instruments; task attention; self-restraint.

- **Organization of Environment:** organize task; environmental depth perception; arrange instruments.

- **Cognition and cognitive association** through visual/auditory resources (number/letter shapes and colors songs, picture-song books, cause/effect activities); imitation; generalization.

- **Social awareness**, development of affect, choice, likes/dislikes, awareness of self-other; personal boundaries; sharing; turn-taking; etc.; interests, conversations.

- **Relatedness** to task, stimulus, activities requiring specific hands-on participation addressing eye-contact, assess at this time, the exact processing of auditory information. Imitation of therapist's facial expressions and affect will be primary focus, in order to elicit sound imitation paralleling facial expressions and instrumental sounds.

- **Attention/Focus** extended attention to task; self-regulation; extended focus and repetition.

Summary

Child A seems to be taking the world in on his own terms, and is basically content. He is very motivated by music, listening astutely, allowing prompting, and generally enjoying the experience. He displays a readiness to take in cognitive information, and is willing to attempt a task with physical prompting. He is aware of the music environment, anticipates and attends to sounds, has been providing continuous and extended eye-contact, and has the ability to sustain self through a longer session of music therapy. The inclusion of Individual Music Therapy Services into his IEP will contribute an important and holistic therapy treatment which can address many of the issues which seem to predominate, including helping him sustain focus and attention, physical coordination, sensory integration, relationships, system organization through rhythmic internalization, functional adaptation and cognitive development, language development, and a general sense of "belonging" and well-being.

Since music – especially rhythm – is an important stimulant and motivational tool for Child A, it is recommended at this time that 45 minutes three times a week of individual music therapy be provided.

Submitted April 24th, 2000

Dorita S. Berger, MA MT-BC

Board Certified Music Therapist

The Music Therapy Clinic

DORITA S. BERGER MA,MT-BC

INVOICE

ACCOUNT #: PVT 1042

DIAGNOSIS: PDD/Autism

DATE: Jan. 6th 2000

TREATMENT CODES: 97770, 92506, 97112, 97799 Cognitive Development, Sensory Integration Language Development; Physical Coordi-
SERVICES TO: Child A nation;
Neuromuscular Reeducation; Coordination;
Visual and Auditory Tracking

D.O.B. 00/00/00

DESCRIPTION OF SERVICES: 90-minute individual Music Therapy Sessions @ $00/per 45-min session Twice weekly

Invoice for sessions as follows:

Wednesday,	Jan. 6th	1:45PM	45-minutes
Monday,	Jan.11th	11:30AM	45-minutes
Wednesday,	Jan 13th	1:45PM	45-minutes
Monday,	Jan.18th	11:30AM	45-minutes
Wednesday,	Jan.20th	1:45PM	45-minutes
Monday,	Jan.25th	11:30AM	45-minutes
Thursday,	Jan.28th	1:45PM	45-minutes

Total Sessions in January   Seven (7)

Total Due for January: $ 000

TREATMENT PLAN: Auditory integration, discrimination and tracking tasks

Random Sound imitation; pre-language development

Vocalization-random vocal sound articulation

Vestibular regulation/rhythmic activities for motor planning and purposeful, controlled movements

Strengthening of musculoskeletal activities

Relatedness and purposeful interaction with therapist

Creative self-expression

Following of simple 1-step and 2-step commands

Development of imitation skills

Breath control, blowing, and oral-motor stimulation

(through blowing instruments and similar activities)

PLEASE NOTE: Payments are due no later than 7 days from date of invoice. Cancellations with 24-hour advanced notice, or emergencies, weather, therapist unavailability, will be credited or made up at a later date. THANK YOU FOR YOUR COOPERATION AND PROMPTNESS

DORITA S. BERGER MA MT-BC

Board Certified Music Therapist

MUSIC THERAPY GOALS AND TREATMENT

CLIENT NAME: *Child B*   Diagnosis: *PDD/Autism*

D/O/B: *7/8/86*   Date of Report: *January 30, 2000*

CURRENT TREATMENT FOCUS: *Development of social skills including: organization of self and environment in relation to group activity; meeting needs of self and others; identifying feelings of self and others in relation to self; making choices relative to group participation; problem solving; conversation; interpretation of body language; asking and answering questions relevant to ongoing dialogue; creative self-expression both verbally and non-verbally; leadership skills; and a variety of auditory/cognitive sensory needs as presented.*

Overview and Update of Group Music Therapy

Group Music Therapy establishes a socially interactive environment based on a non-competitive setting. While it is a clinical intervention, Music Therapy nonetheless encompasses a wide range of music creativity, self-expression, self-organization and environmental organization, non-verbal and interactive co-dependent behavior, the continuous responsibility of understanding and relating to behaviors and needs of others, problem solving for self and group, and many other aspects of interpersonal and social skills development.

Group Music Therapy sessions flow within the alternation between pre-structured activities suggested by therapist, and improvisational musical playing emanating from the group as a whole and each member individually. As a group, members conform to pre-assigned tasks and roles developed by leader, and as individuals, members have the opportunity to redesign tasks and roles both for themselves and the group, designating roles and tasks of others, choosing activities, discussing self needs, likes and dislikes, identifying moods and feelings as expressed in the music being improvised, and more.

It is important to understand Group Music Therapy as a clinical intervention that differs from a general music class or recreational activity. During our Music Therapy sessions, group members have the opportunity to self-explore in a creative way, but with consideration of others, who are also exploring in creative improvisational ways. Thus, when the elements of tonality, rhythm, dynamics, timbre, form, harmony (or dissonance) permeate the environment, something is happening: feelings are being experienced, awareness of others cannot be escaped, personal choices and self-organization are taking place, as well as likes and dislikes of what others may be doing, playing, saying, and so on. There is no chaos in the Group Music Therapy session which does not become an immediate opportunity to organize and re-organize the self. Because music seeks order, form and closure, each member of the group experiences the need to solve and resolve in the moment.

There are five members in Child B's group, ranging in ages from 13–15. The Norwalk Public School is currently contracting this service for several group members, and Easton is contracting for the participation of Child B. Child B has been a participant in this Group Music Therapy during 14 weeks of the Fall, 1999–2000 semester. Sessions are 45 minutes in length, held once a week at The Music Therapy Clinic in Norwalk, Ct. Dorita Berger, a Board Certified Music Therapist, conducts the sessions.

The following will provide your administration with a very brief overview of Child B's excellent progress in developing social, cognitive and sensory (auditory) skills and personal relationships as a direct result of this Group Music Therapy intervention.

Social Skills

The area of Social Skills Development in the music therapy setting includes the following emphasis:

a)   Observing and identifying self needs and feeling states under current circumstances (likes, dislikes, interests, current feelings and moods, energy level, desires, other persons of particular interest within group, and similar self-observations)

b)   Observing and identifying needs and feeling states of others under current circumstances

c)   Problem Solving; Conflict Resolution; Cooperation; Alternative responses.

Child B is becoming quite verbal and interactive in letting therapist and group friends know how he is currently feeling, and in which aspects of the activity he would like to take part. Example: if he becomes unfocused and bangs on the gong to his heart's content while group is attempting to organize, he will describe his out-of-sync behavior by stating the he has the need to "hear the loud vibrations because it makes me excited and happy".

When a group member shouts that the sound is too loud, and begins to agitate as a result of Child B's banging, the entire group is asked to discuss the situation based on how each is feeling and reacting to the confrontation. Child B has, in more recent sessions, been able to explain his behavior, hear the complaint, listen to recommendations from other group members, develop his own conclusion and self-alter his actions. All of his responses, as those of other members of the group, are unsolicited from therapist! When similar events occur due to behavior of others, Child B takes his place among the group members in discussing and recommending alternative possibilities. Child B has made impressive progress at being fully aware of the consequences of his actions upon himself and others.

One recurring activity which takes place in the session is an improvisation (on piano and keyboard) involving one member "asking a question" on his instrument, and the other member (seated at another keyboard instrument) "answering the question". This is quite a complicated non-verbal activity. LISTENING is key to responding! Child B has been absolutely amazing in this activity, whether he asks the questions, or is the respondent. As this task evolves, other group members are asked to observe what "feeling" might be being expressed by the keyboard dialogue. There is no right or wrong answer to this question. The objective is learning to associate feelings with moods and how these might be expressed through music and behavior. In all cases, Child B has enjoyed exploring such observations, and coming up with a variety of moods and feelings beyond simply "happy" and "sad". In addition, the aspect of how one's own actions can influence those of another is discussed: in this case, how one's music material influenced the other's musical response! (Cause/Effect of behavior.)

In these aforementioned social skills (see above) it is quite apparent that the music therapy environment contributes to Child B's ability to focus, listen, understand how to identify the feeling states of himself and others, help derive resolutions, and take part in interactive dialogue. Bravo! for his progress in this area. Continuation of this kind of activity will absolutely contribute to his continued awareness of himself and others.

    d)   effectively participate in group activities

    e)   develop organizational and leadership skills.

Following a), b), and c), are the goals of developing effective participation skills within a group, developing organization and leadership qualities. In the Music Therapy environment, where many of the activities are self-motivated improvisational, non-directed tasks, Child B has shown an amazing capacity to follow the leadership of a peer. His personality is less assertive than those of several other members in the group, and Child B has learned to recognize this about himself. On the other hand, he has been encouraged, by other group members, to speak his mind, express his interest, and "take charge". In turn taking activities, Child B is right in there keen on being one of the group! Some of the activities involve taking turns directing and leading the music activity. For instance, assigning instruments to other members, providing rhythmic themes, and "conducting" the flow of the playing: who comes in when, with whom, and who drops out when, according to the "conductor's" choosing. Child B has shown amazing assertiveness in this task, as well as a great deal of joy being able to "lead" and have others do exactly as he assigned! Each member of the group has this opportunity, and each member then becomes a willing participant in the leadership of another. This has become one of Child B's favorite activities. He is progressing quite well, although he still needs encouragement to lengthen his "conducting" time.

This is a non-verbal activity encompassing the wide realm of skills required to organize this music environment: developing task(s), making choices and decisions, following another, becoming leader. It is spontaneous and creative, allowing full body language and mannerisms to be focused toward communicating ideas to others.

It is obvious by Child B's response, that this kind of activity allows him to self-explore and learn about himself in ways that other situations might not offer. Continuation of this kind of activity obviously will impact other areas of his functional social development.

g)   auditory discrimination, auditory tracking and figure-ground improvement

h)   auditory memory and accurate imitation

i)   sequential memory and sequential repetition of extended patterns.

One of the areas to which music therapy contributes extensively for PDD and other diagnosed populations is the area of auditory integration, memory and sequential processing. Music, by nature, is sequential, and in order to process this stimulus, memory and sequential processing is imperative! Auditory figure-ground (being able to hear the foreground sound while putting unnecessary sounds in the background) is a major component of this focus. With all the activities presented to the Music Therapy group, the majority is auditory, non-verbal. Thus it is all the more important to focus the auditory, in order to hear, follow, repeat, and retain musical information.

Many of the Music Therapy tasks involve each member providing a rhythmic pattern of several beats to the group, which the group then has to accurately repeat. As each member takes turns providing a rhythmic pattern, it requires not only remembering one's own rhythmic pattern which needs to be presented, but tracking whether the others are accurately repeating "your" pattern!

In the beginning, Child B was less adept at this task, predominantly because of his inability to self-organize his auditory focus. By now, however, Child B has become quite capable of focusing auditorily for an extended length of time, repeating the information, and developing one of his own. This has become a crucial activity for each member of this group (all with forms of PDD and Learning Disabilities). Since this is a high-functioning group, and all are verbal, much verbal interaction takes place as the members help each other produce the exact repetition of a presented rhythm. Memorizing "strategies" are offered by members to each other!

Child B's progress has been very swift, and continuous. In addition, his auditory processing and memory seem to be increasing. He is developing longer rhythmic patterns for presentation, as well as imitating longer patterns (which I may present from time to time). Development in this area will eventually become evident in academic areas as well. I am very pleased with Child B's progress thus far. It needs to continue and develop as he is developing.

General Progress

Because the Group Music Therapy environment is quite motivating and stimulating, and because Child B has bonded with the group and has developed several personal relationships with some members of the group, I have observed an increasing sense of creative self-expression in Child B. Not only has he become quite verbal and focused in his interactions with other "musicians" in this group, but he has also become aware of his "role" as a member of this music group, and the sense of how each member depends on the presence of the other, both in attendance, musical interaction, and social "fun". The environment is conducive to self-expression, learning, non-competitive interaction. It is the nature of this intervention to elicit spontaneity, organization, eye contact, auditory and cognitive focus. Many of the activities are developed to address these and other issues. Since the members of the group are in the same age range, but come from different areas of the county, it offers the opportunity to "play" and make music as a result of evolving social skills and common interests. Child B has made wonderful progress in this setting. He depends upon, and seeks members of the group for enjoyment, both in the group, and (according to parent), outside of group time. He spontaneously greets his friends, they bond with him, as he has bonded with them.

As a therapist, I am gratified in knowing that Child B is being given the opportunity to excel and "feel good about himself" because he can be self-directed, self-sufficient, and part and parcel of a fun yet learning creative activity. His movements are much more organized, and he feels good inside his body.

In addition to the above mentioned social and auditory skills, Child B is learning to organize cognitive information in the opening activity of this group therapy: playing recorder, which involves eye tracking of rhythmic notation, breath control, and group sound. The therapy component of recorder playing addresses rhythmic internalization, organized breathing, visual/auditory/physical coordination for tracking of notation, and more. In his IEP, I noticed one of the music class goals is to have Child B recognize music language. Each member of this therapy group reads recorder notation, and rhythms. The presentation of this task is for therapy purposes rather than music learning, addressing sequence retention, auditory memory, eye-hand coordination, fine-motor skills (in fingering the recorder holes), pitch and auditory tracking, eye-focus and visual tracking, and other aspects of sensory integration issues. Child B's skills are increasing, as is his ability to remain focused visually and intellectually, as well as physically.

Finally, one of the best results of Child B's participation in this Music Therapy Group is the fact that he has established a solid social relationship with one of the other members of this group. I understand that these two "musicians" speak to each other on the phone, often leave my session to have dinner together and socialize further. In addition, I understand that, recently, another group member encountered Child B in an outside setting, and they held a lengthy dialogue about their mutual interest and contributions to the Music Therapy group! So this common, self-explorative, creative experience has contributed well beyond any written goals, to the social awareness and development of Child B.

I recommend continued participation for Child B in this Music Therapy Group. Goals for the Spring semester will include, in addition to those focuses mentioned above, further in-depth verbal interaction, identification of feelings and social circumstances; behavioral cause/effect, discussion and sharing with others, both musically and verbally, strengths, weaknesses, feeling and circumstances experiences during the week the group does not see each other, and continued emphasis on sensory issues, logic, sequence, organization, and more.

The Group Music Therapy group meets for 45 minutes, once a week. Over the 14-week period, that totals a mere 10 and a half hours of treatment! One must conclude that in just over 10 hours, an amazing amount of goals can be addressed and progress made addressing important developmental issues for Child B. I am very proud of his participation and progress and look forward to including him in further sessions.

Dorita S. Berger, MA, MT-BC

Submitted January 30, 2000

DORITA S. BERGER MA MT-BC

Board Certified Music Therapist

GOALS AND TREATMENT

CLIENT NAME: *Child C*   Diagnosis: *Autism/Down Syndrome*

D/O/B: *12/8/95*   Date of Report: *December 6, 1999*

CURRENT SELECT TREATMENT OBJECTIVES: *Language/communication; Following of 1 and 2-part directions; movement coordination–vestibular/upper-lower body coordination; visual and auditory tracking & integration; sensory coordination and proprioceptive stimulation; rhythmic internalization for organized physical control of movement; sequencing; association and cognition issues.*

Overview of Music Therapy Treatment

Child C has received weekly music therapy for the past 15 weeks at 45 minutes per week, totaling a mere 11 and a quarter hours of music therapy to date (including Monday, Dec. 6th). Judging by the progress being made in such a short time, it can only point to the effectiveness of this particular therapy for Child C. The following will give you a brief overview of some of the areas being addressed in Child C's music therapy, and the progress being made in these very few hours. Please understand that Music Therapy is unlike standard cognitive instruction, being neither instructional nor cognition-based. It is a cumulative process; thus, "results" are not always clearly visible in academic terms. However, we understand brain physiology and physiologic accommodation enough to understand that a process is taking place which ultimately alters for the better, neurologic repatterning, cognitive potential, physical coordination, and social interaction.

1. Vestibular coordination

Several tasks are being presented to Child C, to encourage reorganization of balance potential, reduction of "fear" of falling, and encouragement of balanced coordination. Among these include jumping on the trampoline to the beat of the song being played. At first, Child C could only stand still on the trampoline and simply shake the maracas (given to her as a means of maintaining balance by holding onto something, as well as providing auditory input in sync with the beat and bounce). After several sessions, perhaps after some 3 hours of contact, Child C was able to display jump "preparation" by bending knees, flexing at the waist while leaning forward in the pre-jump position! She continues to attempt to jump to the music, while having graduated from holding maracas to clapping hand cymbals in rhythm to the music while "pretend jumping" while bouncing in the exact rhythm of the music. In addition to this task, Child C has been presented with a task requiring her to "jump over the candle sticks". She clearly has learned to await the appropriate moment, make physical preparation to "jump" over the sticks…but takes a step over the stick instead. I fully antici- pate that before long, Child C will, in fact, jump over the stick! As her ves- tibular system becomes more comfortable and secure, she will suddenly disconnect from the ground while curling her legs beneath her! She loves the jumping tasks and looks forward to practicing these with music. Rhythmic internalization is part of this area, and is important in control- ling the pace in which the system physically responds.

2. Upper-lower body coordination

When first we met, Child C was unable to actually beat a hand drum while "marching" to the beat – simultaneously. It's amazing to observe her now! She is clearly able, in these short weeks, to maintain two separate activities in sync with the music. The music does drive her into motion, and her brain has learned how to coordinate the activity in order to keep up with the music! We are also working on running, and will introduce skipping. The developmental aspect of these coordination tasks is also to increase control of body dynamics (heavier motion when marching, lighter movement when running, etc.). Body dynamics are generally synchronized with music dynamics of louds, softs, high/low registers, etc. I am also looking to organize flow of energy and control in her arms.

3. Upper body and arm dynamics

This is being addressed through proprioceptive stimulation from drumming with heavier mallets, and playing of a variety of hand instruments of varying weights and sound qualities: triangle, bells, small light-weight mallet for xylophone tones, lifting of light bells alternating with heavier stick for larger drum, and so on. In addition, Child C is asked from time to time to play either very loud, or quite soft, and always, her arms are alternated, so that each arm has the opportunity to experience varying dynamics. These activities will eventually translate into the manner in which Child C uses writing implements, lifts books and other items, etc. She has been so extremely cooperative in these tasks, enjoying the "Old MacDonald Had a Band" game in which she must play a variety of instruments according to what the song requires.

4. Following commands, locating objects, reacting in appropriate amount of time

In addition to upper/lower coordination and body dynamics, Child C is enduring a difficult task as mentioned above (Old MacDonald) attempting to coordinate the sound cue for the instrument being called for (e.g., high-pitched piano crashes for the hand cymbals; low-pitched slow beat for the drum, etc.). Total time spent on this task, to date, might total 30 minutes over the past several weeks! Not much time, yet she is making amazing progress in understanding the multi-step requirements of this task. Her sound location is good…her memory for where the items being called for are located is excellent, and her energy for continuing the task over several repetitions is also excellent! This is a developmental task, which will eventually include more than the three–four items we are currently using.

5. Control of self; control of environment

Child C was given a task to "hear" the words being sung, play the sounds that go with those words, and wait until the appropriate time to play the instrument. "Coo Coo" is a song in which Child C is required to play two bell tones (across mid-line), to make the "coo coo" of the bird; play two castanets for the "quack quack" of the duck; jingle the bell for the chirping of the little bird… It took Child C exactly one sitting to master this task! She was able to hold off playing until the appropriate time (as she now does in waiting to "jump" at the appropriate time). And, Child C can flow in and out of the activity as per my recommendation. Child C can also arrange instruments of her interest and play these in conjunction with my playing. Her ability to self-organize as well as organize her environment in music is excellent!

6. Visual tracking and visual/auditory/physical coordination

This is coming along quite well. She is asked to play only certain pitches on the full xylophone. Those pitches have stickers on them in order for her to seek and play these, and they are spaced apart in order for her to use her visual tracking to locate the pitches. This task also involves having to coordinate her arms to her visual, to the auditory (I'm playing too, after all), in order to comply. For the most part, she has been doing quite well in this task. At times, it may take her a few minutes to become organized and "willing", but we have had little problem arriving at the task. In fact, she has been exploratory in playing the various registers in which these tones are found.

7. Communication, language, breath control, cognitive association, sequencing

Every session begins with the recorder and kazoo as our "hello" song. This is to coordinate and organize breathing, bring focus to mid-line, pace the system through breath control, and "awake" the cognitive processes. Child C does very well with this, imitating my blowing rhythms (while I also play the piano), making sounds on the kazoo, etc. The kazoo stimulates vocal pitch and inflection, which might otherwise not be present. In singing, Child C uses less pitch inflection than when playing the kazoo (we're fooling the brain!). In order to arrive at good vocalization for language inflection, both the recorder and kazoo are encouraged for use at home as well as in sessions. We also employ many nonsensical sounds…squeals, etc., to "stretch" her vocal cords, her pitch memory, and her imitation of inflection. She is doing quite well in this area, and is having lots of fun! Understanding certain associative logic is still difficult (for instance, when asked to look at a picture, find it elsewhere and push that picture in order to hear the song play, she seems confused as to what she is being asked to achieve). We are working on this as well. Fill-in songs in which Child C must provide the missing lyric is fun for her, and addresses some of these language responses.

8. Cognition, association, sequencing

Musically, Child C displays the ability to sequence when hearing a song. However, she has not, as yet, attempted to sequence tones in order to "find" a song on the xylophone or the piano. She is young yet, however, and the idea is evolving in her mind. She plays individual tones on the keyboard/piano, rather than simply banging clusters, and will play orderly, scale-like tones one following the other. As stated above, her association with words, meaning of words, and logic of response requires some work, and we are addressing this issue as well. The song book which plays the tune by pushing the correct button, is one task we have been using. Drumming by imitating, on several instruments is another kind of task to address this, and singing fill-in songs in which she will provide the words, even when nonsensical, is another.

Summary

In the very short time that Child C and I have been working together, I have had absolutely no problem in directing activities and having Child C comply. She is willing, eager, and happily motivated to undertake whatever tasks with which she is presented, without resistance! There may be moments when she is unwilling to attempt something, and this, I have found, coincides with the difficulty of the task! (That's surely normal for anyone!) Since this therapy is child-centered, I do not insist or force Child C to undertake a task, but will rather redirect her into another activity, and perhaps present the earlier activity once again at a later time. This works extremely well, and she is happy in this environment. I also believe we have established an excellent rapport with each other, in which we are comfortable taking or leaving a task and moving into some other area. I can address my goals in many different ways. Creating a stressful environment is not one of these!

When Child C is comfortable with herself, her environment, the activity, and the person directing these, she is completely congenial, compliant, and actually performs on a very high level! I believe she is quite adaptive, and very quickly conforms to what is required. I look forward to each session we spend together, and am very proud of her progress and abilities in music!

Dorita S. Berger, MA, MT-BC
Board Certified Music Therapist
December 6, 1999

DORITA S. BERGER MA MT-BC

Board Certified Music Therapist

GOALS AND TREATMENT

CLIENT NAME: *Child C*   Diagnosis: *Autism/Down Syndrome*

D/O/B: *12/8/95*   Date of Report: *September 25, 2000*

CURRENT SELECT TREATMENT OBJECTIVES: *Language/communication; Following of 1 and 2-part directions; movement coordination—vestibular/upper-lower body coordination; visual and auditory tracking & integration; sensory coordination and proprioceptive stimulation; rhythmic internalization for organized physical control of movement; sequencing; association and cognition issues;*

Music Therapy Progress Report

Child C has continued to receive weekly music therapy sessions throughout the year, at 45 minutes per week. She has made incredible progress in many areas of our focus. Child C continues to enjoy her music encounters very much.

1. Language/communication progress

Child C has become very verbal and fluent in expressing her desires and options for music activities. We have many exchanges of "how are you", "what would you like to do today" and the like. She is asking for what she wants, and is also asking for the implements she needs in order to make music. Child C is also quite articulate in singing song lyrics audibly, and has been attempting a variety of inflections. Her inflective melodic contouring of odd sounds is increasing, thus adding affect to her verbal statements. It is typical of Down Syndrome persons to have limited vocal inflections. However, with the use of the kazoo, Child C instigates some rather diverse and contoured inflections, sliding up to high tones, and down to low tones much better than when she first began our sessions. In music therapy, Child C is as verbal as any other child in this setting, and provides good visual contact when she addresses me.

2. Vestibular coordination progress

This area has proven to have brought about the most progress! Child C now jumps on the trampoline quite fearlessly, with both feet off the trampoline! She also jumps across the room, over 4 or more sticks, to the tune of "Jack be Nimble", and clearly loves her new-found sense of balance! Jumping while propelling forward is not an easy task! Yet Child C will jump over the sticks, regardless of what position they are placed in on the floor, including jumping over sticks placed in a circle!

Her newly discovered sense of vestibular security has reached across much of her movement activities. She propels across the room more securely, when marching and running. We are now exploring pre-skipping activities such as hopping on one foot. This is just at the beginning, but will no doubt be achieved as well as was her jumping with both feet in the air. Since rhythm is her driving motivator, Child C's body rhythms drive her into movements, and she executes movement fearlessly as long as music rhythm is present.

3. Upper-lower body coordination

This area is also progressing quite adequately. She is much better organized rhythmically to march and beat the drum simultaneously, sustain rhythm well. That means she will beat the drum at the same time she takes a step in sync with the drum beat...a difficult task at the beginning. She also responds immediately to changes in speed and directions as dictated by the musical elements. In this respect, her mid-line orientation is ever stronger, and since her vestibular is more secure, she undertakes challenging maneuvers quite well using arms and legs in a very coordinated manner.

4. Upper body and arm dynamics; bilateral coordination

Child C was introduced to the violin during the late Spring of our sessions. This was done in order to assist with centering of vision, and strengthening of bilateral upper body coordination. The result has been most astounding! Child C absolutely loves the violin! Parent was urged to rent a violin appropriate in size for Child C. This was done, and Child C has since been playing on a violin size one-sixteenth! (Almost the size of a jewelry pin!). However, the violin has become an extension of Child C's arm! She has the most incredible coordination in being able to hold the violin steady, under her chin, with her right arm, and bow back and forth with her left arm, keeping the bow exactly even and at the center of the playing area on the fiddle. Her eyes fully focus down on her finger board (center and slightly to the left of mid-line!). She holds the instrument absolutely correctly, and sings away as she plays the open strings. It is amazing to observe Child C in this task. She can sustain this coordination for an unlimited amount of time, as long as the piano is playing along with her; she will play for the full 45-minute session, if I were to allow it!

She never seems to tire of holding the instrument up under her chin (something that tires even me!). And is completely adept at taking out, and replacing the instrument in its case. The violin IS Child C, and it appears that she has clearly found her identity. (She is quite possessive of this instrument.)

In drumming loud and soft, Child C is able to modulate the muscular dynamics required when exerting more or less force onto the drum. She is given heavier, bulky mallets in order to provide good proprioception. She is displaying no problems in this area, and has made incredible progress very quickly!

5. Following commands, locating objects, reacting in appropriate amount of time.

In the music therapy environment, Child C has little difficulty following commands, locating appropriate objects and reacting in the appropriate amount of time. Many of her directives are sung and placed in quick rhythmic succession, causing the brain to attend and process within the rhythm of the music. She seems to do much better when given instructions which are sung and rhythmic, than when they are spoken. Her system is so attuned to musical responsiveness that it is then easy to transfer this disciplined listen/do action to the spoken words. Child C has good auditory/mental processing in this environment. When she does not respond to a directive, it is more that she either is not interested in what she is being asked to do, or has not focused on what was being said to her. Otherwise, I find that she is able to respond immediately. Many tasks are undertaken, involving 2 and 3-step directives (play the drum, the triangle, and the gong). This involves the ability to retain sequential information long enough to reproduce the requested sequence. Although Child C has not yet perfected this, she has made very fine progress, and has required little repetition or prompting. These are difficult tasks because not only are the words to follow, but the brain is also occupied with the music behind the words. Yet Child C is not thrown by the activity, and is working on following the directions as well as can be expected.

6. Control of self; control of environment.

Child C has excelled in this area, but is now becoming a bit feisty! In many respects, this is being encouraged by the independence which music therapy nurtures. In this respect, she is making wonderful progress. She actually does control herself…and when she refuses to undertake a task, that can be viewed as an awareness of her ability to control her desires (even though it may not be compliant with what is being asked of her). She does not throw tantrums, nor act out in any other way. But she can refuse to undertake a task…and in this therapy, this is acceptable. However, she is then asked to come up with another task (control of environment), and she usually is quite specific at telling me what she would like to do. The only contentions are when I ask her to undertake something which is difficult for her to do. At that point, she shuts down ("I'm so tired."). She is progressing well in this area, and is developing a fine sense of self!

7. Visual tracking and visual/auditory/physical coordination

Work on the xylophone, playing on specific tones, is greatly improved. She is quite comfortable tracking visually. The violin work has influenced her visual coordination. In general, although we continue to employ tasks which address this area, it is not a very problematic one in the music therapy environment at this point. She finds any instrument around the room, gets to it in time to play it with the music, and is generally well focused and coordinated in delivering the results. In this area, she is performing better than many "typical" children I have worked with! Tracking from the blackboard is still problematic to a certain extent. She requires the benefit of my pointing to the items, letters, or numbers she is being asked to track. This will take more time to develop.

In the task where she is asked to see the letter A, or G, or other, and find the A or G tone on the xylophone in order to play the sequence, she is still finding it difficult to track, find, and deliver. But we continue to work in this area.

8. Cognition, association, sequencing

I find Child C to be an extremely intelligent, very teachable child. She learns quickly, and retains information very well. Many of the earlier tasks devoted to this area are successfully completed. In books in which a picture is to be found, then the button bearing the same picture is to be found and pressed in order to extract the song which goes with the picture, Child C now has no problem associating and responding to the task appropriately. She is describing what she sees in the picture. We are still undertaking some difficult cognitive tasks, and have introduced pre-writing skills…drawing circles, straight lines, to music rhythm. She resists these tasks – they are difficult, requiring much visual focus and motor coordination, but it will be continued throughout this year.

Conclusion

Child C has made incredible progress in many areas of our work! And all indications are that she will continue to progress because she is highly motivated to participate in the music therapy sessions. The violin and the recorder have added to her ability to self-control, coordinate movement and breathing, and gain a strong sense of self. She is fearless in her explora-tion of vestibular movement…even daring at times! She jumps with glee "like a big girl"…and is willing to undertake any physical activity now. She's grown in height and no longer needs a step to reach the drum. Her coordination is excellent, as is her auditory processing. Attention factors rely on motivation factors and focus. When she focuses, she responds appropriately. (Don't we all). I'm delighted with Child C's growth and look forward to more and more exciting developments.

Dorita S. Berger, MA MT-BC
Board Certified Music Therapist
September 25, 2000

DORITA S. BERGER MA MT-BC

Board Certified Music Therapist

MUSIC THERAPY
TREATMENT REVIEW

CLIENT NAME: *Child D*   Diagnosis: *PDD / Asperger*

D/O/B: *0/0/00*   Date of Report: *February 2001*

CURRENT SELECT TREATMENT OBJECTIVES: *Self-organization; Mental organization; Taking responsibility for self and behavior; Self-actualization and realization; Cooperation and accepting directives; Acknowledgment, awareness and expression of feelings; Self-pacing and physical control; Visual Tracking; Eye-Hand coordination; Flow and Modulation; Rhythm Internalization and Slowing of Body Rhythm; Flexible body dynamics; Breadth and rhythmic movement pacing; Self-Esteem.*

Brief Overview of Current Music Therapy Objectives and Progress

Child D is 13 years old, and has made excellent progress in Music Therapy sessions over the past year. He comes to Music Therapy once a week for a 45-minute session, and has been coming since the Fall of 1999. In general, Anonymous has shown growth in the following areas of Music Therapy sessions:

- enters and exits sessions with less resistence and redirection needs

- recalls and organizes favorite activities

- general comfort with the disciplined nature of music structure (rhythm, patterns, melodic flow and contour; etc.)

- more cooperative in willingness to undertake prescribed tasks

- becoming more relaxed and comfortable with creative musical self-expression and use of instruments to express feelings and states of mind.

Music Therapy objectives for the academic year of 2000–2001 have been structured within three basic areas of need:

1. The physiologic needs including:

- sensory integration and modulation
- visual tracking and extended visual attention
- eye-hand coordination
- pacing of movement rhythm (slower) and body dynamics
- breathing and vocal pacing; modulation of speaking voice
- fine-motor skills enhancement
- rhythmic internalization for controlled upper/lower body movement
- spontaneous and appropriate physical response to stimuli
- auditory integration; auditory tracking and focus; auditory memory.

2. Behavioral/psycho-emotional needs, including:

- creative appropriate spontaneity and/or shut-down
- self-initiation vs. cooperation with rules and needs of others
- self-management of behavior – ability to flow and modulate emotionally
- appropriate negotiation skills (compromising, etc.)
- taking charge of self and self-control (of incessant talking, for instance)
- self-discipline and responsibility for tasks and behaviors
- expression of needs; recognition of feeling states
- self-recognition (who am I?)
- self-esteem

- achievement and self-pride.

3. Mental / cognitive / intellectual needs, including:

- mental organization and focus for appropriate information processing
- problem solving: thinking and planning ahead; developing solutions appropriate to problem issue(s) and/or confrontations
- spontaneous and appropriate thought organization
- sequential memory and recall of information (accurate imitation)
- abstract information processing, retention, recall

The above areas are being addressed throughout this academic year through music improvisation tasks and song-writing opportunities targeted towards self-recognition and self expression. Encounters include imitation of movement and instrumental tasks, sundry music games; music improvisations on drums and various instruments, task organization for self. Also included as a portion of music therapy particularly addressing self-discipline and accountability is recorder and kazoo playing leading toward the structured learning of music elements. In addition, the playing of kazoo and recorder addresses issues of breath control and mid-line orientation of eyes and arms.

Other music therapy activities addressing the above objectives involve Child D's directing of session, selection and organization of specific tasks, developing and executing rhythmic patterns addressing abstract thinking and planning (problem solving issues), and the most difficult discipline of matching pitches in singing and instrumental playing (which requires solid auditory focus, memory, recall, and understanding of accuracy!). Child D has made some progress in this area of abstraction, and has shown a greatly improved ability to focus, understand the requirement, and follow through. However, when he is unwilling to cooperate, all bets are off!

Overall, the main concern for this young man is that he recognize and take charge of his responsibilities and behaviors without needing modification with "rewards". Intentions are to address the difference between being taught (or told by others) to "behave appropriately" and judging and initiating appropriate actions for himself. This has been the predominant theme of our sessions, and will continue to play a role in music therapy objectives. He has learned to choose his instruments according to what he knows is "allowable", and is learning to "ask for permission to use" those which he knows require permission. The continuing objectives are to help Child D discuss and learn, through our music therapy encounters and role-playing techniques, how to develop self-initiative and self-determination skills.

General Observations

It is my opinion that this child's Oppositional Defiance type of disorder, perhaps part of the PDD diagnosis which in his case includes autistic and attention deficit behavioral characteristics, is predominantly due to Child D's sensory system's inability to appropriately register and modulate emotional/sensory information. His need to "control" others in his environment may be the result of his inability to process information sequentially enough to feel comfortable with what is being expected of him in compliance with the needs of others. (In other words, if one is being continually talked at, and meanings (especially unspoken assumptions) are not being processed quickly or adequately in order to make compliant modulations deferring self needs to those of others, then one will feel safer commanding rather than cooperating with others.)

In addition, Child D's seeming inability to remain visually focused for any length of time could be a contributor to his inability to focus his thought processes. He is more absorbed in his own, albeit erratic, thought processes rather than intuiting the state-of-mind of another. This makes him less able to understand and "read" someone else's mind in order to quickly adjust his own thoughts to conform with others. In the music therapy session, Child D is perseverative with "Can I ask you something...?", "Can we do..." "No, I want to do...", and other standard evasive, inappropriate, off-the-subject statements as an avoidance mechanism to undertaking a prescribed task. This occurs even if the prescribed activity is something he has preferred to undertake in the past! This would indicate that Child D's ability to remain focused on one idea and follow it through to completion is being interrupted by sensory input which he cannot modulate, and which commands his immediate attention.

Thus, Child D's emotional reactions parallel the erratic nature of his thought process. In fact, Child D may not actually know his own mind! Nor what other thought options are available. He also seems unable to generalize one circumstance and apply the problem-solving formula to another. Trying to use psycho-philosophic reasons does not work, because again, it involves using words and logic – things Child D's system is unable to register and absorb, retain and call to use consistently.

Child D's inability to sustain attention may also be due to an atypical ability to focus auditory/visual information in an integrated manner. His habit of repeating or dwelling on a past idea is consistent with his inability to modulate from one sensory/emotional need to another; from one visual or auditory input to another; from one task to another. I often feel as if he is not quite seeing/hearing things simultaneously. Therefore, while I have moved on to something else, his system is still processing information given awhile back. In effect, it becomes a kind of time-warp event. (It is like one of us "typical" persons having difficulty relinquishing feelings of love, anger, disappointment, although others have moved on. How often have I heard, "Haven't you gotten over that yet?".)

Some recommendations

I am of the opinion that Child D would benefit greatly from more extensive OT, in addition to Music Therapy and other interventions. His visual-tracking, his constant use of peripheral vision, his inability to remain visually focused for any length of time is greatly impacting his ability (as stated earlier) to remain cognitively focused. In addition, a daily dose of SI interventions could greatly reduce his sensory coping issues. In music therapy, Child D focuses and responds extremely well after an opening segment of non-verbal quiet time with soothing music and dimmed lights reducing sensory input. This seems to enable his system to calm down first before undertaking heightened sensory processing. It is has been my experience that Child D will "perform" admirably after at least 15 minutes of simply being in the stillness of the music environment. Once his system has "relaxed", he becomes much more amenable to flowing in and out of tasks and thoughts. In general, I suggest that steps be taken to slow Child D's body rhythms! Fast language, fast music, fast movements, fast changes appear to heighten his erratic behaviors. I recommend that he is spoken to in slower, lower tones. I also do not recommend loud, extremely stimulating music which tends to put him "over" his sensory limit.

In addition to more OT and Music Therapy aimed at reducing the speed of Child D's biorhythms (which are always ahead of his thought processing rhythms), and addressing issues involving his eye-hand coordination deficits, his visual/auditory integration, and his generally "fight-or-flight" response to visual information (peripheral vision, etc.), I suggest that perhaps a reduction or even elimination of medications for a period of time will provide an opportunity for Child D's system to readapt naturally (through growth, therapy, education, his changing chemistry). It seems that a reassessment of Child D's psycho-pharmacological interventions could clarify whether the medications are indeed helping to reduce the system's stresses, and whether combining medications is warranted.

Summary

In general I feel comfortable stating that if Child D *could* "behave" and control himself, he would. I do not think his system understands and accurately processes the information it receives. This results in erratic thoughts, unruly behavior and perseveration, in addition to cognitive deficits. Just as we cannot blame a patient for coughing in public, we cannot blame Child D for behaving in atypical ways. His sensory system is non-compliant with what we consider to be "norm". This could be contributing to his behaviors. (In fact, his behavioral responses can be considered to be his system's adaptive responses to messages it is receiving and processing! If there are errors in this processing, there will surely be errors in "acceptable" behaviors.) As music therapist, my goals are to assist this child's system in investigating new options for dealing with his situation. This is obviously a slow and cumulative procedure. Adapting to the "norm", for Child D, may become a life-long learning process. Basically I experience him as a good kid who wants to feel accepted and typical. I think he has made great strides towards reaching this goal.

Respectfully submitted February 15, 2001.

Dorita S. Berger, MA, MT-BC
Board Certified Music Therapist
The Music Therapy Clinic

Bibliography

Altenmuller, E.O. (2001) 'How Many Music Centers are in the Brain?' In J.R. Zatorre and I. Peretz (eds) *Biological Foundations of Music*. New York: Annals of the New York Academy of Sciences, Vol. 930, pp.273–280.

Austin, J.H. (1999) *Zen and the Brain*. Cambridge, MA: The MIT Press.

Aylward, G.P. (1997) *Infant and Early Childhood Neuropsychology*. New York: Plenum Press.

Ayotte, J. and Peretz, I. (2001) 'Case Study of Dysmusia: As a Developmental Disorder of Pitch Perceptions.' In J.R. Zatorre and I. Peretz (eds) *Biological Foundations of Music*. New York: Annals of the New York Academy of Sciences, Vol. 930, pp.436–438.

Ayres, A.J (1979) *Sensory Integration and the Child*. Los Angeles: Western Psychological Services (WPS).

Balter, M. (2001) 'Language, Brain, and Cognitive Development Meeting: What Makes the Mind Dance and Count.' *Science 292*, 5522, 1 June 2001, 1636–1637.

Barron, J. and Barron, S. (1992) *There's a Boy in Here*. New York: Simon & Schuster.

Bauman, M.L. and Kemper, T.L. (eds) (1994) *The Neurobiology of Autism*. Baltimore, MD: Johns Hopkins University Press.

Begley, S. (2000) 'Music on the Mind.' *Newsweek*, 24 July 2000, 50–52.

Berard, G. (1993) *Hearing equals behavior*. New Canaan, CT: Keats Publishing, Inc.

Berger, D.S. (1997) 'Are you listening?' In J. Schneck, D.J. and J.K. Schneck (eds) *Music in Human Adaptation,* 209–214. Blacksburg, VA: Virginia Tech Press.

Bharucha, J.J., Tillmann, B., Janata, P. (2000) 'Cultural Adaptation of the Brain to Music and Speech: An FMRI Study of Listening to Indian and Western Music, Hindi and English.' In Abstracts, *The Biological Foundations of Music*: A New York Academy of Sciences Conference. New York.

Blood, A.J., Zatorre, R.J., Bermudez, P. and Evans, A.C. (1999) 'Emotional Responses to Pleasant and Unpleasant Music Correlate with Activity in Paralimbic Brain Regions.' *Nature Neuroscience 2*, 4, April 1999, 382–387.

Bregman, A.S.(1990) *Auditory Scene Analysis: The Perceptual Organization of Sound*. Cambridge, MA: MIT Press.

Brewer, C.B. (1997) 'Learning Progress through the Use of Music in the Creative Process and in Critical Thinking Skills.' In J.D. Schneck and J.K. Schneck (eds) *Music in Human Adaptation*, 317–318. Blacksburg, VA: Virginia Tech Press.

Brown, T.S. and Wallace, P.M. (1980) 'Audition.' In *Physiological Psychology* chapter 6, 117–146. New York: Academic Press Inc.

Bruer, J.T. (1999) *The Myth of the First Three Years: A New Understanding of Early Brain Development and Lifelong Learning.* New York: The Free Press/Simon & Schuster.

Brust, J.C.M. (2001) 'Music and the Neurologist: An Historical Perspective.' In J.R. Zatorre and I. Peretz (eds) *Biological Foundations of Music.* New York: Annals of the New York Academy of Sciences, Vol. 930, pp.143–152.

Carroll, D.H.L. and Erickson, C.A. (1992) *Brain Gym for Educators: Student Manual.* Ventura, CA: Educational Kinesiology Foundation.

Cross, I. (2001) 'Music, Cognition, Culture and Evolution.' In J.R. Zatorre and I. Peretz (eds) *Biological Foundations of Music.* New York: Annals of the New York Academy of Sciences, Vol. 930, pp.28–42.

Dallos, P. (1986) *The Search for the Mechanisms of Hearing.* On-line reprint: http://www.cscd.nwu.edu/public/ears/mechanisms.html (April, 2001).

Damasio, A.R. (2001) 'Emotion and the Human Brain.' In A.R. Damasio, A. Harrington, J.Kagan, B.S. McEwen, H. Moss and R. Shaikh (eds) *Unity of Knowledge: The Convergence of natural and Human Sciences.* New York: Annals of the New York Academy of Sciences, Vol. 935, pp.101–106.

Damasio, A.R. (1999) *The Feeling of What Happens: Body and Emotion in the Making of Consciousness.* New York: Harcourt Brace & Co.

Damasio, A.R. and Moss, H. (2001) 'Emotion, cognition and the human brain.' In A.R. Damasio, A. Harrington, J. Kagan, B.S. McEwen, H. Moss and R. Shaikh (eds) *Unity of Knowledge: The Convergence of Natural and Human Sciences.* New York: Annals of the New York Academy of Sciences, Vol. 934, pp.98–100.

Davis, W.B., Gfeller, K.E. and Thaut, M. (1992) *An Introduction to Music Therapy: Theory and Practice.* New York: McGraw Hill.

Deacon, T.W. (1997) *The Symbolic Species: The Co-evolution of Language and the Brain.* New York: W. W. Norton and Co.

de Fockert, J.W., Rees, G., Frith, C.D. and Lavie, N. (2001) 'The Role of Working Memory in Visual Selective Attention.' *Science 291* 5509, 2 Mar 2001, 1803–1806.

Deliege, I. and Sloboda, J. (eds) (1997) *Perception and Cognition of Music.* East Sussex, UK: Psychology Press Ltd.

Dennison, P.E. and Dennison, G. (1986) *Brain Gym.* Ventura, CA: Educational Kinesiology Foundation.

Dennison, P.E. and Dennison, G. (1989) Brain Gym handbook. Ventura,CA: Educational Kinesiology Foundation.

Dennison, P.E. and Dennison, G. (1989) Brain Gym for educators: Teachers edition. Ventura, CA: Educational Kinesiology Foundation.

Dess, N.K. (2000) 'Music on the Mind.' *Psychology Today,* September/October 2000, 28.

Drake, C. (2001) 'The quest for universals of temporal processing.' In J.R. Zatorre and I. Peretz (eds) *Biological Foundations of Music.* New York: Annals of the New York Academy of Sciences, Vol. 930, pp.17–27.

Drayna, D., Manichaikul, A., deLange, M., Sneider, H. and Spector, T. (2001) 'Genetic Correlates of Musical Pitch Recognition in Humans.' *Science 291,* 5510, 9 March 2001, 1969–1972.

Engelein, A., Stern, E. and Silbersweig, D. (2001) 'Functional Neuroimaging of Human Central Auditory Processing in Normal Subjects and Patients with Neurological and Neuropsychiatric Disorders.' *Journal of Clinical and Experimental Neuropsychology 23,* 1, February 2001, 94–120.

Findlay, E. (1971) *Rhythm and Movement: Applications of Dalcroze Eurhythmics.* Miami, FL: Summy-Birchard, Inc. (Distributed by Warner Bros. Publications, Miami, Fl.)

Fink, B.F. (undated). *Sensory-motor Integration Activities.* Catalogue #4160. Tucson: Therapy Skill Builders/Div.of Communication Skill Builders.

Fisher, A.G. (1991) 'Vestibular-Proprioceptive Processing and Bilateral Integration and Sequencing Deficits.' In A.G. Fisher, E.A. Murray and A.C. Bundy (eds) *Sensory Integration: Theory and Practice,* 71–107. Philadelphia: F.A. Davis Company.

Fisher, A.G. and Bundy, A.C. (1989) 'Vestibular Stimulation in the Treatment of Postural and Related Disorders.' In O.D. Payton, R.P. DiFabio, S.V. Pares, E.J. Protos and A.F.VanSant (eds) *Manual of Physical Therapy Techniques.* 239–258. New York: Churchill Livingstone.

Fisher, A.G., Murray, E.A. and Bundy, A.C. (1991) *Sensory Integration: Theory and Practice.* Philadelphia: F.A. Davis Co.

Fries, P., Reynolds, J.H., Rorie, A.E. and Desimone, R. (2001) 'Modulation of Oscillatory Neuronal Synchronization by Selective Visual Attention.' *Science 291,* 5508, 23 Feb 2001, 1560–1563.

Frith, U. (1989) *Autism: Explaining the Enigma.* Cambridge: Blackwell Publishers.

Fukui, H. (2001) 'Music and Testosterone – A Hypothesis for the Biological Foundations and Origin of Music.' In J.R Zatorre and I. Peretz (eds) *Biological Foundations of Music.* New York: Annals of the New York Academy of Sciences, Vol. 930, pp.448–451.

Gaddes, W.H. and Edgoll, D. (1994) *Learning disabilities and brain function: A neuropsychological approach.* 3rd Ed. New York: Springer-Verlag.

Gardner, H. (1994) *The Arts and Human Development.* New York: Basic Books.

Gardner, H. (1985) *Frames of mind: The Theory of Multiple Intelligences.* New York: Basic Books.

Gazzaniga, M.S. (1998) *The Mind's Past.* Berkeley, CA: University of California Press.

Getman, G.N. (1985) 'Hand-eye coordination.' *Academy Therapy 20,* 261–275.

Gillingham, G. (1995) *Autism: Handle with care! Understanding and Managing Behavior of Children and Adults with Autism.* Arlington, TX: Future Education, Inc.

Goleman, D. (1995) *Emotional Intelligence: Why it can matter more than IQ.* New York: Bantam Books.

Gossard, T. (1997) 'Structures for Listening.' In D.J. Schneck and J.K. Schneck (eds) *Music in Human Adaption.* 215–217. Blacksburg, VA. Virginia Tech Press.

Grandin, T. (1995) *Thinking in Pictures and Other Reports from My Life with Autism.* New York: Vintage Books.

Grandin, T. and Scariano, M.M. (1986) *Emergence: Labeled Autistic.* Novato, CA: Arena Press.

Gray, P.M., Krause, B., Atema, J., Payne, R., Krumhansl, C. and Baptista, L. (2001) 'The Music of Nature and the Nature of Music.' *Science 291,* 5501, 5 Jan 2001, 52–54

Greenfield, S. (2000) *The Private Life of the Brain: Emotions, Consciousness and the Secret of the Self.* New York: John Wiley & Sons, Inc.

Greenspan, S.I. and Benderly, B.L. (1997) *The Growth of the Mind: And the Endangered Origins of Intelligence.* New York: Addison-Wesley Publishing Co.

Greenspan, S.I. and Wieder, S. (1998) *The Child with Special Needs: Encouraging Intellectual and Emotional Growth.* Reading, MA: Addison-Wesley Longman, Inc.

Halpern, A.R. (2001) 'Cerebral Substrates of Musical Imagery.' In J.R Zatorre and I. Peretz (eds) *Biological Foundations of Music.* New York: Annals of the New York Academy of Sciences, Vol. 930, pp.179–192.

Hargreaves, D.J. (1986) *The Developmental Psychology of Music.* Cambridge, UK: Cambridge University Press.

Hart, C.A. (1993) *A Parent's Guide to Autism: Answers to the Most Common Questions.* New York: Pocket Books/Simon & Schuster.

Hayek, F. (1963) *The Sensory Order.* Chicago: Univ. of Chicago Press.

Helmuth, L. (2001) 'Dyslexia: Same Brains, Different Languages.' *Science 291,* 5511, 16 March 2001, 2064–2065

Hero, B. (1997) 'Some Effects of Whole Number Ratio Intervals in Music.' In D.J. Schneck and J.K. Schneck (eds) *Music in Human Adaptation,* 107–132. Blacksburg, VA: Virginia Tech Press.

Hero, B. and Foulkrod, R.M. (1999) 'The Lambdoma Matrix and Harmonic Intervals.' *IEEE Engineering in Medicine and Biology 18,* 2, March/April 1999, 61–73.

Hodges, D. (ed) (1996) *Handbook of Music Psychology.* Second edition. San Antonio, TX: IMR Press.

Holden, C. (2001) 'How the Brain Understands Music.' *Science 292,* 5517, 27 April 2001, 623.

Huron, D. (2001) 'Is Music an Evolutionary Adaptation?' In J.R Zatorre and I. Peretz (eds) *Biological Foundations of Music.* New York: Annals of the New York Academy of Sciences, Vol. 930, pp.43–61.

Hyde, K., Peretz, I., Ayotte, J. and Clement, J. (2001) 'Determination of Pitch and Temporal Discrimination Thresholds in the Adult Dysmusic.' In *Abstracts, Biological Foundations of Music Conference,* May 20–22 2000. New York: New York Academy of Science.

Jacques-Dalcroze, E. (1930) *Eurhythmics, Art and Education.* London, UK: Chatto & Windus.

Jacques-Dalcroze, E. (1921) *Rhythm, Music and Education.* New York and London: G.P. Putnam & Sons, The Knickerbocker Press.

Jordan, R. and Powell, S. (1995) *Understanding and Teaching Children with Autism.* New York: Wiley & Sons.

Jourdain, R. (1997) *Music, the Brain and Ecstacy: How Music Captures our Imagination.* New York: William Morrow and Co., Inc.

Kaas, J.H., Hackett, T.A. and Tramo, M.J. (1999) 'Auditory Processing in Primal Cerebral Cortex.' *Current Opinion in Neurobiology 9,* 2 April 1999, 164–170.

Kartha, D.K.M. (1997) 'Magic of Hand Drumming: Hand Drumming as an Activity Promoting Human Adaptation through Enhancement of Skills.' In J.D Schneck and J.K.Schneck (eds) *Music in Human Adaptation,* 199–202. Blacksburg, VA: Virginia Tech Press.

Kaye, M. (1997) 'Music of the Spheres: Mystic Probability becomes Implemental Reality.' J.D. Schneck and J.K. Schneck (eds) *Music in Human Adaptation,* 291–299. Blacksburg, VA. Virginia Tech Press.

Kivy, P. (1990) *Music Alone: Philosophical Reflections on the Purely Musical Experience.* Ithaca, NY: Cornell University Press.

Kohn, A. (1993) *Punished by Rewards: The Trouble with Gold Stars, Incentive Plans, A's, Praise, and other Bribes.* Boston: Houghton Mifflin Co.

Kozak, F.M. (1986) *Autistic children: A Working Diary.* Pittsburgh: Univ. of Pittsburgh Press.

Krumhansl, C.L. and Toiviainen, P. (2001) 'Tonal Cognition.' In J.R Zatorre and I. Peretz (eds) *Biological Foundations of Music.* New York: Annals of the New York Academy of Sciences, Vol. 930, pp.77–97.

LeDoux, J. (1998) *The Emotional Brain: The Mysterious Underpinnings of Emotional Life.* New York: Touchstone Book/Simon & Schuster.

Legge, M.F. (1997) 'Hypnocise – A Rehabilitative Modality using Pentatonic Scales and Octotonic Modes.' In J.D. Schneck and J.K. Schneck (eds) *Music in Human Adaptation,* 379–394. Blacksburg, VA: Virginia Tech Press.

Legge, M.F. (1999) ' Music for Health: The Five Elements Tonal System.' *IEEE: Engineering in Medicine and Biology 2,* March/April 1999, 80–88.

Lipscomb, S.A. and Hodges, D.A. (1996) 'Hearing and Music Perception.' In D.A. Hodges (ed) *Handbook of Music Psychology,* Second edition, 83–132. San Antonio, TX: IMR Press

Lowrey, G.H. (1986) *Growth and Development of Children.* 8th edition. Chicago: Yearbook.

Margoliash, D. (2001) 'The Song Does Not Remain the Same' *Science 291,* 5513, 30 March 2001, 2559–2561.

Martin, R. (1994) *Out of Silence: A Journey into Language.* New York: Henry Hold and Co.

Maurice, C. (1993) *Let Me Hear Your Voice: A Family's Triumph over Autism.* New York: Alfred A. Knopf.

Meyer, L.B. (1956) *Emotion and Meaning in Music.* Chicago, IL: The University of Chicago Press.

Nakkach, S. (1997) 'Into the Core of Music Healing.' In J.D. Schneck and J.K. Schneck (eds) *Music in Human Adaptation,* 441–458. Blacksburg, VA: Virginia Tech Press.

Ornstein, R. (1997) *The Right Mind.* New York: Harcourt Brace & Co.

Parsons, L.M. (2001) 'Exploring the Functional Neuroanatomy of Music Listening, Discrimination, and Performance.' In J.R Zatorre and I. Peretz (eds) *Biological Foundations of Music.* New York: Annals of the New York Academy of Sciences, Vol. 930, pp.211–231.

Patrick, G. (1999) 'The Effects of Vibroacoustic Music on Symptom Reduction.' *IEEE: Engineering in Medicine and Biology.* Vol.18 (2), March/April, 1999, pp.97–100

Paulesu, E., Demonet, J.F., Fazio, F., McCrory, E., Chanoine, V., Brunswick, N., Cappa, S.F., Cossu, G., Habib, M., Frith, C.D. and Frith, U. (2001). 'Dyslexia: Cultural diversity and biological unity.' *Science 291* (5511), March 16, 2001, pp.2165–2167.

Peretz, I. (2000) 'Brain Specialization for Music: New evidence from congenital amusia.' In J.R. Zatorre and I. Peretz (eds) *Biological Foundations of Music.* New York: Annals of the New York Academy of Sciences, Vol. 930, 153–165.

Peretz, I. (2001) 'Autonomy and Fractionation of Musical Processes.' In *Abstracts, Biological Foundations of Music Conference,* May 20–22 2000. New York: New York Academy of Sciences.

Pinker, S. (1994) *The Language Instinct: How the Mind Creates Language.* New York: Harper Perennial.

Powers, M.D. (1989) *Children with Autism: A Parent's Guide.* Rockville, MD: Woodbine House.

Recanzone, G.H. (2000) 'Spatial Processing in the Auditory Cortex of the Macaque Monkey.' *Proceedings of the National Academy of Sciences of the USA,* 97, 22, 24 October 2000, 11829–11835.

Repp, B.H. (2001) 'Effects of Music Perception and Imagery on Sensorimotor Synchronization with Complex Timing Patterns.' In J.R. Zatorre and I. Peretz (eds) *Biological Foundations of Music.* New York: Annals of the New York Academy of Sciences, Vol. 930, pp.409–411.

Rivlin, R. and Gravelle, K. (1984) *Deciphering the Senses: The Expanding World of Human Perception.* New York: Touchstone Books/Simon & Schuster, Inc.

Rolls, E.T. (1999) *The Brain and Emotion.* Oxford, UK: Oxford University Press

Romanski, L.M., Tian, B., Fritz, B., Mishkin, M., Goldman-Rakic, P.S. and Rauschecker, J.P. (1999) 'Dual Streams of Auditory Afferents Target Multiple Domains in the Primate Prefrontal Cortex.' *Nature Neuroscience 2,* 12 Dec 1999, 1131–1136.

Royeen, C.B. and Lane, S.J. (1991) 'Tactile Processing and Sensory Defensiveness.' In A.G. Fisher, E.A. Murray and A.C. Bundy (eds) *Sensory Integration: Theory and Practice.* Chapter 5 108–133. Philadelphia: F.A. Davis Company

Sacks, O. (1994) 'An Anthropologist on Mars.' *The New Yorker.* Dec/Jan 106–125.

Sacks, O. (1995) *An Anthropologist on Mars: Seven Paradoxical Tales.* New York: Alfred A. Knopf, Inc.

Samson, S., Ehrle, N. and Baulac, M. (2001) 'Cerebral Substrates for Musical Temporarl Processes.' In J.R Zatorre and I. Peretz (eds) *Biological Foundations of Music.* New York: Annals of the New York Academy of Sciences, Vol. 930, pp.199–178.

Schatz, H.B. (1997) 'The Chord of Nature and the Evolution of Music theory.' In D.J. Schneck and J.K. Schneck (eds) *Music in Human Adaptation,* 423–436. Blacksburg, VA: Virginia Tech Press.

Schlaug, G. (2001) 'The Brain of Musicians: A Model for Functional and Structural Adaptation.' In J.R Zatorre and I. Peretz (eds) *Biological Foundations of Music.* New York: Annals of the New York Academy of Sciences, Vol. 930, pp.281–299.

Schneck, D.J. (1997) 'A Paradigm for the Physiology of Human Adaptation.' In D.J. Schneck and J.K.Schneck (eds) *Music in Human Adaptation.* Blacksburg, VA. The Virginia Tech Press, 1–22.

Schneck, D.J. (1990) *Engineering Principles of Physiologic Function.* New York: New York University Press.

Schneck, D.J. (1990) 'The Sensory Systems of Environmental and Somatic Perception.' *Engineering Principals of Physiologic Function,* 51–60. NewYork: NYU Press.

Schneck, D.J. (1987) 'Feedback Control and the Concept of Homeostatis.' *Mathematical Modeling 9,* 12, 889–900

Schneck, D.J. and Berger, D.S. (1999) 'The Role of Music in Physiologic Accommodation.' *IEEE Engineering in Medicine and Biology Magazine 18 ,*2, March/April 1999, 44–53.

Schneck, D.J. and Schneck, J.K. (eds) (1997) *Music in Human Adaptation,* Proceedings of International Conference, Virginia Polytechnic Institute and State University. Blacksburg, VA: Virginia Tech Press.

Schneck, D.J. and Tempkin, A.R. (1992) *Biomedical Desk Reference.* New York: New York University Press.

Schopler, E. and Mesibov, G.B. (eds) (1987) *Neurobiological issues in Autism.* New York: Plenum Press.

Schopler, E. and Mesibov, G.B. (eds) (1983) *Autism in Adolescents and Adults.* New York: Plenum Press.

Schroeder, C.D., Lindsley, R.W., Specht, C., Marcovice, A., Smiley, J.F. and Javitt, D.C. (2001) 'Somatosensory Input to Auditory Association Cortex in the Macaque Monkey.' *Journal of Neuphysiology 853,* March 2001, 1322–1327.

Seashore, C.E. (1967) *Psychology of Music.* New York: Dover Publication, Inc.

Sessions, R. (1950) *The Musical Experience of Composer, Performer, Listener.* Princeton, NJ: Princeton University Press

Siegel, B (1996) *The World of the Autistic Child: Understanding and Treating Autistic Spectrum Disorders.* Oxford, UK: Oxford University Press.

Siegel, D.J. (1999). *The Developing Mind: Toward a Neurobiology of Interpersonal Experience.* New York: The Guilford Press.

Slawson, W. (1985) *Sound Color* Berkeley. CA: The University of California Press.

Sloboda, J.A. (1985) *The Musical Mind: The Cognitive Psychology of Music.* New York: Dover Publications, Inc.

Sperry, V.W. (1995) *Fragile success: Nine Autistic Children, Childhood to Adulthood.* North Haven, CT: Archon Books.

Stehli, A. (1991) *The Sound of a Miracle.* New York: Avon Books.

Steiner, R. (1983) *The Inner Nature of Music and the Experience of Tone: Selected Lectures from the Work of Rudolf Steiner.* Hudson, NY: Anthroposophic Press.

Sternberg, E.M. (2001) 'Piecing Together a Puzzling World.' *Science 292,* 5522, 1 June 2001,1661–1662.

Stewart, L., Walsh, V., Frith, U. and Rothwell, J. (2001) 'Transcranial magnetic stimulation produces speech arrest but not song arrest.' In J.R Zatorre and I. Peretz (eds) *Biological Foundations of Music.* New York: Annals of the New York Academy of Sciences, Vol. 930, pp.433–435.

Storr, A. (1992). *Music and the Mind.* New York: The Tree Press/MacMillan, Inc.

Stryker, M.P. (2001) 'Drums Keep Pounding a Rhythm in the Brain.' *Science 291,* 5508, 23 February 2001, 1506–1507.

Szonyi, E. (1973) *Kodaly's Principles in Practice· An Approach to Music Education through the Kodaly Method.* New York: Boosey & Hawkes.

Talwar, S.K., Musial, P.G. and Gerstein, G.L. (2001) 'Role of Mammalian Auditory Cortex in the Perception of Elementary Sound Properties.' *Journal of Neurophysiology 85,* 6, June 2001, 2350–2358

Tannenbaum, B. and Stillman, M. (1973) *Understanding Sound.* New York: McGraw Hill Book Co.

Tchernichovsky, O., Mitra, P.P., Lints, T. and Nottebohm, F. (2001) 'Dynamics of the Vocal Imitation Process: How a Zebra Finch Learns its Song.' *Science 291,* 5513, 30 March, 2001, 2564–2569.

Thaut, M. (1997) ' Rhythmic Auditory Stimulation in Rehabilitation of Movement Disorders: A Review of Current Research.' In D.J. Schneck and J.K. Schneck (eds) *Music in Human Adaptation,* 223–229. Blacksburg, VA: Virginia Tech Press.

Thaut, M., Kenyon, G.P., Schauer, M.L. and McIntosh, G.C. (1999) 'The Connection Between Rhythmicity and Brain Function.' *IEEE Engineering in Medicine and Biology 18* ,2, March/April 1999, 101–108.

Thaut, M., Miller, R.A. and Schauer, M.L. (1997) 'Rhythm in Human Motor Control: Adaptive Mechanisms in Movement Synchronization.' In D.J. Schneck and J.K.Schneck (eds) *Music in Human Adaptation,* 191–198. Blacksburg, VA: Virginia Tech Press

Thompson, B.M. and Andrews S.R. (1999) 'The Emerging Field of Sound Training.' *IEEE: Engineering in Medicine and Biology 18,* 2, March/April 1999, 89–96.

Thorpe, S.J. and Fabre-Thorpe, M. (2001) 'Seeking Categories in the Brain.' *Science 291,* 5502, 12 Jan 2001, 260–263.

Tian, B., Reser, D., Durham, A., Kustov, A. and Rauschecker, J.P. (2001) 'Functional Specialization in Rhesus Monkey Auditory Cortex.' *Science 292,* 5515, 13 April 2001, 290–293

Tomatis, A.A. (1991) *The Conscious Ear: My Life of Transformation through Listening.* Barrytown, NY: Station Hill Press.

Trainor, L.J., McDonald, K.L. and Alain, C. (2001) 'Electrical Brain Activity Associated with Automatic and Controlled Processing of Melodic Contour and Interval.' In J.R Zatorre and I. Peretz (eds) *Biological Foundations of Music*. New York: Annals of the New York Academy of Sciences, Vol. 930, pp.54–56.

Tramo, M.J. (2001) 'Music of the Spheres.' *Science 291*, 5501, 5 Jan 2001, 54–56.

Tramo, M.J. (2001) 'Neurobiological Foundations for the Theory of Harmony in Western Tonal Music.' In J.R Zatorre and I. Peretz (eds) *Biological Foundations of Music*. New York: Annals of the New York Academy of Sciences, Vol. 930, pp.92–116.

Trehub, S.E. (2001) 'Musical Predispositions in Infancy.' In J. R. Zatorre and I. Peretz (eds) *Biological Foundations of Music*. New York: Annals of the New York Academy of Sciences, Vol. 930, pp.1–16.

Valentinuzzi, M.E. and Arias, N.E. (1999) 'Human Psychophysiological Perception of Musical Scales and Nontraditional Music.' *IEEE Engineering in Medicine and Biology 18*, 2, March/April 1999, 54–60.

Wallin, J.L., Merker, B. and Brown, S. (eds) (1999) *The Origins of Music*. Cambridge, MA: The MIT Press.

Weiss, C. (1997) 'Thought Forms and Music.' In J.D. Schneck and J.K. Schneck (eds) *Music in Human Adaptation*, 277–288; Blacksburg, VA: Virginia Tech Press.

Wheeler, L. and Raebeck, L. (1972) *Orff and Kodaly Adapted for the Elementary School*. Dubuque, IO: Wm. C. Brown Co., Publishers.

Wickelgren, I. (2001) 'Working Memory Helps the Mind Focus.' *Science 291*, 5509, 2 Mar 2001, 1684–1685

Williams, D. (1998) *Autism and Sensing: The Unlost Instinct*. London: Jessica Kingsley Publishers.

Williams, D. (1996) *Autism: An Inside-Out Approach*. London, Jessica Kingsley Publishers Ltd.

Williams, D. (1992) *Nobody, Nowhere*. New York: Avon Books.

Wilson, F.R. and Roehmann, F.L. (eds) (1990). 'Music and Child Development.' *Proceeding of Conference on The Biology of Making Music 1987*. Denver Co., St.Louis, MO: MMB Music, Inc.

Zatorre, R.J. (2001) 'Neural Specializations for Tonal Processing.' In J.R Zatorre and I. Peretz (eds) *Biolgical Foundations of Music*. New York: Annals of the New York Academy of Sciences, Vol. 930, 193–210.

Zatorre, R.J. and Peretz, I. (eds) (2001) *Biological Foundations of Music*. New York: Annals of the New York Academy of Sciences, Vol. 930.

Index

melody 122
objectives, Child D 194,
    231–6
progress report, Child C
    193–4, 220–30
Randy 20–1
resources 195–
sensory adaptation goals
    152–65
sensory integration 130–51
sensory interpretation 33
    sensory
systems 75–6
    auditory system 89, 96,
        108–10
tactile defensiveness 70
timbre 125
vestibular system 64–5
see also group music therapy
music-movement exercises 109

needs
    mental/cognitive/intellectual
        233–4
    physiologic 30, 178, 232
    psycho-emotional 232–3
neo-cortex 38, 44–5
    cognitive function 43–4, 46
    filing information 43
    music interpretation 131
    physiologically-based therapy
        55
neurobiological impairment 28
neurons 35
neurotransmitters 190–1
norepinephrine 190
normal behaviour, determination
    of 19
norms, of behaviour 17, 21–2

occipital lobe 45
occupation therapy 63–4, 66,
    141
ocular-motor activity 65–6
off-beats 116
olivary complexes 81
olivo-cochlear bundle 84
oppositional defiance disorder
    (odd) 166
Orff-type instruments 142
organ of Corti 79
otoliths 64
outer ear 79
oval window 79

pacing
    body movement and breath
        159
    physiologic 155
paleoencephalon 38, 40, 45, 46,
    49, 53, 59, 68, 182
parietal lobe 45
patterns
    hearing for 85–6
    rhythmic 116–17
PDD see pervasive developmental
    disorder
perception, auditory 80
perceptual interpretation 180
percussion 141–2
perfect pitch 97
periodicity 187
peripheral vision 73
permanent physiologic
    accommodation 57–8, 59,
    185–6
perseveration 117–18
pervasive developmental disorder
    (PDD) 26, 91, 97